JOURNEYING
TO THE END OF LIFE

Shannon

Blessings on

Your Journey to the

End of life

Tom

JOURNEYING
TO THE END OF LIFE

*Discovering the Ancient Hospice Way
of Companioning the Dying*

Rev. Dr. Kenneth Patrick

authorHOUSE®

AuthorHouse™
1663 Liberty Drive
Bloomington, IN 47403
www.authorhouse.com
Phone: 1-800-839-8640

First published by AuthorHouse 2/18/10

ISBN: 978-1-4490-5475-5 (sc)

Printed in the United States of America
Bloomington, Indiana

This book is printed on acid-free paper.

> I invite all to shift their gaze, their thoughts, from worrying about health care to cultivating the art of living. And, today, with equal importance, to the… art of dying.
>
> ~ Ivan Illich.
> Brave New Biocracy: Health Care from Womb to Tomb
> – 1994

All the stories and reflections by patients, family, and hospice staff in ***Journeying to the End of Life*** are true. The names and other identifying details have been changed significantly to protect the privacy of those involved. In one case, the accounts of several hospice patients' experiences have been merged into one story. If any persons or experiences described in this book seem familiar to you, it may be that this ancient way of hospitality has at some time in your life touched your heart and soul.

> "Love begins by taking care of the closest ones- the ones at home. If we have no peace, it is because we have   forgotten that we belong to each other."
>
> ≈Mother Teresa of Calcutta ≈

Dedication

This book is dedicated to all the patients and their families, both living and those past, as well as the staff of Blue Ridge Hospice. Thank you all for your gracious presence, and revealing to me through your lives true hospitality. It has been a privilege to have you as my teacher on my journey through life.

In the Hospice Way of
companioning
those at the close of life
I experience each day
Light
being brought into darkness,
Hope
created in the midst of despair, and
Comfort and Care
being offered when it is needed most on
life's fragile journey.
May God bless this ongoing work of
companioning the dying
through the beautiful eons old wisdom
tradition
called Hospice.

A portion of the proceeds from the sale of each book is donated to the Patient Care Fund at Blue Ridge Hospice to assist the dying and their families who are in financial need.

.

Acknowledgements

An old proverb goes, "A journey in life is best measured in the friends made along the way, rather than the distance traveled or the final destination."

I wish to thank all those at Blue Ridge Hospice in Winchester, Virginia, who have been special friends on my journey to research, write, and edit this book. It has been an incredible undertaking spanning several years and I deeply appreciate your acts of kindness.

Special thanks to Lynn Gray, Vice President of Patient and Family Support Services, who was willing to hire me as a chaplain and patiently bore with me as I stumbled along and found my way in hospice work. Dorothy Harriman, Medical Social Services Coordinator, has also been a true friend and a wonderful clinical supervisor.

Thank you to Susan O'Kelly, Chaplain's Associate, who read the first notes and early manuscript of the book. I appreciate your encouragement to go forward with publication.

Susan Jarvis, Volunteer Coordinator and Kelly Bucher, Director of Volunteer Services, also commented on the later manuscript. Thank you for the wonderful discussions on medicine, hospice work, and spiritual enlightenment.

Evan E. Knighting, IT Manager, provided technical assistance with formatting the final manuscript into PDF file.

Catherine Wolniewicz, Clinical Administrative Assistant, took on the daunting task of being a creative technical editor. She reviewed the manuscript and re-formatted the text and endnotes. Thank you for your professional assistance.

Lisa Wilt, Coordinator of Special Events, contributed her artistic talent in helping design the cover of the book.

I am grateful to three former Blue Ridge Hospice patients, Reuben H. Hulver, Mildred L. Brannock, and Lee S. Bielski, as well as the current hospice patient Eleanor H. Talbert, who shared with me in detail their journey to the end of life. They all allowed an interview to be tape recorded for this book. Special thanks to Monica Stevens,

Business Office, for transcribing the interviews.

Lawrence Muller, the son of a former hospice patient, has carefully proofread the manuscript, and provided helpful editorial suggestions.

My deepest gratitude goes to Ernie Carnevale Jr., President and CEO. He is dedicated to providing the highest quality of patient services possible. Ernie works tirelessly to ensure that Blue Ridge Hospice is, in his words, "a world class organization."

I benefited from the kind hospitality of the monks at Holy Cross Abby, a monastery of the Catholic Order of Cistercians of the Strict Observance (OCSO), near Berryville, Virginia. The important distinction between Augustinian and Benedictine forms of hospitality in early hospice care comes from discussions with Father Vincent at the monastery.

The library reference staff at Villanova University, a Roman Catholic Augustinian University, was gracious in providing research material on hospitality in the writings of St. Augustine.

Thank you to my wife LuAnne. She put up with years of late night writing and editing of the manuscript. I appreciate your presence on my journey of life. Also thanks to our "Noah's Ark" of six children: McKeon, Logan, Madigan, Jordan, Nancy, and Brevin. It has been a blessing to share the gift of life with all of you.

Contents

Dedication iii

Acknowledgements v

Introduction

The Challenge of Death and Dying Today ix

Part One

The Journey to a Beautiful Death

1. The Path 3

2. Being a Spiritual Companion on the Journey 43

3. Companioning the Dying as a Spiritual Art 61

4. Journey's End: A Beautiful Death 69

5. A Vision for the Journey to a Beautiful
   Death In America 81

Part Two

Stories of Companioning on the Journey

6. Stories From the Path 93

7. The Dying Speak To Us as Companions 107

Part Three

Wisdom for the Journey
The Ancient Path Stretching from the Middle Ages

The Historical Roots of Hospice Companioning 133

Hospice Companioning in Modern Times 181

A Spiritual Manifesto 211

Appendix

A. Historical Time Line of Hospice Companioning in the West 220

B. Reflections on St. Augustine and Companioning the Dying 222

C. Reflections on St. Benedict and Companioning the Dying 227

End Notes 229

Select Bibliography 263

Introduction

The Challenge of Death and Dying Today

As Gomer Pyle on the Andy Griffith television show might say, Surprise! Surprise! In the year 2006, the oldest of the Baby Boomers, the generation born between 1946 and 1964, turned age sixty.[1] This group of Americans represents about 78 million people. In 2006 there were about 330 Americans becoming age 60 every hour.[2] How is such a large, active, politically involved generation to face dying a natural death, both for themselves and their mothers and fathers, husbands, wives, life partners, and other loved ones? A health care crisis of pandemic proportions is looming in our land, considering that there are currently only 16,100 nursing homes in America, with 1.7 million beds available, and an 86% occupancy rate.[3]

The leading edge of the baby boomers is at this moment dealing with the physical decline and the death of their mother and father, or has faced this reality very recently. In the next few years, baby boomers will need to face, for better or worse, the issue of death and dying of their spouse or life partner, and also how they themselves will cope with the fast approaching reality of a natural death.

According to the Last Acts study *Means to a Better End. A Report on Dying in America Today,* 75% of Americans express a wish to die at home, while only 25% actually realize that wish.[4] Instead about 50% of Americans 65 years and older die in a hospital while another 20% to 25% die in nursing homes.[5]

The Last Acts study points to the reality that persons often prefer to die at home because they feel they have a better quality of life. Individuals dying at home enjoy "being with families, enjoying more normal life, having greater autonomy, and being surrounded by familiar and comfortable home environment." The study quotes an elderly man dying of leukemia who stated that he preferred to die at home:

I want to be with my family. Home is always the place you can rest and the place that you spend your whole life…Your spirits will be with your family, and they will take care of you. I enjoy [watching] my grandchildren run in and out of the house.[6]

Persons state over and over that home is, as the saying goes, "where the heart is" and a natural place to be at the end of life. This is where they will not be bothered by the routine and lack of privacy of a hospital or nursing home. Home is a place of pets as companions, meals cooked the way you like, and someone to say "good night" to you at the end of the day and perhaps give you a kiss.

As one individual said of his desire to be at home:

[In a hospital] You will never have decent sleep at night. People talk, carts run, equipment beats….people come into my room no matter what you are doing. You do not have any privacy. You need to give up your plan to fit their schedule….that will not happen at home….When I sleep, my wife will tell my grandson not to come into my bedroom and be quiet. When I need to go to the bathroom, no one will be allowed to come in without permission, and no one will hurry me up. You can be in control.[7]

We could summarize the findings of the study by saying that home is the place of heart and the spirit, and for that reason the place that people overwhelmingly desire to be at the close of life. At the end of the journey of life, a great majority of individuals want to be at a place that is safe and comfortable for them, where they are companioned by those who have walked with them through the emotional mountains and valleys of life. They long for a place where they can slip into comfortable routines and old patterns of life. This place is called home. Here, people want their physical, emotional, and spiritual needs of life to be met. And yet in spite of such deep, heartfelt desires, only 25% of Americans currently experience the end of life at home.

So, in what direction do we as a nation need to go to with our healthcare system to enable untold millions of baby boomers to die a natural death at home? How can they die with care provided for the physical needs of their body, with the emotional needs of their heart heard and responded to in compassionate ways, and with their spiritual needs met? How can this large generation, and all their loved ones, be companioned in body, heart and spirit at home at the end of this natural journey of life?

The great question facing the generation of baby boomers is simply, "Can the face of dying change in America?" Can dying at home, companioned by those we love and who love us, become as it was for our grandparents and ancestors, the norm for people in the United States? By "home" I want to include hospice residential units, where a warm, "homelike" setting is provided, and families are free to come and go. Home can be a tastefully decorated room in a hospice residential unit that speaks of comfort and care. Within these units can be caring nurses well trained in pain management, volunteers who fix homemade meals, and the companionship of pets. Trained staff can attend to the needs of the body, the heart, and the spirit. So what will it take for this to be the way the natural journey of life draws to a close at homes all across our land? How can we make the deep longing to die at home come true for millions of Americans?

This question calls us to see beyond the issue of death itself. It is also as the face of dying changes in America that the face of living changes in our land, as was pointed out to me so beautifully by the Blue Ridge hospice social worker Gina Caudill. As the dying are in our midst in our homes, they become our spiritual teachers. They teach us how to value, respect, and honor the elderly, and the vast wisdom from their life experiences. The dying teach us that life is a natural journey and each step of the way, from birth to death, is to be held in wonder and awe. As little children come once again to see the elderly in our homes, they can come to know in their heart and soul that life indeed comes to a natural end. It is a knowing of death and dying that is beyond simply intellectual knowledge. We need the elderly among us to help us cope with the great denial of death in our culture. As one highly educated baby boomer said to me at a conference on health care for boomers: "The baby boomers believe that they are not going to die."

The dying in our homes can teach us the importance of family and basic human compassion. As a child helps mommy make a plate of cookies for granny, and then takes them in to the senior citizen, the child can be taught a life lesson that no books can teach so deeply: making room in your heart and soul for another person is one of the things that life is most about What a different world we would live in

XI

if each person lived out this simple life lesson day by day.

The dying as our teachers call us back to the importance of community, and how much we depend on community for our quality of life. As we see an elderly person struggle with steps going into the house, we suddenly realize that perhaps our home is not handicap accessible. As an elderly member of our family who no longer drives has to wait on a bus, we realize how important is transportation for the elderly A natural death at home provides the opportunity for the elderly as teachers to be among us and for us to learn from early childhood some of life's greatest lessons.

I believe that the path to this compassionate way of dying at home with holistic care is what I call the ancient "Hospice Way" of companioning the dying. It challenges us to fundamentally shift our understanding of hospice work today. This way of eons old spiritual wisdom of companioning the dying first emerged with the fall of the Roman Empire in the later part of the fifth century. From the time of the so-called Dark Ages, Roman Catholic monks and nuns offered a spiritual hospitality to the dying in hospices, hospitals, monastic infirmaries, and leper houses. The Hospice Way took shape from this spiritual care for those at the end of life. This way of being with the dying is profoundly holistic, and offers companionship for the dying in body, heart, and spirit.

The modern hospice movement has evolved in a highly medicalized way, and has today all but lost the emotional and spiritual companioning of patients and their families. The ancient Hospice Way teaches us the lost dimensions of being with the dying; companioning the heart and spirit as well as the body to the end of life in a place called home. To companion patients and families at home and care for their physical, emotional, and spiritual needs, we must listen once more to the rich wisdom of the ancient Hospice Way.

This book is a journey I invite you to take with me. Together let us discover the incredible wisdom of this Hospice Way, so ancient and yet so new. May we hear in our times another story of how to face death and dying. Our journey can transform both us as caregivers, those we companion, and the nation in which we live. The Hospice Way is eons old, and can literally show us the way home.

As an aging baby boomer myself, I have the immense privilege of being a chaplain at Blue Ridge Hospice in Winchester, Virginia. I see death and dying every day. Death has personally come knocking at my door a few times. On a 2,139 mile hike from Georgia to Maine on the Appalachian Trail to help raise money to open a homeless shelter, my pack was struck by lightning in a violent thunder storm. After losing my sight and hearing, I recovered and finished the trek. While writing this book, I experienced paralysis of my body and immense pain caused by the rare Guillain-Barre Syndrome. As many people prayed for me, I felt my whole body bathed in a cone of light while in the neurological intensive care unit of a local hospital. The syndrome began to reverse itself, and I knew that the way forward would be difficult but would not be life threatening.

For those who have know the nearness of death and how fragile this human life is, and for those who will soon find out, I send this book to you as a spiritual resource for those "end times" that come. They indeed can be a challenge on life's journey.

This book shares the ancient wisdom of the hospice tradition that has provided comfort and care for millions and millions when it was needed most. This eons old Way has taken many twists and turns in the 1,500 years or so that it has been around. Especially in the modern era of the 1960's till today the Hospice Way has been given a unique medicalized face. However, no one to my knowledge has ever shared the whole story of this beautiful Hospice Way to journey to the end of life. As you search individual hospice web sites today and read their literature, you find information that seems to say that hospice is, for all practical purposes, a modern movement, founded by such figures as Elizabeth Kubler-Ross and Cicely Saunders. However, the Hospice Way is truly an ancient wisdom tradition that traces back to the beginning of the Middle Ages. All modern hospice work is simply another chapter of this centuries old story. I have set out to share with you the ancient Hospice Way and the incredible wisdom and ways of caring that it teaches, so that it may be a compassionate guide for you and your loved ones on the path to the end of life.

The first chapter of our story presents the ancient wise path of journeying to the end of life in direct and simple terms. In this chapter, we come to know exactly how it is that we can be companioned in this Way. What I call "the spiritual art of hospitality" is presented as the heart and soul of hospice companioning as it has been practiced through the ages. We will glimpse, I hope, the power of this Way to transform both the dying and their companions along the journey. The spiritual power of hospitality is profoundly revealed in the life of Maximilian Kolbe, the saint of the death camp Auschwitz.

We then consider how we as caregivers can enable those at the end of life to experience a Beautiful Death. The powerful spiritual teaching of Eckhart Tolle is one of our guides. Being with the dying is a true art form that is an important part of this story. As a hospice chaplain and spiritual teacher, I have found an immense spiritual power in sharing this ancient way of being with the dying. We will consider the importance of spiritual presence and ways we can companion in heart and soul on this final journey of life.

The stage is then set for how baby boomers and others may experience the true fullness and richness of what I would like to call a "Beautiful Death" through this Hospice Way. The term a "Beautiful Death" is taken from Mother Teresa of Calcutta, and distinguishes death in the Hospice Way from a "good death" that occurs after medical care without holistic hospice companioning, such as may occur in an acute care facility or nursing home.[8] We will reflect on how preparing and going through a Beautiful Death may truly change the face of dying in the United States. Changes in our lifestyle and the healthcare system are called for to prepare ourselves for a "Beautiful Death."

In reflecting on a Beautiful Death in America, we will consider the vast technological resources of our land. If we can put a man on the moon and develop highly accurate "smart weapons" such as those used in the Gulf War, why not apply technology specifically to end of life care? The possibilities of technology are truly endless, and could provide a vast improvement in quality of life for the terminally ill. One example is creating a physical place in our daily lives for companioning the dying. It might be adding a "Green" handicap accessible suite onto an existing home, incorporating the latest in technology. This "hospitality house" (the term was suggested by the Blue Ridge Hospice social worker Joanna Tutwiler) could reflect a new face of companioning the dying in America. Technology applied to safety, entertainment and communication devices for companioning the dying has rich possibilities. Given the buying power of millions of baby boomers, a new industry could spring up from the application of modern technology to end of life care.

The Hospice Way saga continues with personal stories from the lives of patients that illuminate the depth and richness of companioning on the journey to the end of life. To further illustrate the power of the spiritual art of hospitality to touch the body, heart and soul in deeply moving ways, I share verbatim interviews with four hospice patients I have been privileged to companion. I want us to hear what they speak from their hearts, and what they have experienced as they have walked in this path of companioning. They have kindly given me written permission to share their stories.

In the final section we explore the rich history of this story of companioning the dying. Here we find the fountain of wisdom from which modern hospice companioning has flowed. The Hospice Way emerged from the Dark Ages into the Middle Ages through such spiritual giants as St. Benedict and St. Augustine. Both individuals have decisively shaped our understanding of modern hospice care. However, their contributions have yet to be recognized. In the appendix will be found further reflections on these early Christians' contribution to a spiritual understanding of care offered on the journey to the end of life. As our story of companioning unfolds, we will re-create how it was that death and dying may have first been experienced in hospice care in these medieval times. The writings of the great French scholar Philippe Aries will guide us. This serves as a model for our understanding of holistic care for the dying today. We will also consider a recently discovered book that relates in great detail how the sick and dying were cared for by Christians during the period of the Crusades.

The story then unfolds how companioning the dying has taken place in modern times. The Hospice Way was shaped and reformed by such charismatic pioneers as Kubler-Ross and Cicely Saunders. We will also consider in some detail how the medicalzing of hospice care has occurred in our time and especially the dominant role of both the National Hospice and Palliative Care Organization and the Medicare legislation of the federal government.

A Beautiful Death for baby boomers will require a cultural shift in American society to accept death as a normal part of the process of human life. It will require that we move beyond denial of our mortality and allow this natural part of the life cycle to unfold in the personal space of our own homes. In the coming years, our national health care resources will need to be increasingly directed toward a companioning of the dying at home and in residential hospice units, with the family enabled to be caregivers, as well as in local hospice residential units.

Above all, we will need a deep spiritual awareness of the power and wisdom of the ancient way of **hospes**, which is true hospitality expressed through a Beautiful Death. Such an awakening of hospitality can dramatically shift the experience of natural death from taking place in nursing homes and hospitals to occurring with families and loved ones in the home.

Companioning a loved one at home on the journey to the end of life can be the most powerful life experience we may ever have. In the search for life's meaning, our society has become a veritable supermarket of spirituality. From New Age thought, such as the best selling book *The Secret*, to Buddhist meditation, to talks on the *Power of Now* by Eckhart Tolle, to Roman Catholic centering prayer, to "born again" Christians who accept the authority of Scripture as "God's Word," we can find an almost endless variety of ways to pursue enlightenment, peace, and prosperity. However, when we are faced with companioning a dying loved one at home, our spirituality is put to the ultimate test. It is truly a time when "the rubber hits the road," so to speak. When the dining room furniture goes into storage, and a hospital bed is rolled in to take the place of our cherished possessions, can we still be at peace? Can we feed a loved one who spills most of their food all over themselves and is dirty and still find joy in the present moment? When we hear the same story repeated over and over, can we still be kind and gracious and listen to it "one more time" without expressing our irritation?

Companioning the dying "up close and personal" in our own homes can itself be a powerful spiritual teacher. It can teach us the greatest lessons of life. It can teach us of the burden of our ego and pride, and in doing so may open the door to true spiritual liberation. It can teach us, and all in our family, about the natural course of birth, life, and death that can take place in our very bedrooms and living rooms. Companioning at home those on this final journey can unlock for us the great teachings of this ancient hospice wisdom tradition.

For a Beautiful Death to occur at home as the normal course to the end of the journey of life, the family needs to be empowered. This empowerment of the family will need to occur at the national level.

Suppose that a spouse, a child or grandchild or other immediate relative is willing to take an unpaid leave of absence from a job to become a full time hospice home companion. Could this leave, with the job guaranteed upon returning to the work force, be available as a new benefit of the Family and Medical Leave Act of 1993? Perhaps such a leave could be extended month by month, up to a one year maximum (the concept of family leave to companion a loved one at the end of life comes from conversations with David Gray, the son of a former hospice patient).

Also, could a sliding scale tax credit be provided the caregiver's family for this care as a new form of a hospice Medicare benefit? Reflect on the fact that according to a recent study conducted by Met Life, the average cost of nursing home care in 2007 in the U.S. is $213 per day.[9] This amount varies by region and types of care required. At $213 per day, a one year stay in a nursing home will cost $77,745. Could the Medicare cost, or at least a portion of it, that is saved by having the patient stay at home be kept by the family as a direct credit on their federal and state income tax? This credit would empower a family in providing care at home for the dying. The direct savings to Medicare would be in the billions of dollars for the millions baby boomers who would choose to die at home (this idea of a tax credit for hospice companioning at home comes from the RN at Blue Ridge Hospice, Debbie Olsen). Such a tax credit could also be given, at an adjusted rate, for families whose loved one needs the care of an assisted living facility, but chooses instead to be companioned at home. Perhaps for those of very low incomes a direct payment of the current Medicare hospice benefit, on a sliding scale, could be made directly to the families who provide a hospice certified full time end of life companion in the home.

This national provision for an extended leave of absence to serve as a hospice family companion at home, as well as a sliding scale tax credit with provision for direct payment of hospice companions at very low family incomes, could help emerge in America the reality of dying at home as the normal way the natural journey of life ends in our nation. I call this way of families being with the dying at home "Hospice Home Companioning", or HHC. This could complement, and not replace, the existing short term (six month) hospice Medicare Benefit. Ideally, key features of this new Hospice Home Companioning Medicare Benefit would include family members receiving required training, certification, and supervision in palliative end of life care by current hospice professionals, longer lengths of stay in hospice companioning (one year or more) and hospice staff available on an "as needed basis" (prn) to the patient and family. Hospice residential units in America could be a valuable resource for those using the Family Companioning Benefit, as a place for short-term respite care as well as brief care for those ending the journey of life. Millions of baby boomers who might choose to die at home but may not be eligible for the current hospice form of care could potentially benefit from a new Hospice Home Companioning Program.

The HHC Program fits well with the changing trend in our nation's supply of long-term care. The demand for home and community based services is growing, while a smaller proportion of elderly and disabled people live in nursing homes today compared to 1990.[10] Above all, a Home Companioning form of hospice care could be truly holistic care that would empower the family to serve as end of life caregivers and bring a new awareness of death and dying in our land.

The envisioned Hospice Home Companioning Medicare Benefit would also compliant several successful existing programs which assist elderly citizens in continuing to live in their homes and communities. Since 1968, LIFE (Living Independently for Elders) has been providing a lifetime plan for all-inclusive care to help frail elderly residents of West Philadelphia, Pennsylvania.[11] The LIFE Program "promotes independence and the highest level of functioning while allowing choice and dignity for our members and their families".[12] This program provides all needed preventive, primary, acute and long term health care services so that eligible older individuals continue to live in their homes as long as possible. LIFE is a service of the Penn Nursing Network (PNN), a division of the University of Pennsylvania's School of Nursing.

LIFE follows the national PACE Model (Program of All-inclusive Care for the Elderly), which has a 30 year track record of successfully enabling elderly individuals to remain in their home.[13] The program requires that members be in need of nursing home care to enroll. However, only about 7% of PACE members live in a nursing home nationally.

The PACE program serves individuals who are aged 55 or older, certified by their state to need nursing home care, able to live safely in the community at the time of enrollment, and reside in PACE service areas. The program provides a range of care to seniors with chronic needs while allowing them to remain in their own homes for as long as possible. Many other successful care delivery models now exist for seniors in our land.[14]

While these successful programs meet the needs of many older citizens for palliative care at home, none of the programs exist as a form of holistic end of life companioning, nor do they include the financial support to the family of the envisioned Hospice Medicare Home Companioning Benefit. Above all, this new Hospice benefit is unique in that it seeks to empower the family to serve as trained caregivers at home with the dying, while working as part of team with skilled and trained hospice professionals. Such a new hospice Medicare benefit, focused on long term companioning at home by the family, would allow end of life patients to easily transition in and out of existing short term hospice palliative care services, and also provide for hospice residential units as a resource for patients and families at the end of life. The current hospice program of care also has a national scope in its services, which other programs lack. The proposed Hospice Home Medicare Benefit may well not replace existing home care programs for seniors, for many situations exist where no family members are available as companions, or the family may choose to not server in the role of trained caregivers.

Companioning the dying at home by a spouse will require that affordable health insurance be available for those in Home Companioning care. If a spouse is to be with a loved one at home, then the spouse will need to be able to purchase affordable health insurance, as there may be no employed family member with health insurance. The empowering of the family will require a spouse being able to have access to an affordable health insurance plan, perhaps as a benefit of the leave benefit of the Hospice Home Companioning Program.

This cultural shift to dying at home as the norm in our society will challenge, as we have said, even the present hospice movement. There is a crucial need to expand (and not replace) hospice services from a highly medicalized form of end of life care, with endless paperwork and computer forms dictated by the federal government, to a more holistic form of companioning, including hospice care given by local faith communities. The end of life care for the baby boomer generation presents an incredible opportunity for religious communities to touch the lives of millions that are now outside of organized, institutional religion. As a parish minister myself, I see that faith communities in our nation represent an amazing pool of largely untapped volunteer resources.

What if a local religious community would form a "partnership" with a hospice in its area? The faith community could provide an amazing variety of services for families that are companioning the dying at home. It could begin with a simple act of kindness, such as taking the flowers that were on the altar at worship to the family each week. The partnership could expand to include hosting a monthly appreciation and support group dinner for the family caregivers in the fellowship hall of the faith community. It might include training faith community members as volunteers to offer respite care for families, and also offering prayer vigils in the sanctuary for the dying and their families. I have seen over and over how much handmade birthday cards and heartfelt letters can touch a life. A partnership with a faith community could be a powerful resource for the Hospice Home Companioning program.

The current state of hospice care in the United States is that hospices have been established less to provide an alternative self-directed choice to traditional health care and more as another program of existing health providers, such as hospitals, home health agencies, nursing homes, and for-profit and not-for-profit healthcare systems. Providers have bought into an increasingly inflexible business orientation that stands in sharp contrast to the spiritual heritage of hospice in the West. Companioning at home by families with hospice professionals enabling the families would be a movement toward end of life care which is a true alternative to traditional health care in this country.

Another great challenge companioning at home by families would bring to hospice today involves the crisis nature of current hospice care. The median length of stay is regarded as the most accurate way of showing the length of stay of most hospice patients. According to data from the National Hospice and Palliative Care Organization the median length of stay for hospice patients is a little over three weeks. As Paul R. Brenner writes in *"Spirituality in Hospice- The Challenge of Success,*" hospice programs are doing crisis management because death is imminent, "....rather than facilitating a thoughtful, intentional progressive experience of the end of life that stresses it spiritual dimensions and meaning."[15] Companioning the dying at home could increase the length of stay in hospice programs as dying at home is accepted more and more as the normal way that the journey to the end of life takes place in our country.

It is essential that the most modern advances in medical palliative care be incorporated into the modern hospice movement. However, when companioning the terminally ill is left primarily to the "professionals," such as doctors, nurses, and social workers, with the dying placed in nursing homes and acute care facilities where they are "out of sight and out of mind," there becomes no realistic way to contain the soaring cost of medical care paid for primarily by Medicare.

The answer to affordable holistic care for the natural death of millions of baby boomers lies in the Hospice Way: empower the family to companion the dying at home. Our society at all levels, both local faith communities and the federal government, needs to be companions in this task of enabling the family. Such an empowering is a "win-win" for everyone.

This "bottom up" approach to end of life care is not new. The social critic Ivan Illich proposed such a view of health care a quarter century ago, although in a radical form. He saw modern medicine as launching an inhuman attempt to defeat pain, suffering, and death. In the process, the immense social resources of the family, the community, and the individual are destroyed as the respected resources of "professionals" are brought forth to companion the dying on the journey to the end of life.[16] From the thought of Illich, we learn to value and treasure the eons old "traditional way" of making sense of death and dying. This is the Hospice Way of hospitality (*hospes*); of valuing our families, our faith communities, and respecting the dying among us as our teachers.

The modern hospice movement needs to find its way to a more holistic and less medically driven companioning of the terminally ill. The role of hospice needs to embrace empowering companions as well as providing direct services. I suggest a way to a more holistic hospice companioning of the dying in the final chapter, *"A Spiritual*

Manifesto: A Call for Medical Palliative Care to Embrace Our Spiritual Heritage in Modern Hospice Work." It is my hope that we can begin exploring, as another step in the eons old hospice story, a way of hospice care that is more faithful to our ancient hospice tradition while also incorporating the advances of modern medical palliative care.

The time has come, I believe, to write a new chapter in the history of the hospice movement. This chapter needs to be shaped around a refocused vision of hospice care; one of hospice companioning as an empowering presence on the journey to the end of life. Such an empowering of families needs to flow from a holistic model of care at home for terminally ill patients and their families, and also engage the vast resources of our nation and faith communities *so that natural death at home is possible as the norm in the United States.* Hospice needs to be envisioned as a movement of enabling families as they companion the dying, and not one of simply being the sole or primary provider of care. The spiritual art of hospitality is the great legacy of the ancient Hospice Way, and we will reflect on it as a holistic model of care adequate for our time. This new chapter in the unfolding of the hospice story is one of making the dream come true of ending the natural journey of life in the safety and comfort of home, companioned by those who hold us in their heart.

Baby boomers have shown that they are up to the task of changing the way we live and experience life in American society. This generation of Americans has set cultural landmarks at every stage along the way. The war in Vietnam galvanized many to action in the 1960's and early 1970's. Serving in the Peace Corps was an expression of their concern for a life that was more than simply materialistic and self-centered. The stirring speeches and marches of Martin Luther King Jr. challenged many to work for civil rights.

It may well be that the greatest social issue of all is now coming into view for baby boomers: how will this generation face the natural death and dying of both loved ones and themselves? Will it be with dignity at home, surrounded by those whom they love, able to make decisions of life style and or will it be perhaps in a cold and anonymous place, such as we find in many hospitals and nursing homes? Do we have the spiritual wisdom as a nation to set a course that leads to a Beautiful Death for this generation of 78 million Americans? I believe that this wisdom may be found through hearing the ancient story of the Hospice Way of a Beautiful Death. The baby boomers have the opportunity to leave, as a great legacy of their generation, the dignified companioning, in body, heart, and soul, of loved of ones at home as the normal way the journey to the end of life takes place in the United States.

Dr. David H. Gustafson, after the death of his mother with Alzheimer's, reflected on her pain and suffering in an intensive care unit before she died.[17] He came to the conclusion that the problem with end of life care in this country is not with the people, but with the way we seek to deliver care. He writes:" Healthcare providers are good people. I have seen my sister, a critical care nurse, come home from her job at a leading teaching hospital so tired she can barely move. I have seen doctors so frustrated with the health system that they can barely see straight. Providers are trained to cure at all costs but the incentives are to ensure that they spend as little time as possible with individual patients. The problem is the system, not the people."[18]

His views are powerful for baby boomers and all providing care for a loved one at the end of life. He discerns, very wisely, that "in the final analysis it is up to us (the families) to take more responsibility for the dying person and for ourselves. We are the ones who care the most about what happens. We are the ones that will make the time. We need to know what to look for and what to expect. We need to know how to care for a patient at the end of life."[19] Gustafson points to the crucial importance on this journey to the end of life of patients having their family as empowered advocates. Families need to be taught how to provide care for the activities of daily living, and be involved in deciding what level of care is appropriate for the patient at any given time.

This writing is for all who serve as hospice caregivers, and especially for family members of dying loved ones in hospice care. As much as possible, hospice patients and caregivers share their personal experiences and stories of this journey to the end of life. The book is my way of sharing with you the reader practical ways we can be ever more present with the dying.

My deepest hope and prayer is that when the final days of life on this earth come naturally for you or your loved ones, that all of you may know the blessing of a Beautiful Death in the ancient hospice wisdom tradition of **hospes**, of true hospitality. The powerful tradition of the Hospice Way can truly change how you live and how you die. May your life be as enriched by hearing this story as much as mine has by telling the incredible saga of how companioning of the dying has unfolded through the ages in Western society.

Peace,

Rev. Dr. Ken Patrick

Winchester, Virginia

Part One

The Journey to a
Beautiful Death

Chapter 1

The Path

The patient was an elderly lady who lived out of a deep Quaker faith. As a hospice chaplain, I found her a wonderful person to visit. Her family had built a pleasant addition to the back of their home in the country so that this senior citizen could live out her final days in comfort and dignity. As the patient's illness progressed, she withdrew more and more from the presence of her loved ones. She increasingly found comfort and care by being with those friends from early childhood and family that had ended this earthly life. I asked the family if they had an old photo album of the patient's early life. It resulted in a delightful rainy afternoon spent with the patient lovingly reflecting on all the old, tattered memories of the past. The conversation was quiet and subdued and took a spiritual bent. With each photo, she reflected on how "the light" had come into her life with this person. It seemed as if she were going over her spiritual life story of what lessons her soul had learned on this earth. The light of awareness, of being awake, of enlightenment, was seen clearly as coming into her life through each person she had encountered. All were her spiritual teachers and she recounted for me what lessons she had learned in this school for her soul. I was startled that such a simple thing as gazing at dusty old photos could be so profoundly a spiritual art in an awakened soul's hands.

As her death approached, the patient went into a coma state. She was without communication with anyone for a few days when I went by for a final visit. As she lay quiet and still in her bed, I could hear the distinctive open mouth breathing that announced the end of life. For no real conscious reason that I could explain, I felt compelled to say to the patient, "I want you to do something for me. I want you to find the light. I know you know the light. It will lead you; it will guide you where you need to be. Find the light and follow it." A startling event took place. The patient opened her eyes for a brief second and looked at me. Although the daughter was in the room, I don't think she picked up the look of her mother. The look communicated so much from an old soul. It said, "Thank you, I can go now. I have found the light and it is leading me where I need to go." The patient died soon after that final visit.

This encounter and others like it have convinced me that care for the dying in hospice is a deeply spiritual art. Spirituality is rooted in the Latin word *spiritus*, which means "breath of life." [1] As breathe gives life to the body, so spirit gives life to the heart and soul. Spirituality has been understood as "the courage to look within and to trust. What is seen and trusted appears to be a deep sense of belonging, of wholeness, of connectedness, and of openness to the infinite." [2] The essence of spirituality is a view of human nature that recognizes the human longing for a relationship with a reality that is beyond the physical, finite world of form, and in this longing is the search for a deep and abiding meaning to life.[3]

In essence, the very nature of spirituality is to connect. Spirituality connects us, in living vital ways, to what is most real in life. Spirituality serves to connect us to what gives life meaning, purpose, and value. Spirituality is the connecting link to those experiences in body, heart, and soul, that makes life deep and rich, and truly worth living. Most of all spirituality connects us to experiences of peace, grace and forgiveness, both in the mundane everyday experiences of this life, as well as in our dying, and at the moment of our death.

For me, the connecting nature of spirituality can be illustrated in the image of a beaded necklace. Inside the necklace is an invisible thread that holds all the many beads together. That unseen thread in life is spirituality. It holds together all our connections to what we believe are sacred and holy, to what is valuable and gives our life true meaning. The necklace is more than simply the sum of the connecting thread and the many beads. It has a value of it own that is unique and special. The necklace is a good image for our spiritual journey. It represents what we have strung together in this life to form our spiritual walk on earth. Religion becomes, in this image, a beautiful bead on our necklace. True vital religions may perhaps be what Jesus called the "pearl of great price." For Christians, the great pearl on the necklace of our spiritual journey is salvation. For Buddhists, the great pearl on this journey is enlightenment. Religion is the precious pearl that is strung on the necklace of our spiritual walk. The pearl has the ability to give the necklace its worth and make it a thing of value. The invisible thread of spirituality holds the necklace together; it connects it all and makes it a whole.

As I visit hospice patients, I try to discern what is the nature of their thread, their spirituality. For some, it is weak and tattered, and perhaps a frayed string. For others, it is a strong, robust cord. And then I ponder with patients, "What are the beads that you have strung together on your spiritual necklace through your journey in life?" It may be a job, a career, a family, a special hobby; the possibilities are endless.

I remember simply asking an elderly hospice patient about a framed picture of a child by her bed in a nursing home. Her answer revealed the spiritual thread that connects her life together. She shared that she is a grandmother, in her heart and soul, and that is her great grandchild in the photo. As she talked about her family, the sleepy patient's eyes lighted up and begin to sparkle, and a gentle smile came across her deeply wrinkled face. Her voice became happy and excited. The words seem to tumble out of her as she shared what connected her heart to the depths of life; it was the sacred experience of having given birth and lived as a mother. A thread was revealed that connected her ninety years of life experiences of body, heart, and soul. That is the true nature of spirituality; to connect us with the sacred and the divine in the depths of life.

It is impossible to know ahead of time the nature of the thread of spirituality that connects a person with how they experience the infinite mystery of life. For some, spirituality may lie in times in nature, such as hiking, fishing, or camping, gardening, or walks in the woods. For others, spirituality may be found in experiences with buddies in military combat, when they shared harm and danger together as a "band of brothers." Others may express their spirituality in more traditional Western religious ways, such as "a walk with Jesus as their Lord," or in experiencing the presence of Christ in receiving the consecrated host in the Blessed Eucharist. Whatever way spirituality may be expressed, though, it always serves to connect us to the depths of the mystery of life.

One way to discern the spirituality of a patient, as we companion them in their final days, is to employ a simple spiritual practice that I call the "Innocence of the Present Moment." Spirituality is revealed by what gives a sparkle in the patient's eyes or a smile to their lips. It is shown by what they naturally want to talk about, by the pictures and little mementos they surround themselves with. If we bring the innocence of a child to our companioning of the dying, this same wonder and curiosity that children have, then the spirituality of the patient will often naturally be revealed. A childlike spirit sits and listens to stories, sometimes for hours, and wonders about them. A childlike spirit enjoys looking at pictures and souvenirs, and has fun being silly and laughing. A child will ask from the heart, "Who's that old person in the picture with you?," and really want to know the answer. The Innocence of the Present Moment is a beautiful way to companion the dying on their spiritual journey. When a loved one at the end of life is talking to the saints or angels, or someone long gone, our first impulse may be to correct them and set them straight or increase their medication. It is usually far better to simply sit with them as if you were little child full of inquisitive wonder about what is happening to them. After all, I seldom have visits from the angels or someone that has passed. What a great opportunity to ask questions about this mystery of life! The connecting thread of spirituality, though hidden, is the link to the deeply cherished experiences of the patient's life. It connects with the sacred depths of life.

The ancient Hospice Way is a spiritual companioning of the dying. As the spiritual writer Eckhart Tolle has said, "at death a door to the sacred is open for a brief time."[4] We find ourselves in the presence of the divine mystery.

I have set out to write down the essence of this eons old Hospice Way and make it available to other hospice workers and those who have charge of the care for the dying. Companioning the dying has long been recognized as a spiritual art in the East, as we see in the **Tibetan Book of the Dead and Dying,** and the publications and workshops of the Zen Hospice in California.[5] However, the spiritual nature of hospice in the West has yet to be fully recognized. Various hospice workers, such as the nurse Kathy Kalina in her writing, **Midwife for Souls, Spiritual Care For the Dying,** have expressed their personal experiences of the spiritual nature of death.[6] Yet there still remains the need to set out the spiritual foundation of hospice as a movement in our Western society, and to show how companioning the dying may be spiritually understood in a Western mind-set. The story of the Hospice Way needs to be told.

In our culture, it is difficult to engage the issue of death and dying. The personal philosophy of Woody Allen towards death is very much in vogue in our society today. Woody once quipped, "I don't mind dying; I just don't want to be there when it happens." We who live in a Western culture find death is the last great taboo, and it seems that none of us want to be there when "it" happens to us or our loved ones.[7] Death in this society may be the greatest personal challenge of our life. It seems that in our haste to embrace technology in the West, we have lost the art of how to companion the dying at the end of their spiritual journey in this earthly life. As a chaplain at Blue Ridge Hospice in Winchester, Virginia, I have observed day in and day out, skilled nurses, social workers, music therapists, and volunteers who have an incredible ability to practice this beautiful art of being with the dying in ways that bring deep comfort and compassion to those who need it most.

And yet it seems that this art is more an oral tradition than anything written. This book is an attempt to make available the very ancient hospice "spiritual tradition of the heart" of how to companion the dying.[8] In the midst of a society that lives in dread of death, we need signposts along the way to guide us as we walk with those who are taking the final steps of their journey on this earth. Companioning the dying has been recognized as a way to offer care and comfort to those at the end of life. Such writers as Greg Yoder and Alan D. Wolfelt have emphasized the importance of companioning in their book, *Companioning the Dying: A Soulful Guide for Counselors & Caregivers*.[9] However, as we will see, the Hospice Way has a unique and very special way of companioning the dying. There is a centuries old tradition of hospice companioning that we will explore.

Attitudes toward death and dying have changed dramatically from early civilizations, through the middle ages, and into our modern world of technology.[10] Hospice exists in our world today as a unique movement that takes as its mission that of allowing terminally ill persons to die with dignity, surrounded by those who are closest and most dear. Not to run away from death in fear or to deny the natural place of death at the end of life, but to face death with all the courage of the human spirit, with a concern for the individual and their entire family of caregivers as what needs to be nourished and cherished. United in this mission are people from all walks of life who provide comfort and care when it is needed most at the end of life. It is an amazing story to tell.[11] The saga unfolds as a tale of how to truly companion the dying in their final days, as perhaps the most profound spiritual art that a human being can practice.

The Hospice Way stretches from the time of monasteries of the middle ages, when the comfort of hospices was first given to weary, dying, travelers returning from spiritual pilgrimages, to Dr. Cicely Saunders' residential medical center in London dedicated to the care of the dying in the 1960's, to the pioneering work of Kubler-Ross, to care for the terminally ill in homes and residential centers today throughout cities, villages, and hamlets in the United States and throughout the world. So many faces and so many places make up this spiritual story of extraordinary hospitality extended with courage, hope, and vision to those at the end of their life.

The abiding spiritual theme of this Hospice Way through the years is expressed in the Latin root for the word **hospes** which means both host and guest.[12] The hospice spiritual tradition is a caring between practitioner and recipient, a radical sharing of hospitality. The Latin word emphasizes a dynamic interaction, or a process that is taking place between fellow humans, and not simply a physical location or one event. We see hospitality in hospice as dignified acts of caring that flow from a welcoming and inviting heart of the caregiver and shared with the dying and their loved ones. Marjorie J. Thompson, in her work, ***Soul Feast, An Invitation to The Christian Spiritual Life,*** has a beautiful understanding of the spiritual essence of hospitality. She writes that:

> *"Hospitality means receiving the other, from the heart, into my own dwelling place. It entails providing for the need, comfort, and delight of the other with all the openness, respect, freedom, tenderness, and joy that love itself embodies."*[13]

This profoundly spiritual concept of hospitality has unfortunately been thoroughly trivialized in our day to day world in Western society. We often see hospitality as a "meek and mild" caring that is reserved for simply social graces. A popular view is that of "southern hospitality." This brings to mind an image of a grandfatherly man like Colonel Sanders. Hospitality is visualized as a gracious old gentleman in a gleaming white suit with a straw hat and a cane. He is sitting out on the veranda of a stately old southern mansion having a mint julep and engaged in pleasant conversation. Inside is a beautiful table adorned with a fine lace table cloth, family china and generations old silver. There are servants bustling back and forth, taking care of every need. Hospitality is simply being nice and polite, and saying the correct thing, so that no one is upset or even mildly ruffled. The spiritual view of hospitality is totally different from this secularized image.

Spiritually, hospitality is a radical concept that demands our heart and soul. While social graces may be a part of spiritual hospitality, there is a much deeper and more profound dimension. Spiritual hospitality calls us to truly make room in our heart and soul, our very lives, for the needs of another person. It is a putting others first and yourself second in order to make another person feel loved and accepted. It is easy to be nice to be people when they are nice to you. However, spiritual hospitality is extending our heart in times and situations and with people that may not be pleasant or likeable.

We may contrast the image of southern hospitality and Colonel Sanders on the veranda with an image of radical spiritual hospitality that is drawn from a death camp in Nazi Germany during the holocaust. The depths of spiritual hospitality are revealed in the life of Saint Maximillian Kolbe, priest hero of Auschwitz.[14]

Kolbe was born on January 7, 1894 in Zdunska Wola, Poland. After suffering tuberculosis during his youth, he was a frail man for the rest of his life. Yet, he became a Doctor of Theology and also founded the Immaculate Movement. He fostered the growth of his movement through a magazine promoting Marian Spirituality, The Knight of the Immaculate. As a Franciscan Priest, he served in missionary work in Japan, but because of poor health he found it necessary to return to Poland.

At the City of Mary Immaculate, Father Kolbe and other friars began to organize a shelter for three thousand Polish refugees, including two thousand Jews. As an act of spiritual hospitality, the friars shared everything they had with the refugees. They housed, fed, and clothed them, and brought all their resources into use in their service. Father

Kolbe wrote, "We must do everything in our power to help these unfortunate people who have been driven from their homes and deprived of even the most basic necessities. Our mission is among them in the days that lie ahead."[15]

In 1941 he was arrested by the Nazis, on charges of aiding Jews and the Polish underground. Father Kolbe was eventually sent to the concentration camp at Auschwitz, one of the principal death camps of the holocaust. There he was branded as prisoner number 16670. He was assigned to a special work group staffed by priests and supervised by guards who were especially vicious and abusive. It is said that his calm dedication to the faith brought him the worst jobs available, and more beatings than anyone else. At one point, he was beaten, lashed, and left for dead. It was his fellow prisoners who were able to smuggle him into the camp hospital where the priest spent his time in recovery hearing confessions. When he returned to the camp, Father Kolbe ministered to the other prisoners, including conducting mass and ministering communion using smuggled bread and wine. Father Kolbe wrote: "Every man has an aim in life. For most men it is to return home to their wives and families, or to their mothers. For my part, I give my life for the good of all men."[16]

Eventually in July 1941, there was an occasion in which a man in Father Kolbe's cell block had escaped. All of the men from that block were brought out into the hot sun and made to stand all day with no food or water. At the end of the day, the man that had escaped had not yet been found.

Commandant Karl Fritsch, the camp commander, told the men that ten prisoners would die in place of the one that had escaped. Some men were chosen to die in reprisal for a prisoner's escape. The Commandant relished walking along the ranks. "This one, that one," the camp commander said as he issued orders. The Polish Sergeant Franciszek Gajowniczek was selected. When the sentence of doom had been pronounced, Gajowniczek cried out in despair, "Oh, my poor wife, my poor children. I shall never see them again."[17] As they were being marched away to the starvation bunkers, prisoner Number 16670 dared to step from the line. The commandant asked, "What does this Polish pig want?" Father Kolbe pointed to the Polish Sergeant, saying, "I want to die in place of that father of a family, I beg you to accept the offer of my life."[18] There was no mention of a name, no statement of fame. Silence. The commandant was dumbfounded. His only reply was: "And why?' The answer was very simple. "Because I am old and useless. My life is not worth anything, while he has a wife and family."

Fritsch asked, "Who are you?" His eyes toward the ground, the Franciscan quietly answered: "A Catholic priest." There was a moment of silence, and then Fritsch motioned with his hand, showing that the offer of one life for another had been accepted.[19] Father Kolbe went with the nine prisoners. In the "block of death" they were ordered to strip naked and the slow starvation began in darkness. But there was no screaming—the prisoners sang.

Bruno Borgowiec was an eyewitness of those terrible last days, for he was an assistant to the janitor and an interpreter in the under grown bunkers. He tells us what happened:

In the cell of the poor wretches there were daily loud prayers, the rosary and singing, in which prisoners from neighboring cells also joined. When no SS men were in the block, I went to the bunker to talk to the men and comfort them. Fervent prayers and songs to the Holy Mother resounded in all the corridors of the bunker. I had the impression I was in a church. Father Kolbe was leading and the prisoners responded in unison. They were often so deep in prayer that they did not even hear that inspecting SS men had descended to the bunker; and the voices fell silent only at the loud yelling of their visitors.

When the cells were opened the poor wretches cried loudly and begged for a piece of bread and for water, which they did not receive, however. If any of the stronger ones approached the door he was immediately kicked in the stomach by the SS men, so that falling backwards on the cement floor he was instantly killed; or he was shot to death ... Father Kolbe bore up bravely, he did not beg and did not complain but raised the spirits of the others. ...Since they had grown very weak, prayers were now only whispered. At every inspection, when almost all the others were now lying on the floor, Father Kolbe was seen kneeling or standing in the centre as he looked cheerfully in the face of the SS men. Two weeks passed in this way. Meanwhile one after

11

another they died, until only Father Kolbe was left. This the authorities felt was too long; the cell was needed for new victims. So one day they brought in the head of the sick quarters, a German, a common criminal named Bock, who gave Father Kolbe an injection of carbolic acid in the vein of his left arm. Father Kolbe, with a prayer on his lips, gave his arm to the executioner. Unable to watch this I left under the pretext of work to be done. Immediately after the SS men with the executioner had left I returned to the cell, where I found Father Kolbe leaning in a sitting position against the back wall with his eyes open and his head dropping sideways. His face was calm and radiant."[20]

They burned his body in the camp oven with all the others and scattered his ashes. Father Kolbe was beatified by the Roman Catholic Church in 1971 and canonized in 1982.

It is reported that the heroism of Father Kolbe went echoing through Auschwitz.[21] In that desert of hatred he had sown love. Through this incredible act of spiritual hospitality even such a place as the infamous Auschwitz death camp was changed.

Mr. Jozef Stemler, former director of a cultural institute in Poland, comments: "In those conditions ... in the midst of brutalization of thought and feeling and words such as had never before been known, man indeed became a ravening wolf in his relations with other men. And into this state of affairs came the heroic self-sacrifice of Father Maximilian. The atmosphere grew lighter, as this thunderbolt provoked its profound and salutary shock."[22] Mr. Bielecki declared that Father Kolbe's death was "a shock filled with hope, bringing new life and strength. ...It was like a powerful shaft of light in the darkness of the camp."[23]

There is indeed a redeeming and profoundly transforming quality to spiritual hospitality that is far beyond social graces, one that is radical in its ability to change individual lives and even entire communities. In the great depths of suffering and misery at Auschwitz, the spiritual hospitality of St. Maximilian Kolbe had a powerful effect. It was truly a "light that shines in the darkness."

St. Kolbe shows us the true nature of spiritual hospitality, which contrasts so starkly with simply being nice to others as a form of social politeness. While we may not experience spiritual hospitality to the incredible depths of this saint, the spiritual nature of hospitality calls us to truly make room in our hearts for the needs of others. It is the transformation of the heart that is needed most. As St. Kolbe writes: "The real conflict is the inner conflict. Beyond armies of occupation and the hecatombs of extermination camps, there are irreconcilable enemies in the depth of every soul: good and evil, sin and love. And what use are the victories on the battlefield if we ourselves are defeated in our innermost personal selves?"[24]

Contrasted with gracious southern hospitality is the image of a sick, beaten priest in the midst of a death camp freely offering up his life so that another prisoner may live. In the midst of unspeakable horror is an act of hope and compassion that truly makes room for another. This is the character and the transforming power of spiritual hospitality, although the depths of this hospitality are rarely glimpsed in our world today. The full revelation of spiritual hospitality, such as in the life of St. Maximilian Kolbe, is understood by the Christian community as sainthood.

It is this transforming spiritual hospitality that is the driving force and the true power of the Hospice Way through the ages. Hospice reveals to the world the incredible depths of *hospes*. It has the ability to change lives and even the nation in which we live in ways that are beyond the ability of words to express. In the first centuries of western history, monks and nuns cared for the sick and dying who were on spiritual pilgrimages as an expression of monastic spiritual hospitality, and here we find the birth of hospice. The contemporary monk, Father Daniel Homan, states that we have lost today the radical character of spiritual hospitality that infused the monastic life of early Christians. We see hospitality as "safe and cozy, even productive, rather than revolutionary, risky, and world rattling."[25] In their care of strangers on pilgrimages, "monasteries saved lives when they opened their doors to strangers. It was not about comfort and entertainment- it was about saving lives."[26]

While we may never be called to be like St. Maximilian Kolbe and give our life for a stranger, all who companion those at the end of life following this ancient Hospice Way are called as caregivers to open themselves to another who is dying. Can we let a dying person bring their pain and discomfort into our neat, ordered lives, and change our schedules and priorities? Can we companion them in all the messiness and disorder of dying? Can our heart and soul, indeed our very lives, be opened up that much? When we have the courage to do this, the awesome power of spiritual hospitality and this Hospice Way will be revealed in our midst as a life-changing presence to both the host and the guest.

To be involved in serving in the Hospice Way today is to stand in a long lineage of hospice caregivers who have practiced what I call *"the spiritual art of hospitality."* This spiritual art can be expressed in terms of every religion professed by mankind on the earth, for hospitality is one of the common threads that weave us together as one humanity expressing our belief in the infinite. This common way of hospitality for all the world religions is considered in an endnote.[27]

As we have seen, spirituality is the direct experience of that which gives our lives meaning and purpose, a meaning that goes beyond merely material experience, however successful. Religion is not the same thing as spirituality. Religion may be one way that persons give expression or have an experience of spirituality. The essence of religion is the organization of belief which is common to a culture or subculture, "the codified, institutionalized, and ritualized expressions of peoples' communal connections to the Ultimate." [28] Hospice today embraces the spiritual nature of companioning the dying, while it does not identify with, or promote, any particular religious belief system. Spiritual hospitality offers a gracious acceptance of patients and families in hospice, regardless of religious stance. They are free to believe and practice (or not practice) whatever religious beliefs that serve to connect them spiritually to the Ultimate. It is this spiritual thread of hospitality that weaves the Hospice Way together through the ages.

The spiritual art of hospitality is a true spiritual art that flows from the welcoming and inviting heart of the caregiver. This art graciously provides nurture for the needs of the body, heart, and soul of the dying, and those most precious to them, through seven spiritual practices.

The purpose of this book is to present the companioning of the dying through the centuries old Hospice Way as a *spiritual work* and indeed as a true *spiritual art*. Regardless of the role of the hospice caregiver, be it nurse, social worker, music therapist, or healer in other fields, it is the spiritual art of hospitality that most deeply touches the life of a dying person and their family, and brings comfort and care when it is needed most. It is this very ancient spiritual art that is the true vitality of the hospice movement and the very reason for its existence in the world today.

As the modern hospice worker fills out countless forms, reports, and a computer generated "Plan of Care" with carefully stated patient interventions, the reason for this blizzard of paperwork can easily be forgotten. It all goes back to *practicing the spiritual art of hospitality in our modern technological world.* How much we need to recover the spiritual foundation of hospice! As Kathleen Dowling Singh writes in *The Grace in Dying, A Message of Hope, Comfort, and Spiritual Transformation,* "It is my observation that the average hospice, now moved solidly within the Medicare system and thus increasingly concerned with cost effectiveness, has virtually no capacity-and often no inclination or adequate understanding-to provide transpersonal care or guidance."[29] She also emphasizes, "Many hospices, in fact, give no more than lip service to the possibility that dying is other than a medical event." [30]

This book is a response to a very practical need to set forth the ancient tradition of hospice work for those who are both guests and hosts in hospice today. As we will seek to show, it is upon the eons old spiritual art of hospitality that the entire hospice movement today rests as it provides care for those at the end of life.

Hospice has been defined by the Hospice Education Institute as "….a philosophy of caring which respects and values the dignity and worth of each person, and good hospice care is the practical expression of that personal and professional commitment. Hospice cares for people approaching death, but hospices cherish and emphasize life, by helping patients (and those who love and care for them) live each day to the fullest."[31] It is the spiritual story of this hospice philosophy of caring that we will tell.

This story is shared not just to satisfy idle curiosity, but to enable us as hospice caregivers to face death with courage.   It is as we stand in the face of death that we learn how seasoned we truly are in this spiritual work. We find again and again the need for the spiritual art of hospitality in our lives.

The greatest of all hospitalities is toward ourselves, as we say "Yes" to our own finite, mortal life. I call this *"practicing the spiritu-*

al art of self-hospitality." Far from being a sad and depressing story, the hospice spiritual story unfolds as one that brings to us what Christ called "the fullness of life." The dying have many lessons to teach us, but above all they show us how precious life is, and how we may live our lives filled with wonder, depth, and beauty.

However, amid all the business of modern, everyday living, the beauty of each moment easily escapes us. We slip into a world of regrets called "past" or a world of anxiety and fear called "future." But it is in the present moment where life truly is lived as joyful. The dying come into our lives to teach us this lesson. They show us that at each moment we have all that we need to be fully alive. As we say "Yes" to our suffering, death, and mortality as a practice of the spiritual art of self-hospitality, we experience an eternal dimension of our existence that unfolds in a simple, mysterious way.

Elizabeth Edwards, whom *Time Magazine* calls, "A courageous role model for the millions who live with cancer," speaks of her lessons regarding the way cancer changed her life as she faced her own death.[32] She shares the insights learned from practicing the spiritual art of self-hospitality. She finds that "Cancer is powerful. It can stop whole lives and start new ones. It is the ultimate dark drama. Cancer brings a crisp urgency to every hour: Live right, live well, live now. Take each day and create. Create good, create love. Cancer touches everyone around it and can bring wisdom and learning. Learning to love and let go."[33] For Elizabeth, the beauty in a courageous saying "Yes" to her finite life is the great lesson cancer teaches. This beauty in life flows from the spiritual practice of the art of self-hospitality.

The hospice movement is an unfolding story of spiritual hospitality. It speaks of those through the centuries who have practiced a fearless hospitality as they opened their homes, their hearts and souls to fellow brothers and sisters facing their final days on earth.

Through being with the dying, we can discover for ourselves seven spiritual practices that form the spiritual art of hospitality. As we unfold the hospice story, we will explore each of these practices and show how they are rooted in the history and tradition of the Hospice Way. These spiritual practices express the face of hospice both down through the centuries as well as today. They are the heart of the Hospice Way.

> The first spiritual practice of the art of hospitality is observing the dignity of the patient above all else.

"Death with dignity" is the spiritual foundation of all hospice care for the dying. Death can be difficult and messy. It may be perhaps one of the most difficult things to experience. As one dying patient told me, "I haven't had much practice with this." As a spiritual art, hospice care respects the many ways that death unfolds for the patient, and honors that unfolding with dignity. Very simple things can bring dignity to the patient, such as simply giving them a measure of control over their life. It may be just letting them choose their own meals, or changing the channel on the remote. As you look for ways to honor the dignity of a dying person, the spiritual practice unfolds.

In a nutshell, this first spiritual practice calls the hospice caregiver to respect the dying for the unique person that they are, regardless of their race, religion, beliefs, gender, sexual orientation, nationality or social status. Hospice respects the dying.

Even now I vividly recall meeting with one terminally ill lady. She looked very sad and unhappy. It was past nine in the morning, and she was still in her bathrobe. This patient was always up early and prided herself on her looking attractive. I simply said, "You look unhappy," and she replied, "I'm disgusted." "What about?" I asked. "It's past nine and I'm still not dressed. The nurses have just left me here." "O.K." I said, leaving the room, "I'll go get an aide to help you get dressed." A simple thing, to go get an aide, but it is a deep spiritual practice to honor the dignity of a dying person. This is truly the Hospice Way of companioning the dying.

> The second spiritual practice in the art of hospitality is providing palliative care, focusing on pain management and symptom control.

This second spiritual practice is a unique art, as hospice provide end of life *care* and not medical *cure*. Palliative care is understood in the broadest sense as care that alleviates pain, discomfort and distress for the body heart and soul of the patient.[35] A major focus of hospice care is the management of pain and physical symptoms as the body makes the journey to the end of life. It is a beautiful experience to observe skilled hospice nurses, social workers, music therapists and chaplains at Blue Ridge Hospice bring this sacred gift to patients. Palliative care is often associated with just pain management, but it can be so much more than this. It can be a powerful, yet simple experience, such as just getting a drink of water for a patient, or careful hand feeding of a meal from the food tray. Just the awareness that a patient is uncomfortable in bed and finding another pillow for them can be a practice of this spiritual art.

What a profound opportunity there is to practice this spiritual art as we provide palliative care in companioning the dying. I watched a spiritually awake hospice nurse get a straw for a patient with a smile. As she said, "Here you go sweetie," I was reminded of the Japanese tea ceremony that in Buddhism is used to reveal an awakened presence in the world. The nurse revealed a deep presence of compassion and gentle care as she brought "one pointed" attention to picking up a straw and making it available to the patient. It was as if the world stopped for that moment in time, and all that mattered was this act of being fully present to the simplest need of the dying person. That is the practice of the spiritual art of hospitality, and the opportunities for this practice are virtually endless in palliative care for the dying.

The World Health Organization points to this spiritual nature of palliative care in their definition of this healing art: "Palliative care improves the quality of life of patients and families who face life-threatening illness, by providing pain and symptom relief, spiritual and psychosocial support from diagnosis to the end of life and bereavement. Effective palliative care requires a broad multidisciplinary approach that includes the family and makes use of available community resources..."[36]

One particularly powerful expression of spiritual care through the use of palliative therapy has emerged in music therapy. Historically music has deep, ancient roots, and can provide a "peaceful holding environment" that makes for effective palliative care.

In a recent *"Physician Newsletter"* Dr. Mai Amy Ha, medical director at Blue Ridge Hospice in Winchester, Virginia stated some of the important palliative effects of music therapy. She writes that this therapy can "…help relax patient's symptoms with live music, through the manipulation of tempo and volume to correspond to the patient's breathing pattern or to the rise and fall of the patient's chest."[37] Another significant effect of music therapy in palliative care is in the management of pain. Music therapy has the benefit of helping relax patients' symptoms of pain with live music, through distracting and refocusing patients through relaxation techniques and guided imagery.[38] Music therapy may also help patients produce music time lines of their lives or help compose songs about their lives. This "Life Review" for the patient can recount life experiences, successes, and sometimes failures that may bring for closure in their lives.[39]

Modern research has shown a significant difference for quality of life for those patients at the end of life who received music therapy.[40] It has been shown that the more music therapy sessions a patient received, the higher their quality of life, even as their physical health declined.[41] Music therapy has also been demonstrated to increase spiritual well-being for the terminally ill.[42]

As a hospice chaplain, I have observed in working with patients the powerful palliative effect that music therapy has for many individuals. This may extend to the families as well, for many spouses and loved ones find music therapy a vital resource for their dealing with grief and loss.

Another crucial aspect of palliative care in hospice is what I call **gracious listening**. This is a way of being present by a caregiver that places the needs of the patient first in a conversation. It brings the simple yet powerful message to the companioning process that "this is about you and your needs and not about me and my needs." Gracious listening creates space in the relationship for the patient to be truly heard and known as a unique human being. It allows a person to express what Cicely Saunders calls "total pain; the emotional and spiritual dimensions of suffering." Through gracious listening pain felt in the heart and in the soul can be brought into the companioning process on this journey to the end of life.

I still visit a patient who has loved for many years to walk her dog down the lane of her house out in the country. Because of the progression of her physical decline, she has to remain inside these days. It is real suffering for her not to be able to go to the mailbox with her dog each day. This is the emotional face of "total pain." Spiritually, she asks why this awful disease happened to her when she reads the Bible, prays to Jesus each day, and tries to be a "good person." This is the spiritual face of "total pain." The emotional and spiritual nature of her pain is just as real and just as debilitating as the physical pain of her body's decline. The ancient Hospice Way embraces palliative care as a truly spiritual art that cares for the physical, emotional, and spiritual pain that may be a part of the journey to the end of life.

> The third spiritual practice of the art of hospitality is compassionate care for the entire family of the dying person and empowering the family to companion the patient.

Hospice seeks to have no terminally ill person die alone unless it is of their own choosing. At the end of the day, it is natural to long to be surrounded by those who have been our caring companions on this life's journey. The family in hospice care may be the traditional family as we know it, but it may also include an extended family such as pets or social acquaintances. Who are we judge the boundaries of the human heart? A beloved dog or cat may hold a place of honor in the heart of the dying, and be in the inner circle of family members. We practice the art of spiritual hospitality as we extend care and concern to the family of the dying, however this family may be expressed.

Hospice companioning invites the family to become involved in the care of the patient, and be an advocate for this care. The hospice nurses are available to empower the family to provide essential palliative care in the home. Hospice social workers also work closely with family members to enable them to be a vital part of the companioning of the patient. The family is not on the sidelines in hospice companioning, unless they choose to be.

It comes as no surprise that hospice traditionally provides bereavement care for the family of the dying person, because the needs of the family extend beyond the death of the patient. Unlike a modern hospital setting, in hospice there is care intentionally offered to the whole family of loved ones as an integral part of the practice of spiritual hospitality, and the family is graciously invited to take part in this journey to the end of life with a loved one.

A family member of a patient who had been in Blue Ridge Hospice shared with me that she was so thankful that "hospice care always comes with a warranty." I asked her what she meant by that. She explained that "hospice doesn't forget the family when the patient dies. There's a hospice warranty for giving care that goes on beyond the life of a loved one." This was well said. The family of the dying person is cared for in the practice of this spiritual art called hospice.

> The fourth spiritual practice of the art of hospitality is providing care ideally in the home of the patient or a home-like residential facility.

Unlike traditional Western medicine, the Hospice Way provides patient care that is focused on the home, or a facility that is as much like a home as possible. The home is the place where we experience life with our family, which has so many different ways of being expressed today. Home and family are often hard to separate in the spiritual practice of hospitality, for they blend into one another as places of care.

There are profound implications for health care in America today in this Hospice Way of intentionally including the home and family in the care of a terminally ill person. Once the home and the family are removed from the picture, and no longer are the primary place of care and the means of care for a loved one dying a natural death, the nature of death changes radically. Care is then left to "the professionals," such as certified nursing assistants, nurses, and doctors. The cost of this care for the 78 million Baby Boomers as they journey to the end of life is simply beyond the financial capacity of our nation. The ancient Hospice Way makes financial sense today: empower the family to companion the patient on this way to life's end, and use professional caregivers only as they are truly needed on this journey. A combination of federal and state income tax credits for "stay at home companions" of the terminally ill would empower many families to have a loved one at home rather than in a nursing home or assisted living facility. Hospice residential centers could provide another level of care for families who are companioning loved ones. The entire hospice team could serve as a resource for empowering families as they make this journey to the end of life with the dying.

The ancient Hospice Way calls us to care for the family of the dying and enable the family to be care giving companions on this journey to the end of life. From this companioning, a natural death at home may well become the normal way of death in our country. This leads us to consider the special place of home in the Hospice Way.

The home is the normal and natural place for hospitality in our lives. Our deepest experiences of hospitality in life are usually found in the places where, since childhood, we were provided food, shelter and care. For most of us, for better or worse, this is our home. The spiritual art of hospitality in hospice unfolds as care in the home, or an institutional setting that is made to be as close to the home as possible.

At Blue Ridge Hospice, each patient's room in the residential unit has been professionally decorated to make it seem like a cozy room in a warm and inviting house. All of the rooms have special color schemes and furnishings, and each one speaks of home and family. Patients bring into their rooms pictures of loved ones and often little mementos, such as an embroidered pillow. A happy golden retriever and her gentle owner (a hospice volunteer) as well as other dogs come to visit patients and make them feel at home. Most everyone seems to enjoy petting a dog with a wagging tail and bright, sparkling eyes. Both staff and volunteers sometimes make special treats for patients, like a plate of warm cookies that fills a room with a delightful aroma. (They taste good too, as they are sometimes shared with the chaplain). A hospice staff music therapist can often be heard playing a guitar and singing in a soft voice. Sometimes a patient will sing along to a familiar song that harkens back to happy days.

Home. What is it? On our hospice residential unit at Blue Ridge Hospice this place of the heart is expressed in a homey room in the *sight* of pictures of people that are loved ones, in the furry *touch* of rubbing a soft dog, through the *smell* of freshly baked cookies, in the *taste* of a special treat, and in the cheery *sound* of the singing of pleasant familiar song. Here we see reflected a dimension of the Hospice Way of companioning the dying through spiritual hospitality. It is a special spiritual art that speaks to our heart and soul.

Hospice spirituality is an embodied spirituality that embraces all of the senses of the human body as we journey with the dying in their final days. We all yearn to find that hospitality of a place called home, and hospice offers this to the dying, either in a companioning in their own homes or in a special residential unit which is as homelike as possible. Hospice spirituality lives out the saying, "home is where the heart is." It is natural to experience death at the end of a terminal illness in a place that we know in our heart and soul as our home. Here we are safe and comfortable. Here we have our routines of life. Here is the most natural place in all the world to find the spiritual art of hospitality lived out. The Hospice Way truly calls us home.

The Hospice Way provides for the companioning of the dying and their families in whatever place might be called home as the journey of life draws to a close: be it a house or apartment, or a hospice residential center that is designed to be as close to a home as possible. Home speaks of what we value in life. This is reflected in pictures and furnishings, in the way space is arranged for our daily living. I always enjoy seeing the pictures and personal mementos that patients and families cherish in whatever place is called home. The home is rich with the spirit of those we companion. Home is a place of stories and rituals. It is not simply a physical place, but a place that tells us of the relationships (or lack of relationships) that have taken place in life. Home can be seen as a space that is bounded by the unique and special values and meaning that the patient and family bring to this journey of life.[43] Home is the natural space in which we come to experience hospitality.

This Hospice Way of empowering the family to companion a loved one at home could change the very face of dying in the United States. As death is seen as a normal and natural part of the life cycle, families would have an incredible opportunity to educate younger generations on death and dying. Rather than being "strange" or creepy," death in our homes could be accepted as a normal part of the course of the journey on this Earth.

Think of the profound consequences in the life of a small child who is with a grandparent day by day as this elderly person makes their journey to the end of life. The life transforming power of the spiritual art of hospitality could be revealed in the care offered by family members. The child could be invited to be part of this care, and the companioning at home of the dying could speak so deeply to a little one's natural curiosity and wonder about life and death. Not only is the nation saved countless expense by enabling families to companion a loved one at home, but we are spiritually and emotionally enriched by sharing the full drama of life and death in our homes. The ancient Hospice Way calls us to care for the family of the dying and enable the family to be care giving companions on this journey to the end of life. Such is the inseparable place of home and family in the Hospice Way.

This brings us to the next spiritual practice of this ancient spiritual art.

> The fifth spiritual practice in the art of hospitality is allowing all care to be determined by the needs of they dying, as much as possible.

In the Hospice Way of companioning the dying, the patient is the one to say how they will make the final journey in this life. No expert has the answers, for the true expert in our dying is the patient and this is embraced in hospice care. In the practice of the spiritual art of hospitality, the patient knows best.

The guiding principle is that we are to be their companions along the way, not the other way around. This requires sensitivity to the patient, a gentle listening to what is being said by the patient through their body, heart, and soul. The patient may decide, for example, to stop eating for a while as death draws near. This decision on the part of the dying needs our respect and support. I have seen more than one hospice patient "chewed out" by a nurse in a nursing home when they pushed away their food tray.

While visiting a dying patient with an older "seasoned" hospice chaplain, I listened as a patient shared how hard it was for her to eat as her life drew to a close. In our conversation in her room, Mary related that when the nurse came in today with a big tray after she already said she wasn't hungry, she told the nurse to "go to hell" and said "I damn well don't have to eat this crap if I don't want to and you can't make me." There was silence in the room after this powerful expression of emotions. I looked at the older chaplain to see what response he was going to make to the patient. He knew well the spiritual art of hospitality. Father Fred's reply was beautiful. He looked Mary right in the eyes and said, "You go girl!" How much we need the practice of the spiritual art of hospitality today which allows, as much as can possible, for the care of the dying to be patient directed.

Sacred palliative care can be profoundly expressed through skilled pain management that meets the patient's needs. Hospice can provide for a "kit" with needed pain medicine in the home of the hospice patient. Not only is medicine for comfort available to the patient as they decide if and when it is needed, but this takes place in the home and the family has a role to play in providing the medicine at the end of life. I have observed hospice nurses working with patients and providing palliative pain relief as a true art form. They are sensitive to the needs of the patient and know the drugs that will comfort most. In my final days, I hope that I can be companioned by a hospice nurse who knows the spiritual art of hospitality and allows me to decide on my care along the way.

The sixth spiritual practice in the art of hospitality is providing holistic care through a health care team.

The dying person is a marvelous and wonderful human being, who brings to hospice the gift of a unique body, heart, and soul. As the **Psalmist** puts it, "We are fearfully and wonderfully made." (**Psalm** 139:14). To be a companion with the dying is to honor and respect all the diversity of their life. Hospice provides a ***team approach*** to caring for the dying. The team of a doctor, nurse, social worker, and other caregivers such as music therapists, chaplains and volunteers are part of the patient care in order to honor and respect all the many dimensions of the patient's life. The team approach is basic to the practice of a holistic hospitality in hospice care. Each team member has their special walk in companioning the dying. The ancient Hospice Way provides for companioning in body, heart, and soul for both the patient and the family.

A hospice social worker once asked me to visit a dying patient who had apparently no place for religion or the church in his life. The patient was asking to see a chaplain. As I went by and sat in the patient's living room, he expressed his desire to get married in his final days. He didn't know if it was possible or not, but that was what he wanted. I gathered for him information on how to get a wedding license and what was involved. And so we had a hospice wedding that took place at the dying person's bed. As he struggled to get his breath, low, faint wedding vows were shared. The "honeymoon" was simply the couple holding each other in the bed. The patient died shortly afterwards in the same bed. The practice of the art of spiritual hospitality in hospice is holistic to the core: it responds to the needs of the patient's body, heart and soul.

> The seventh spiritual practice in the art of hospitality is to foster a sacred presence through nature and all of creation.

Hospice companioning of the dying fosters, as a spiritual practice, a sacred companioning by nature itself and by all of the natural creation. As the authors of **Innovations in Hospice Architecture** have written: "The relationship between nature and the management of the patient's pain is a critical facet of palliative care… ." [44]

There are several important ways that this spiritual practice of companioning through nature forms a basic dimension of the spiritual art of hospitality in the Hospice Way. From the earliest ages in the West, healing gardens have been used as therapeutic interventions designed to provide care of the body, heart and soul. We can trace this hospice spiritual practice of connecting to nature back to the monastery courtyards and cloistered gardens of the Middle Ages. Restorative gardens for the sick and dying were a vital part of palliative care from the Middle Ages to the early twentieth century. A garden provides a place of beauty where renewal and wholeness can occur physically, emotionally, and spiritually. [45] In the long history of the hospice movement, we find that the monastic hospice usually had a garden. The fostering of a companioning through nature has long been a part of the hospice tradition.

In the Middle Ages, a primary means of palliative care for the poor,

Medieval Gardens

In medieval times, a garden could have a symbolic and spiritual dimension. The hortus conclusus or 'enclosed garden' was a sacred area which might represent the Christian soul, enclosed in the body, or the Church formed of the body of the faithful. It was also, in the late Middle Ages, an image of the Blessed Virgin Mary identified with the bride in the Song of Songs in the Old Testament.[47]

the sick, the destitute and the dying was the use of herbs in the practice of monastic medicine. We see this care in the hospices, monastic infirmaries and leper houses of the time. The herb garden was a common link to nature in the palliative care offered the dying.

Modern clinical research has pointed to important therapeutic benefits of gardens in patient, family and staff care. As Roger S. Ulrich has written in "*Health Benefits of Gardens in Hospitals,*" "...there is mounting evidence that gardens function [as] especially effective and beneficial settings with respect to fostering restoration for stressed patients, family members and staff." [46]

In modern times, we see hospice palliative care employing the powerful analgesic natural drug morphine. This has been called the "prototype narcotic drug" and the "gold standard" against which all other opioids are tested. Morphine was first isolated in 1804 by the German pharmacist Frederick Wilhelm Adam Sertuner, who named it "morphium" after Morpheus, the Greek God of dreams. In Greek mythology, Morpheus has the ability to take any human's form and appear in dreams. He is the son of Hypnos, the god of sleep. He sleeps on an ebony bed in a dimly lit cave, surrounded by poppy flowers.[50]

The source of morphine is the opium poppy (*papaver somniferum*).[51] Raw opium contains about twenty alkoid substances, one of which is morphine, in a typical yield of ten percent . In modern hospice palliative care, morphine is used as a powerful anesthetic which has the added benefit of not decreasing consciousness. The drug also suppresses the respiratory system, which can be of great value in relieving distress for many patients at the end of life. In the palliative use of morphine we see again a link to nature through the natural healing powers of the opium plant.

A sacred presence through nature and all of creation is also reflected in modern times in both the natural setting and architecture of many hospice residential units. The grounds of the Connecticut Hospice, the first free-standing hospice in this country, have spacious land for walking, contact with the ocean, and wooded trails.

At the Maitri AIDS Hospice in San Francisco, everyone in the hospice is invited to be involved in the care of the indoor plants. Patients are allowed to adopt one or more plants and provide for their care while they are in the hospice.

At the end of life, the effects of advanced disease and the side effects of medical treatment can bring for the dying anxiety, stress and deep restlessness. A sacred link to nature through a natural setting of peace and beauty, as well as architecture designed to foster the presence of nature, can help provide comfort and care to patients and families in hospice.

Another aspect of this spiritual practice of sacred presence through all of creation is the use of animals as companions with the dying. In many hospices today, dogs and cats become a powerful presence with those at the end of life. All types of animals have been used in Animal-Assisted therapy and applied to companioning the dying in hospice work. These include dogs, cats, elephants, birds, dolphins, rabbits, lizards and other small animals. Companioning with horses is known as equine-assisted therapy or therapeutic horseback riding.

Companioning with animals in a 2007 meta-analysis found that there are many beneficial outcomes from animal-assisted therapy. These included a reduction in anxiety and loneliness, as well as increased attention skills and increased self-esteem.

Through the ages, hospice has fostered a sacred relation with nature and all of creation. This has included gardens and natural outdoor settings as part of hospice care, as well as architecture that reflects a bond to nature.

We have now considered all seven practices that together make up the spiritual art of hospitality. Each practice is foundational to the ancient Hospice Way of companioning the dying on their journey to the end of life, It is important to reflect on how the spiritual practices are shown in hospice care.

> The ancient Hospice Way expresses the practices of the spiritual art of hospitality through the Spiritual Presence of the caregiver.

What do we mean by spiritual presence and how is this important in hospice companioning of the dying? We express hospitality by giving a person our full attention. It is a listening to people's stories, and taking the time to be with them. As Christine D. Pohl writes in ***Hospitality, A Practice and a Way of Life***, spiritual presence may require us to slow down to be with others. She states: "for those of us who feel that time is our scarcest resource, often this requires slowing ourselves down sufficiently to be present to the other person. It means that we view individuals as human beings rather than as embodied needs or interruptions…When we give people time and space, and create an environment that is respectful of them, strangers know that they have found a safe place."[53]

Spiritual Presence

The alertness

which finds everything plain

and grasps it clearly

with entire apprehension

Hugh of St. Victor

A hospice patient I visited today said her neurologist was a brilliant doctor who had been of great help to her in coping with her Parkinson disease, but she lacked any real presence. I asked her to explain, and she said, "When the doctor entered the room, her mind was here but her feet were pointed toward the door." Spiritual presence is having our mind and our feet pointed toward a person. It is being with a fellow traveler on this journey to the end of life in body, heart, and spirit. Spiritual presence is taking the time to abide with another. We are told that over 90% of what we communicate is through body language, and less than ten percent is through speech. If our feet are "pointed toward the door" then the unspoken message comes through loud and clear that we are not treating others as a human being. Spiritual presence is awareness, a true seeing and comprehending.

Spiritual presence is to offer our being as much as our doing in hospice companioning. A great discovery we can make in being present with the dying and their families through the spiritual art of hospitality is that compassion emerges in our midst as we practice the Hospice Way. Compassion comes from *com* and *passio*, which means *"to suffer with."*

In the Hospice Way, compassion is the willingness to "suffer with" or "be in the fire with" the dying and their families. It is true compassion when a caregiver can be present with the suffering and seeming unfairness of suffering and death,

In companioning the dying, we come face to face with suffering. We find it in the life of the patient and in the grief of the family. Those who do this hospice work are by training and by personality people who are doers and fixers. We tend to see suffering as a problem that needs to be dealt with. The medical model of cure has become the de facto model of hospice companioning, although by itself it is at odds with the ancient Hospice Way. In hospice today, professional caregivers must think in terms of problems and interventions. We see this in "grief management." This phrase presupposes that somehow grief is a problem that occurs with those who have the great loss of a loved one, and that with some psychological technique the pain of this loss can be reduced and the natural sorrows of life healed.

The modern hospice movement, as a medically driven movement funded primarily by Medicare and private insurance reimbursements, contains within this movement a deep, fundamental tension in its philosophy. It has been said that hospice is the result of the tension between medicalizing and demedicalizing forces: As Cathy Siebold writes of the history of hospice in the United States:

> In hindsight, we can speculate about ways that the hospice movement's leaders might have better managed the movement's political course. Had they chosen to maintain purity of purpose in their efforts to assert patient and family control over treatment and therefore demedicalized the process, they might have established hospice centers with no ties to the acute health care system... The movement represents a compromise of medicalizing and demedicalizing forces, and its experience in attempting to bring about change reflects an ongoing social struggle.[55]

If hospice is to be viewed as medically driven so that it can operate with Medicare payments, then the proper focus is on *cure* and *intervention,* for this is the accepted way of medicine. However, hospice presents itself as a movement based on *care* and *companioning*. Even the model of medical palliative care does not resolve this conflict. Palliative care still requires intervention in terms of the management and treatment of physical symptoms of the body on the journey to the end of life.

Hospice stands in danger today of being simply a glorified form of home health care, receiving its financial support from reimbursement for medical services, while espousing a philosophy of care and companioning that are actually secondary to its medical character. The root of the problem in modern hospice work is that the medical model is simply not holistic enough to fully embrace the reality of the journey to the end life. While offering an absolutely essential physical companioning of the patient and their family through medical palliative care, the medical orientation falls far short in companioning of the heart and does not even attempt to companion the things of the spirit. The way forward from this impasse of medical *intervention* and cure vs. holistic *companioning* through *care* is found in illuminating the very heart and soul of what has been know as hospice since its beginnings in the early Middle Ages: spiritual presence which is expressed in hospitality.

Hospice through the ages has been, as we have seen, a movement of spiritual hospitality. Each of the seven practices of the spiritual art of hospitality is made manifest through spiritual presence. Medical palliative care has been incorporated into this ancient Hospice Way, but to be true to our spiritual heritage it should not be *the* practice which drives all hospice companioning. It is truly the holistic spiritual art of hospitality which needs to drive the companioning of the dying and patients that is called hospice. The journey to the end of life, as a journey of the body, heart, and spirit, is fully embraced through the spiritual presence of companions who walk with the dying and their families on this path of the spiritual art of hospitality.

The spiritual art of hospitality in hospice companioning is like a brilliant diamond that sparkles and shines in the sun. Each facet of the diamond, and each spiritual practice of this art, reflects the light and serves to add to its radiance. A diamond is not complete in its luster without all its polished facets, and the spiritual art of hospitality is not complete without hospice caregivers undertaking the seven spiritual practices. We can only "separate out" spiritual presence so that we can talk about it and see what it is like in hospice companioning. As hospice care unfolds in the life of a patient and their family, each spiritual practice of hospitality naturally reflects the bright light of spiritual presence that shines on the path to the end of life with the dying. This light often shines without our really noticing it. However, families will occasionally comment on the hospice caregiver that was "an angel to them" or became "just another member of our family" or "we could not have made it without them." I believe that what families are experiencing and giving voice to is the immense power of the light of spiritual presence reflected in the seven practices of the spiritual art of hospitality. It is a light that "shines in the darkness" in the face of death.

In the Hospice Way, our skills as a caregiver, such as nurse or social worker, are not by themselves enough. Hospice calls us to come from behind the role we are in, and be a real, genuine person with the dying and their family. Most of all, spiritual presence calls us to see the other person we are companioning as our equal in every way that really matters. As we hear in the beautiful book, *The Art of Being a Healing Presence*, "Both you and the person you're accompanying are unique, immersed in different life circumstances and roles. If you're the nurse or physician in a caring relationship, you have specialized knowledge and training that exceeds that of the patient. The same is true if you're a counselor, social worker, teacher or clergy person. If you're the parent of an underage child, one of you has more say than the other. But where healing presence is concerned, whoever you are, you're equally human, equally created, equally capable, equally loved."[56]

In the Hospice Way, this equality of spiritual presence is crucial in being with others as they may experience the indignities that may accompany the final journey to the end of life. A loved one may lose control of their bowls, or not be able to walk or talk as a disease progresses. The dying may find it humiliating to be given a bath or have diapers changed. Can we accept how the natural course of life draws to a close for a loved one, and not flee, or refuse to be with one we may have known through the years? Can we honor their sacred humanity with our spiritual presence. As Walt Whitman once wrote: "If anything is sacred, the human body is."[57]

Spiritual presence is found as we say a deep "Yes" to the messiness and unpleasantness that come with a dying body, and living with the situation with as much grace as possible. This is the way to compassion. It is a willingness to be with the dying, in body, heart and spirit, and treat them with dignity regardless of the situation. The Hospice Way is a way of true compassion.

 As we companion the dying, it is not enough to stand on the sidelines and throw ideas, suggestions and platitudes in the direction of those at the end of life. Worse yet are pat answers that mean nothing in the face of the awesome mystery of life and death. What is required for the practice of this ancient art of hospitality known as the Hospice Way is to roll up your sleeves and get involved in a companioning relationship with the dying. In Christian spiritual terms, it is a "dying to self" that gets the needs of the caregiver out of the way, so that the dying can be honored with our presence.

Companioning the dying is truly a spiritual work that demands who we really are to "show up" in the relationship with the dying, and not hide behind the mask of a professional role or identity. The dying ask for our simple presence as a real human being; nothing more, nothing less.

  The spiritual art of hospitality in hospice is a powerful mutual hospitality as a spiritual work. The dying call us to spiritually die to ourselves. As we previously observed, the life of St. Maximilian Kolbe reveals the depths of the spiritual art of hospitality, when we get ourselves out of the way.

To companion the dying in the spiritual way of the ancient Hospice tradition is to offer more than helping and fixing and making things right on the journey to the end of life, as important as doing all this might be. It goes beyond giving answers and providing solutions. This way of companioning the dying calls for our being, our spiritual presence. A powerful gift we can bring to the bedside of the dying is an awakened heart; a heart that knows the spiritual depths of this eons old art of hospitality. Surprisingly in our fast paced world of always doing, this presence of being is exactly what brings comfort and care to those at the end of life.

All simple acts of palliative care, such as careful hand-feeding the patient or giving a drink of water, can take on incredible depth and beauty when they flow from the heart filled with compassion. I have been moved to tears by the simple act of a back rub of a dying mother by her adult daughter in a nursing home. The touch of loving hands spoke so loudly in the quiet room. With each stroke of her gentle fingers, the daughter expressed so powerfully the words she whispered, "I love you, mom. Thanks, mom for all the times we spent together. Sorry I was such a bitch growing up, mom." Even more surprisingly, the awakened heart is exactly what brings comfort and care to us. Life flows in a beautiful way when we bring a "Yes" to each moment, and allow what is to be. When we die to our need to provide answers, we start to get ourselves out of the way, and finally have something genuine to offer those at the end of life. The dying ask for our presence to companion them in their final days.

I remember so vividly talking with a graceful ninety two year old patient who was rapidly declining. We had seen each other about every day for the past few months, and had become real companions. She looked up from her bed, and said simply, "How much longer is it going to be?" I replied, "I don't know. It is a real mystery. I think it may be a mystery even to God. But I do know this. I will be with you all the way through the mystery." "Even when I get so I can't speak?" she asked. "Yes" I said, "I will walk with you all the way." The dying want our presence, not our canned answers. I am convinced that it is the spiritual art of hospitality that provides true comfort and care when it is needed most. Palliative care for the dying can be sacred care when it flows from an awakened heart. What an incredible spiritual work is hospice.

The simple words of the 23rd *Psalm* can speak so powerfully to the dying because they speak of presence that is eternal. Have you noticed how the *Psalm* is written in the present tense, "The Lord IS my shepherd?" It's not in the past, as the Lord has been my shepherd long ago and is no more. It's not in the future; the Lord will be my shepherd one day by and by. But it is here, now, in this present moment that we find a presence. I've often reflected on how the end of the first verse follows so naturally from simple presence, "I shall not want." The reason for not wanting is due to an eternal presence in my life. It is presence that provides comfort as we seek to companion those at the end of life. I think this is the spiritual "secret" of why this passage is read at almost every Christian funeral. Our lives come from the mystery of eternal presence, they are bound up moment by moment in this presence, and it is to this mystery of presence that we all return. There may be no answer to the whys of pain and suffering and death, but there is an Eternal Presence and in that presence "I shall not want."

In the movie, "*Shall We Dance,*" the character Mrs. Clark shares her reasons about why people get married. In a powerful speech, she talks about spiritual presence, without using these words. If we could paraphrase Mrs. Clark, we might ask: "Why would someone want to be a hospice caregiver?" There are, after all, over a billion people on the planet. What does one life matter? We are all going to die, so what does one death really mean in the great scheme of things? We offer companionship through the spiritual art of hospitality in hospice because we promise to care about the last days of a particular person here on earth. About the good things and the bad things, about the simple and mundane things as well the important things. In hospice we are really saying by our spiritual presence what Mrs. Clark said about life. We enter into this caring mutual relationship because our heart and soul want to say to another, "Your life will not go unnoticed because I will notice it. Your life will not go unwitnessed because I will witness it."[58] Our spiritual presence as hospice caregivers is a noticing and a witnessing of a life, and in this hospitality we find the spiritual reason for the hospice movement.

It is the noticing and the witnessing of a life that brings dignity to the dying, that calls us to provide sacred palliative care, that leads us to offer care for the family of the dying, that opens the door to their home as a place of hospitality, that lets all care be determined by their needs as a patient as much as possible, and also it calls us to offer holistic care through a health care team. Our noticing and our witnessing of the patient's life cares about them being companioned by a dear pet, if that is their desire. Our spiritual presence in hospice is not a convenient "option" as a caregiver; it is the true reason for our being a caregiver in the first place. Hospice is founded on the eons old Hospice Way of companioning the dying through the art of spiritual hospitality. This requires our spiritual presence to notice and witness a life that is drawing to a close in this physical form. Hospice care is that simple and that difficult.

35

I find over and over that spiritual presence is the "key" to unlock the power of the spiritual art of hospitality in companioning the dying. For example, the practice of respecting the dignity of the patient is based on spiritual presence by a caregiver. As I am writing this, our family is watching the television program "House." It is based on a doctor who is a caricature of modern medicine. Dr. House is a brilliant doctor who has the ability to diagnose the most bizarre symptoms of patients and cure them. He approaches patients as malfunctioning machines, with no heart or soul. His sole role as a health care provider is to repair a broken mechanical body that is highly complex. He is rude, abrupt, and arrogant with both patients and staff. By contrast, the ancient Hospice Way calls us to spiritual presence as we companioning the dying. This presence mysteriously unfolds the full dimensions of a fellow human being who is suffering in body, heart and soul on this journey to the end of life. The emotional and spiritual dimensions of the patient and family are companioned as well as the dying body. It is precisely this companioning with spiritual presence that creates dignity and respect for the patient, and this is what is lacking in Doctor House.

We will explore the fundamental spiritual practices that form the art of courageous hospitality in more depth, for this is the spiritual fountain from which flows the stream of the modern hospice movement.[59] These practices are truly spiritual. As we have seen, it is the nature of spirituality to provide us connections in life. The spiritual practices that form the art of hospitality offer connecting links in many unique ways. As a spiritual practice, they have the ability to connect us with the ancient tradition of the Hospice Way of caring that has gone for centuries. They also connect as caregivers to patients at a deep and profound level, as we companion them in their final days. These practices can also serve to connect patients to what is holy and sacred in the mystery of life. They also connect us together as caregivers in the hospice movement, as we serve together as practitioners of the spiritual art of hospitality. It is their profound ability to offer us all these many connections that reveals their spiritual nature. Together the practices form a powerful spiritual art.

As the spiritual art of hospitality is practiced in hospice, there is space provided for true nurture of the physical, emotional, and spiritual needs of the patient. It is through this ancient spiritual art that care and compassion is extended when it is needed most. The seven spiritual practices of hospice hospitality normally all flow together in the course of companioning the dying and it is often difficult to separate them out. There is no special order and manner in which they appear in the care of the dying. The World Health Organization, for example, views the seven spiritual practices solely in terms of palliative care.[60] Yet each practice has its own uniqueness and special qualities that together make up the spiritual art of hospitality. They are the heart and soul of hospice.

I find as a hospice chaplain that each spiritual practice of the spiritual art of hospitality supports and strengths the other spiritual practices in a very beautiful way. For instance, a hospice nurse or aide may be primarily concerned with the spiritual practice of sacred palliative care (Practice #2). Yet in the ancient Hospice Way of companioning, this palliative care is not simply given in a vacuum. The caregiver provides patient care that observes the dignity of the patient above all else (Practice #1). So when a patient is being given a bath by an aide, the door to the room is closed, curtains are drawn if necessary, and towels may be placed on the patient to maintain their dignity. Also, the nurse does not talk about the patient as an "it" to other hospice caregivers, especially in the presence of the patient. The dignity of the patient is observed at all times to the greatest extent possible in providing palliative care. The patient is told what treatment or medicine is being given them, and they are provided an opportunity to ask questions and clarify anything they are unsure of.

The palliative care of the patient includes care for the family of the dying (Practice #3). As we have seen, the medical kit of necessary medications may be used by the family under the direction of the nurse.

The palliative care provided by the nurse is normally offered in the home of the patient (Practice #4). The nurse is expected to make regular home visits, and offer care in the setting of the home. The nurses' palliative care is directed by the needs of the patient, as much as possible (Practice #5). The patient's medication may be increased or decreased, with medical approval, as desired by the patient. The nurse assists in providing what is helpful in relieving pain and making the patient comfortable.

The nurse does not work alone in providing palliative care, but companions the patient in hospice as part of a health care team (Practice #6). Other members of the team can contribute valuable information about the patient's progress and condition. The effects of drugs and other medications can be shared in team meetings in hospice.

The hospice nurse may use a natural drug such as morphine (Practice #7) as they seek to control the pain of the patient and make them comfortable. Some hospice patients find herbs to be very helpful.

As a hospice companion of the dying, the spiritual presence of the nurse can be a crucial part of the care of a patient. Patients often have many questions about their illness and their medication. They can develop deep bonds of affection with those that provide care which alleviates pain and suffering. It is natural to want to be with someone that can mean so much in your final time. The spiritual presence of the nurse or aide can be an incredible gift to a patient.

Each spiritual discipline of the spiritual art of hospitality thus incorporates, in a graceful way, all the other spiritual disciplines. As we practice this ancient Way of hospice care, we move to a more holistic and less medicalized form of companioning those at the end of life. It is not that the value of the medical care is in any way lessened, but instead of being medically driven, the hospice care is spiritually driven by the holistic practice of hospitality in following the Hospice Way. The role of medicine is given boundaries and parameters in which to operate, and all members of the health care team are given a valid role in the companioning of the dying. The spiritual art of hospitality is truly holistic companioning of the body, heart and spirit of the patient and family.

Conclusion

The spiritual story of the hospice legacy is one that we all need to hear and embrace, for it is life giving water in the parched desert of our culture's denial of death and dying. As a spiritual wisdom tradition, it teaches us how to be fully present in each moment of our living and of our dying.

The ancient Hospice Way holds out a spiritual path for approximately millions of baby boomers. It calls us to practice the spiritual art of hospitality in our homes, as we companion the dying. Most of all, it calls us to offer them a place in our heart and spirit, indeed in homes and bedrooms across our land.

Hospitality practiced as a spiritual art is a beautiful image that captures so well the work of hospice. It defines hospice, and illuminates what gives beauty and depth to this ancient way of wisdom. The gracious host or hostess is called to accept people as they are in the companioning process. The guest is given the freedom to reveal themselves and their needs as they choose. As a hospice chaplain, I find that some patients choose to remain strangers in the companioning process, while others become dear friends at the end of life. There is no requirement for friendship and deep sharing, although it is available if that meets the needs of the patient.

Every day I meet hospice patients who offer little response in hospitals and nursing homes. I remember visiting an elderly lady sitting in her wheelchair in a nursing home at lunchtime. She had her eyes closed as she sat at the dining table. Before her was her noonday meal. "Hi Susie," I said, sitting next to her. She had no response. "Would you like me to help you with lunch?" I asked. Her response was to slowly open her mouth. And so I fed her by hand as much as she wanted. As the last bite of food was taken, she said softly, "I'm finished." "Okay Susie," I said. "Thanks for sharing lunch with me." The nurse then wheeled her back to her room. The spiritual art of hospitality offers the patient the freedom to share as much or as little of their life as they desire. They may remain largely a stranger in the companioning journey, and that too is ok. ***It is important to not romanticize the companioning process in hospice.*** The life of St. Maximilian Kolbe shows us so vividly what spiritual hospitality may require of a person. There are patients in hospice that may be very unkind or unpleasant to be with. The course of their illness, the presence of pain, the dynamics of their family life, or the nature of their personality may all lead to a difficult path to walk for any companion. Yet hospice caregivers seek to offer spiritual hospitality as well as they are able to under the circumstances.

The hospitality image calls hospice workers to respect the life journey of the patient, and how they wish to be companioned in their final steps. As Parker Palmer writes:

Hospitality means letting the stranger remain a stranger while offering hospitality nonetheless. It means honoring the fact that strangers already have a relationship-rooted in our common humanity-without having to build one on intimate interpersonal knowledge, without having to become friends.

I have a close friend who works as a volunteer in another hospice. She finds that it is difficult for her to offer hospitality to hospice patients who live in dirty, smelly homes out in the country. So she limits her work to those settings where she can provide hospitality that is of value to the patient; where the stranger can be accepted and respected for who they truly are. Hospice is a spiritual movement which offers hospitality of body, heart and soul to a stranger, and this calls hospice caregivers to practice a spiritual art that can challenge a person to the core of their being.

The image of hospitality also encompasses the grieving process of the journey to the end of life. As Elizabeth Kubler-Ross has expressed so well, the stages of denial, anger, bargaining, depression and acceptance are part of the journey of grief. Can I be a gracious host or hostess who companions a person as they journey through each of these stages? If I have deep, unresolved issues toward accepting my own death, for example, then it will be hard to make this pilgrimage with a patient. All the emotions of grief challenge me to face my own personal life with honesty as I make the journey of hospitality with a dying soul. The companioning called for in the spiritual art of hospitality is a profound spiritual work. This hospice companioning is summarized in Table One at the end of this chapter.

Let's go deeper into the spiritual work of this ancient path of companioning the dying. How exactly is it that we can be spiritually present with the dying through the spiritual art of hospitality? What are the qualities of being a spiritual companion on this journey to the end of life? How can we as companions "show up" in heart and soul in the lives of the dying? To these questions we will now turn.

Table One

The Ancient Hospice Way
The Seven Spiritual Practices that Form the
Spiritual Art of Hospitality
In Hospice Companioning of the Dying

1. Observe the Dignity of the Patient above all else.

2. Provide Palliative Care, Focusing on Pain Management and Symptom Control.

3. Offer Compassionate Care for the Family of the Dying and Empower the Family to Companion the Patient.

4. Provide Care Ideally in the Home of the Patient or a Home-Like Facility.

5. Let all Care Be Determined By the Needs of the Patient, as much as possible.

6. Provide Holistic Care through a Health Care Team.

7. Foster Sacred Presence through Nature and all Creation.

Be Spiritually Present as a Companion on the Journey to the End of Life through each Spiritual Practice.

Chapter 2

Being a Spiritual Companion on the Journey

As the story of the Hospice Way has unfolded, we have seen that the spiritual heart and soul of the hospice movement is hospitality, a gracious space that invites others in. Through the ages hospice has extended hospitality to the stranger as a very special and sacred way of companioning the dying. As a historical movement, hospice slowly came into existence through the efforts of Christian monks and nuns who practiced this spiritual art of hospitality. Our story has told of practices that form the basis of hospice spirituality down through the ages.

Spiritual presence has been a basic dimension of this spiritual work of companioning the dying from the beginning. It traces back to the early middle ages. In the ***Rule of St. Benedict***, strangers were to be received in the monastery as if they were Christ.[1] The very foundation of monastic medicine and the incredible outpouring of hospitality through hospitals, hospices, monastic infirmaries, and leper houses was based on the spiritual discernment that the poor and the dying are Christ's presence among us. The words of Christ, "In as much as ye did it to one of the least of these my brethrens, ye did it unto me," were truly taken into the heart and soul of the spiritual work of companioning the dying in the West.[2]

But now our story of hospice spirituality comes home in a deeply personal way. The question the dying bring to us is the simplest and yet perhaps the greatest question that we face in companioning: Do we practice hospitality ourselves? Does hospitality flow through us? Or have we shut off this stream of life giving spiritual water that has touched countless lives across many generations?

Work with the terminally ill brings the opportunity to learn and live out a spiritual art that transforms us as caregivers, as well as those we companion. We become through this art a gracious companion with the dying. So we may ask, what exactly is it that a gracious host or hostess needs to bring to their companioning with the dying for it to be a spiritual art? In this chapter, we will explore ways of being spiritually present in our companioning with the dying. Through stories of companioning, we will let the dying speak of the ways this act of grace occurs.

A fellow chaplain at Blue Ridge Hospice came to this work of companioning the dying from a different path. Susan ran a beautiful bed and breakfast house for several years in a nearby town. I have enjoyed her stories of how romantic is the notion of having your own bed and breakfast in the Shenandoah Valley, and yet how much hard work is involved behind the scenes. Even when you don't feel especially happy or well, you need to be kind and gracious to your guests, for they are what it is all about in a bed and breakfast.

There is a special attitude that you need to have to be successful in running such a place, according to Susan. It is an attitude of the heart and soul. It's an attitude that says with real genuineness, "Welcome, I'm glad you are here. I want you to be relaxed and comfortable and enjoy your stay with us. It's an honor to serve you." As Susan says, people know right away if you are a gracious host or hostess. It's a simple thing, like flowers in the room, which tells guests if you are "for real" in offering hospitality.

In hospice work, we are called to be a gracious host or hostess as we companion with patients and their families at the end of life. As we have seen, our companionship is far more than social pleasantries; it a companionship of body, heart and soul. All hospice caregivers are more than just their given specialty of volunteers, nurses, doctors, social workers, music therapists, or chaplains. We are the gracious companions that will walk with them in their final days on this earth.

Hospice work is about extending hospitality in this role of a companion. Patients and families know quickly if we are for real. Little things, like our body posture or the expressions on our face, show if we really care or are just doing a job.

In this chapter we will reflect on how we can be a gracious host or hostess of body, heart, and soul as we companion the dying in hospice work. What are the qualities that speak of this hospitality? What do the dying need to find in us to know that we are for real? How do we offer this hospitality from our heart and soul as hospice caregivers? To these questions we will now turn.

> One way of being present with the dying is for a gracious hospice companion to bring an inner "Yes" to the companioning with the dying.

Eckhart Tolle is a contemporary spiritual teacher who shares with us the power of saying "Yes" to life.[4] As we face the issue of our own suffering and death, and reflect on the meaning of all that we have experienced in our lives, what attitude do we bring to life and especially our relation with the dying? Is it one of an inner resistance that says "No" and pushes away what we experience? Or are we able to face life with an affirmation of "Yes?" It is the "Yes" that is the path to a life of joy, peace and happiness, while the "No" traps us in pain and suffering. The inner "Yes" opens to us this living stream of hospitality and spiritual vitality.

As we saw in the reflection on grief explored by Kubler-Ross, the attitude we bring to these stages will influence our companioning of the dying. What happens when the dying person is expressing anger at their doctor and perhaps even God? If we are a person of deep faith, do we recoil inwardly and feel that it is wrong to question the ways of our Creator? While we may not express this openly in our companioning, this inner "No" toward feeling anger at God will be very apparent. It will show in our body language and our facial expressions, such as a frown. It will be revealed in our feeling of uneasiness and our desire to change the subject. Perhaps we will even want to end the conversation and flee from the presence of the dying person.

The inner "Yes" we bring to this companioning is a doorway to a caring presence with the dying. It is not simply giving our approval to all that is taking place, but it is simply allowing it to be.

A patient I visited in a nursing home was very feeble and confined to his bed. He had lost a great deal of weight, and could not even sit up without assistance. He shared with me what his needs and concerns were at this time of life as he lived out his final days. One need totally surprised me. He wanted, more than anything else, to have his toe nails clipped. "Take a look, Chaplain," he said. "See for yourself." So I unwrapped the blanket and sheet that covered his emaciated legs that were dark purple and covered with blotchy skin that was as thin and frail as tissue paper. Sure enough, his toe nails were long and jagged and badly needed to be cut. I can," the patient explained, "wear down my fingernails a little on the sheets, but I can't do a thing with my toe-nails." Even though the patient couldn't walk or even move his frail, discolored legs, he had a simple request for palliative care and it was expressed with utter simplicity. As a chaplain with a Doctoral Degree in Christian spirituality, I was challenged by this simple request. Could I put aside all my years of study, prayer, and theological reflection and simply say "Yes" to how this patient wanted to be companioned in this moment? It was all about getting toenails clipped; nothing more, nothing less. I was well equipped to discuss lectio divina and the con-templative tradition of Christian spirituality, but was I up to dealing with toenails? A simple "Yes" was all that was needed.

Over and over again, I find that the door to companioning a fellow human being in the face of death is either opened by an inner "Yes" that I bring to the companioning or it is closed by a firm "No" that I speak in my heart. The dying patient or family ask us as hospice caregivers to speak that "Yes," which truly opens a door into spiritual presence.

> A second way to be present with the dying is to offer "Gracious Listen-ing" in companioning the Hospice Way.

"Gracious Listening" is a powerful expression of Presence in com-panioning those on the journey to the end of life. The other person is allowed "to be" in the companioning.

Eckhart Tolle teaches that the quality of any relationship is deter-mined by the amount of space in the relationship. He points to the amount of baggage that we often bring to the relationship in the form of our ego. We may come to the companioning process with an iden-tity as a son or daughter, a mother or father, or a professional with a role to perform. Yet can we companion as a human being without this identity? In gracious listening we companion from the heart and the soul, and not listen not simply in terms of our identity in society.

I find that the main characteristic of this "soulful" form of listening is the acceptance of another person. It is allowing the other to share their stories and life experiences with an attitude of respect. Perhaps most importantly, gracious listening teaches the great lesson that it isn't about me in companioning the dying. My ideas and my opinions are not the most important thing in life. Even my emotions and my reactions are not what matter most. The other person may at times yell or even scream and I do not have to take it personally. While it may be unpleasant, I know that it is not about me.

Gracious listening involves far more than simply speech. In counseling and psychotherapy, we are taught to listen with the "third ear." This is hearing what is not said in a conversation as well as what is said. Gracious listening goes a step further. It's listening with the heart and soul. It is listening to all the ways that the dying are present in their life as they journey to the end of life.

I visit a patient who has dementia. She is in a nursing home, and calm most of the time except when it comes to bathing. She then becomes agitated and may even be combative at times. The aids in the facility "do battle" with the patient to try and provide basic hygiene for the lady. The hospice approach has been to have a music therapist come in and relax the patient before her baths. The music seems to provide a soothing, gentle presence and the time with the baths goes much better with less tension and agitation.

Such is the nature of gracious listening. It is from the heart and the soul, and provides that crucial empty space for the other person to be in a relationship. I find as a hospice chaplain that the practical value of gracious listening is often in my willingness to hear from the heart and soul the stories that the dying want to share.. "Soulful listening," as the nature of this gracious listening, is an amazing experience that truly opens the door to the true life of another.

Each patient in hospice care is special and unique. Out of the millions and billions of people that have lived on the earth, this person is unlike all the others. This person has a story to share at the end of their life. It is the stories that we know and share that help make us the special person that we are. As the wife of an Alzheimer's patient tearfully shared with me in a nursing home room, "He doesn't remember any of the stories of our life. He doesn't know how it was when we got married and all the great times we had together as a family. He's just gone." Without the stories of our life we are "just gone" in the eyes of many.

As a gracious companion, we have an opportunity to be present with patients in hospice care by helping them bring their life stories to a conclusion and allowing a closure of a chapter of their life... Such is the power of gracious listening.

I remember working with an elderly patient who loved books on tape. She was legally blind and could not read, and had been a first grade school teacher most of her adult life. Literature was a great love of daily life in the nursing home. While her daughter kept her well supplied with books on tape, there was a time that her daughter was sick and no new tapes were on hand. As I visited with her, I came to know what she enjoyed listening to. It was a simple matter to check out a large book on tape at the local library for this patient. She had such a look of joy and happiness when I shared it with her in her room. This in turn led to her later telling me the story of all 24 tapes she had listened to. The tapes all centered on a family and the struggles they were having in life. It was natural for the patient to then share the story of her family and how she felt about everyone. In a powerful way, she was saying goodbye in her heart to those she had loved in her life. Closure was taking place.

The opportunities are endless to help patients write the final chapter of their life if we are spiritually present with them through gracious listening. As we hear the memories of a World War II veteran, we can bring them a military history book and hear them share their war experiences. I had a patient that was from Germany and always loved to share stories of her life in a little village in Europe. Hospice gave her a German Bible, and she enjoyed so much reading to me in German. Our presence through gracious listening allows their stories to be shared.

Gracious Listening as "soul listening" is a soulful listening presence with all the practices of the spiritual art of hospitality in companioning the dying and their families. It listens as a field of awake presence to the needs of the body, heart, and soul. Gracious Listening is a doorway to the heart and soul of those we companion.

It is easy as a caregiver to want to escape or flee the present moment. In the face of death, the present moment may seem chaotic or messy. And yet this is how the spiritual journey of the patient is unfolding, and this is how life is being experienced, for better or worse.

> A third way to be present with the dying is for a gracious hospice companion to Know the Present Moment as Sacred.

One meaning of the word "sacred" is simply "worthy of respect or veneration."[5] The word itself comes from the Latin, sacra meaning "sacred, holy, consecrated," that is, blessed or revered.[6]

I very much enjoy facilitating a Spiritual Life Review with patients. This is simply helping the patient to share their spiritual journey through the years of their life, and letting them reflect on what it has all meant to them. For the Spiritual Life Review to unfold, it requires that I find the life experiences of the patient to be sacred, in that I respect what they have to share.

As I walked into a patient's living room a few days ago, I saw framed pictures that lined every wall of the room. There was a striking photo of a handsome young U.S. Marine in dress blue uniform, photos of babies and young children, of older people enjoying what looked like family reunions and picnics, of tractors and high school graduation. The whole life of the patient, all of her hopes and joys, were there in that moment as I took in the many photos. All that was needed to affirm the spiritual journey of the patient was present. I didn't have to think up something to say or do; the present moment held it all. Just a simple question, "Who's the handsome young Marine?" kicked open the door to a lively spiritual life review. The patient's eyes sparkled and her voice bubbled as she talked about her grandson. She was so proud of her family and you could sense that this was where her heart and soul were poured out in life; in the wonderful love of being a caring mother. The present moment held it all; I didn't have to go looking for some spiritual presence that connected the patient with life. Everything was all right there if I had an open heart to feel it and respect it.

Another patient had in the bedroom of his house a beautiful wooden picture frame that held an American flag and many World War II medals, as well as old faded photos of him in a military uniform. This was a deep look into a precious part of the patient's life. Here in his military service was a truly sacred and holy place and time for this patient. "Were you part of the D Day invasion?" I asked, looking at all the souvenirs. That one question, asked from the heart, led to months of companioning the patient and even helping him plan a military funeral at Arlington National Cemetery. What could be simpler? Everything that is needed to companion the dying is here in the present moment. Again, we don't need to go looking for the patient's spiritual journey; it can be found in the present moment. We are called as hospice caregivers to live with an open heart that responds to the unfolding of this present moment. This present moment is special as it unfolds. It is worthy of our respect, for it is blessed. It is truly sacred.

> A fourth way to be present with the dying is for a gracious hospice companion to stay with the Innocence of the present moment.

We touched on the importance of the innocence of the present moment in the beginning of this book as we unfolded the Hospice Way. It is easy as a caregiver to naturally let our needs, our fears, and our concerns dominate in the companioning process with the dying. It is though, when the needs and concerns of the dying become really important to us, that real companioning of the heart and soul take place.

As patients approach death, it is not unusual for them to relate conversations they are having now with friends and loved ones that have died many years ago. They may share that the deceased are in their living presence. If we are willing to stay with the innocence of their experiences, they have much to teach us. For those of us who practice the spiritual art of hospitality, our response is to not patronize the dying with an invalidating response such as "sure you talked with your husband," or to label them as having serious mental problems. As a gracious hospice host or hostess, we can simply let the innocence of the present moment be what it is.

One time a dying patient shared with me that she had been talking with her husband who had died many years ago, I asked her what she learned from talking with the loved one. I was curious about the life lessons that could be available in such a remarkable conversation. The patient explained it to me this way (as best I can write down the conversation):

"When you are real young, like a little kid, there is kind of a wall or veil that separates this life and the next. Now the wall is like it is made of glass. You can see through it when you are young; it is clear. You really don't know the difference between this side and the next, because the wall of glass is so clear and sparkly. We all play with imaginary playmates when we are kids, but they really aren't imaginary. They are on the other side, but they seem real to us because the other side is so clear. As you get older, the glass wall gets more and more smeared and smudged up. People tell you that the other side isn't real and you stop being able to see through the glass. When you grow up, you swear there is nothing on the other side. The glass wall is so dirty for grown ups that they can't see through it. But a funny thing happens as you get older and nearer and nearer to death. The glass wall starts getting clearer and clearer, just like it was when you were a little kid. Finally it gets so clear that you can see all the way through the glass and you can see everything on both sides at once. That's why I talk about the people 'over there'. I can see them and they can see me. It's all so real to me now; both sides of the glass wall- here and the life beyond."

Is this patient's account fact, fiction, or fantasy? Who knows? We do know that simply staying with the innocence of the present moment often brings deep comfort and care to the dying. It allows their spiritual journey in this life to unfold. There is no need to interpret their stories or find a philosophical or theological truth (or untruth) to what they share. Simply stay with their innocence and let it lead you as a hospice caregiver in the companioning process.

Staying with the innocence of the present moment cultivates a fresh questioning and interest to all that the patient is experiencing. It is seeing with the eyes of a child, and being truly interested in all that is taking place. It is wondering what they are wondering about, and what they are seeing and hearing. Holding in your heart the innocence of the present moment is a wonderful way to companion the dying. It is not judging or rejecting anything, but just accepting it all with a caring heart and soul. It is truly amazing what the dying want to share with us if we have an open heart to receive them with childlike innocence. I have had a World War II combat veteran tell me a story of a friend dying in war that was so traumatic even after all these years that he could not deal with the grief of his own death. It was a humbling experience to have a deep story shared from the heart. It was the innocence of the present moment that allowed this experience to be shared.

> A fifth way to be present with the dying is for a gracious companion to have attention centered in their body.

In order to be spiritually present in hospice work, it is important to have at least fifty percent of the attention focused in how the present moment is being experienced in the body. Caregivers need to be present with their own bodies as they companion the dying.

I visited an elderly patient in a nursing home who would yell and moan anytime she was moved. Any attempt to get her out of bed to go to the dining hall produced a loud cry that could be heard down the hall. In this moment, I could make a number of responses. I could reflect on what I *think* about her pain and discomfort, and have an intellectual discussion with her nurse. I could also reflect on how I *feel* about her pain, and perhaps this would lead to a place of compassion.

A deeper level of spiritual presence, though, is to simply be aware in my own body of how I am present with her pain. I noticed tightness in my stomach when the patient cried out. Simply noticing the tightness helped me discover a presence with the patient more than anything I might think about or feelings I might express. In a real sense, her pain became my pain. Keeping attention in the body is a basic way of companioning the dying with spiritual presence.

I have found the breath a wonderful companion for showing me the way to spiritual presence with the dying. Anytime I become anxious or wonder what I am to say or do in the presence of a patient or family, I turn to my breath for guidance. Just the simple act of becoming aware of the breath is enough to gain a presence in that moment.

Centering attention in the body while companioning the dying also comes naturally through providing simple acts of palliative care for the dying. There is great wisdom in the monastic Benedictine tradition of including manual labor in the journey to God in the contemplative life. For Benedictine monks, work is a normal part of everyday life. Physical labor centers attention in the body. I seek to stay mindful of patients in nursing homes that need to be carefully hand fed, and drop by to visit with these persons at mealtimes. The simple act of getting a spoonful of gooey pudding and gently feeding it to a person is a great release from paperwork and the constant chatter of mental activity. I find centering in the body a beautiful part of companioning the dying.

This way of being with the dying as spiritual presence has also come home to me dramatically since I recently had Parsonage-Turner Syndrome with the intense, "off the scale" pain centered in the upper back. I am often off somewhere in my head during the day, reflecting on how a chapter in a book can be written. After visiting with a patient, I may stop at McDonalds for a coke and write the outline for a chapter on the back of napkins and stuff them in my pocket.

Pain though, has come into my life as an incredible teacher. I am much more aware of my body and each moment as pain calls me to this awareness. While this may not be the path I would choose, pain brings me to a depth of the beauty of each moment. I marvel at the sun reflecting through a leaf on a tree, or the rich texture of bark on a tree. Being brought back to the experience of being the body is a gifted way to be in the present moment.

A sixth way to be present with the dying as a gracious companion is to simply pause for a moment before you enter their room, and offer a brief prayer or have a moment of reflection.

The modern spiritual writer Thomas Merton once said that most of us are not what society would see as evil persons.[7] We are not serial killers or terrorists or rapists. And yet we often find ourselves walking more in spiritual darkness than in light. We are often more asleep than we are awake in our heart and soul. Merton pointed to the incredible busy nature of our modern world as the source of our darkness. Today the relentless ring of the cell phone and the incessant flow of e-mails constantly demand our attention. That high definition wide screen TV is so captivating. Merton teaches us that, "There is a pervasive form of contemporary violence [and that is] activism and overwork. The rush and pressure of modern life are a form, perhaps the most common form, of its violence…to want to help everyone in everything, is to succumb to violence."[8]

It is a beautiful spiritual practice to have "calls to awareness" as we go through the day. In the Middle Ages, the monks and nuns used bells as calls to attention. When it was time to go to the chapel for prayer, a bell would ring out to speak to you in not only your ears, but more importantly in your heart and soul to "wake up." I like using the threshold of a patient's room as a bell. For me, it is a call to attention. I notice the threshold, and hear a medieval bell sound inside me. I am entering a sacred and holy place, and my spiritual presence is requested.

The time that patients stay in hospice care is often brief. This meeting I have with a patient may well be the only chance I will have to be present with this person. My presence is the least I can offer.

> A seventh way to be present with the dying is to know the greatness of small acts done with compassion in the present moment.

Mother Teresa of Calcutta puts it so succinctly, 'We can do no great acts, only small acts with great love."[9] This points to a powerful way to be present with patients in hospice companioning of the dying.

This well known quote was posted on the Community web site of Oprah.com on August 16, 2008. I was touched by one response that said: "I am often struck by the fact that my 'small thing' is another's 'great thing'. I have had people do something tiny that really affected me in a great way."[10]

In the West, we are trained as professionals to be agenda oriented. Our approach to patients is often to have them fit into our agenda that is usually unspoken. In modern hospice care, the medicalized way is to fit patients into a problem, or an intervention, that may be very distant from their real personal life. We decide what are the 'great things' in the companioning of the dying. While this approach is valid in terms of necessary medical care, I have found that when I become attentive to the needs of the patient, I find that they often have a very different agenda from mine. Over and over, I find that patients want to spend time on something that I never would have put on my agenda. A gracious host or hostess can practice the spiritual art of hospitality and true spiritual presence by allowing the 'small thing' to become the 'great thing' of the companioning.

I recall a patient who had worked in a sawmill most of his life in a remote mountain community of southwest Virginia. He left school early to support his family. He was deeply religious, and always had his Bible open when I came by to visit. One week, the patient seemed despondent. I asked him what he was sad about. He shared that his eyesight had declined to where he could no longer read the Bible. He told me his "lifeline to Jesus" was now lost.

The next visit, I brought by a box of tapes of the New Testament and a tape player. There were large brightly colored labels on the stop and play buttons. Eventually, I think the patient just about wore out all the tapes. He had never used a tape recorder before. As he said, "I get the preaching on that machine all the time." I never would have guessed that something as   simple as a tape player would have changed the outlook of a dying person so much. It was a small thing to me, but a great thing to him.   Mother Teresa's life shows us that a powerful way to be present with a dying person is to become aware of the small things in their life and then respond with compassion.

I find that the body of the patient often reveals so many of the small things. I visit regularly one patient in a nursing home who seldom speaks and can sit for hours with his meal. He is often alone in the dining room, and still silently eating long after everyone is gone. I know that his plastic cup will often be empty and he is thirsty. I refill his cup time after time as he quietly gulps down more water or juice. Sometimes he looks at me and sometimes not. It is a small thing for me and a great thing for him.

Having known pain that was intense in a recent hospital stay, I now notice if a patient grits their teeth or continually flinches .The simple question "are you in pain?" often opens the door to the 'great thing' in their life. Holding the hand of a non-verbal patient and saying, "squeeze my hand if are you having pain" is very simple and yet often effective. While I would not wish pain on anyone, it is an amazing teacher that can make you much more sensitive and aware of the needs of the dying.

A few days ago I visited one elderly man who was non-responsive to nurses and staff. He seemed to want to be quiet, so after introducing myself, I held his hand and simply sat in silence for several minutes. In a very soft, gentle voice, he broke the stillness by saying "I am suffering in silence." I asked how he was suffering, and he pointed to his knee. I followed up the visit with a phone call to his hospice nurse. After I told her what the patient said, she asked with real surprise, "he spoke to you?"

The ancient spiritual ways of hospice care may seem at odds with our modern world that is so focused on agendas. Perhaps there is no "billable time" allowed by Medicare for sitting with a patient in silence. Yet there is great truth in knowing that presence may be found with patients through attentiveness to the small things in their lives. It is a powerful way of companioning those at the end of life.

Conclusion

As we live out the art of spiritual hospitality in the unique hospice way of companioning the dying, we are guided by the ways of being present that a gracious host/hostess brings to this companioning. We are called to offer true hospitality, as one who runs a bed and breakfast would offer hospitality. As we walk with the patient in their final days, we are called to bring an inner "Yes" to the journey together. We are challenged to find the present moment as sacred. We are also called to stay with the innocence of the present moment. Attention focused in the body is an ancient way to maintain spiritual presence. The threshold of the patient's room can serve as a call to our attention of the sacred nature of hospice work. We can be present with them in their writing their final chapter of their life.

As we practice the art of being spiritually present, the river of hospitality is allowed to flow through us. Sometimes it will flow with a mighty roar, while other times it is only a trickle. However it flows, the spiritual work of hospice is no longer outside us in an historical or social movement; we are transformed as caregivers to become the living presence of this ancient spiritual art of hospitality.

As I was writing this chapter, I conducted a funeral for a hospice patient. The patient was a very kind, caring lady who lived in a little house with an aluminum screen door in a small town in the Shenandoah Valley. She left behind a deep legacy of love as her life had a profound influence on her children and all who knew her. At the funeral, her son, a high school teacher, shared a moving description of what it was like to companion his mother in the final days. He spent every Friday evening with his mom, as her medical condition required constant care and attention.

The son saw this time with his mom through the eyes of spiritual presence. He wrote a tribute called "A Date With God." It is shared with his gracious permission as a lesson in what it is like to be spiritually present in the Innocence of the Present Moment as we companion the dying.

A Date With God (For Mom)

I have a date with God.
Not Sunday
But Friday at five.
I have a date with God.

No pearly polished gates to enter.
But an aluminum storm door.
I have a date with God.

Never mind the streets paved with gold.
Water Street is the place.
It's 147 North.
I have a date with God.

Two persons,
One voice.
But determined dialogue.
I have a date with God.

Share our time.
Share stories.

57

Laugh like fools.

And shed unwanted tears.
I have a date with God.

Heroic hands to be held.
Pains to be relieved.
Prayers to be whispered.

Memories to relive.
Memories to be made.
I have a date with Mom.

See an inspiring spirit
Within a heart that holds each of us.

See strength
Beyond what we can imagine.

See that amazing smile
Through pain and tragedy.
See that triumphant thumbs up
Every time.

See deeply into hazel eyes.
Beautiful caring wise eyes.
Look closely,
See God.

I have a date with God.
It flew quickly by.
It's okay.

I have made a date with Mom.
And God.
For Later.

Table Two

Ways of Being Present with the Dying in Companioning the Ancient Hospice Way

1. A gracious companion brings an inner "Yes" to the companioning on the journey to the end of life.

2. Offer "Gracious Listening" as you companion the dying.

3. Know the Present Moment as sacred in your companioning.

4. Practice the "Innocence of the Present Moment" in companioning the dying.

5. Keep some attention in your body as you companion the dying.

6. As a gracious companion, pause for a moment before entering a dying person's room and have a moment of silent reflection or prayer.

7. Companion through practicing the "greatness of small acts" done with compassion in the Present Moment.

Spiritual Presence is a healing key that can often unlock the stories held in the heart and soul of patients.

Chapter 3

Companioning the Dying
As a Spiritual Art

Companioning the dying with our presence is a spiritual *art form.* Sharing with the patient as a unique human being present as body, heart and soul and having a relationship with those most dear to the patient is a unique spiritual calling. Regardless of our role in hospice, be it nurse, social worker, doctor, music therapist, volunteer, or other companion, we are involved in a spiritual work in hospice. All we do and say in hospice circles back to the centuries old art of spiritual hospitality as we companion those at the end of this life's journey.

In reflecting on these spiritual practices of the art of hospitality as an art form, my thoughts go back to the work of the music therapists at Blue Ridge Hospice. The story of one therapist's visit with a patient was shared with me by a fellow chaplain. A young and very pleasant music therapist was visiting with an elderly lady who was suffering from dementia at the end of her life. The music therapist was singing in a sweet, soft voice, *"She'll be Coming Round the Mountain When She Comes,"* and trying to get the patient to join in with the song. At the end of each verse the patient looked at the young therapist, waved her finger and said, "God damn you, God damn you." The response of the music therapist was that of a gracious hostess. She simply said, "Oh, I'm sorry that you didn't like that song. Maybe you would like this one." And off she went, playing another song.

The art of the spiritual art of hospitality is very much like that of the art of learning to play a musical instrument. As with any art form, there are basic steps that must be taken to master a true art. Essential knowledge of the musical instrument as well as music itself, such as beat and rhythm, is required. The seven practices of hospice spirituality are essential knowledge to companioning the dying in the ancient Hospice Way. But then the art requires that the instrument be played. At first slowly, and as any parent with a young musician knows, often painfully, the instrument is mastered. Endless hours can be spent learning to play the scales and then simple compositions until the playing becomes second nature. The practices in the art of spiritual hospitality are like the scales in playing an instrument. These practices allow us to companion the dying. As an art form, they can become second nature to us.

Over time, we find that we bring our entire selves to the companioning of the dying without really thinking about it. Actually, the practices are mastered when thinking is no longer dominating the relationship. When we relax and simply **become** the practices, then the art of spiritual hospitality is fully alive. Like playing an instrument, we become one with the music and let it flow through us. It all comes together in our presence of playing. The art of being a musician is a beautiful and mysterious flow of musical knowledge, of skill and technique, and of simple presence in the moment. So it is with the spiritual art of hospitality in hospice. Our knowledge of the seven practices of hospice spirituality and our skill in living them out, can lead to a mysterious simple presence with the dying that truly transforms the process of dying.

As is true with any art form, no two works of art that are created are ever exactly the same. So too with companioning the dying; no two deaths are ever exactly the same. We may find that a patient seeks companioning that draws heavily on one or two particular practices of the art of spiritual hospitality as they journey toward death. For example, there may be a dear friend, or a special nurse on the night shift, or a beloved pet that seems to bring deep comfort and compassion to the patient. In this particular situation, it is the practice of companioning through the extended family that touches the life of the dying most deeply. The other practices of the spiritual art of hospitality may be present, but seem more in the background.

The art of companioning the dying the ancient Hospice Way is to master the spiritual art of hospitality so completely that it becomes a simple and natural gift that we share with those at the end of life. This art disappears, so it seems, and what emerges is what the dying write as the final chapter of their life. This chapter is a work of art that we respect and dignify with our presence. The final chapter they write has never existed before, and it will never exist again on earth in quite the same way.

This work of art cannot be known ahead of time; it can only be revealed in our presence as it unfolds as an act of grace. To observe this new creation requires our spiritual presence with "eyes to see."

As a chaplain, I approach each new hospice patient with an unbounded curiosity in my heart. I enjoy so much the "innocence of the present moment." I wonder what great work of art the patient will write as the final chapter of their life. Maybe this patient is writing a great love story. So often a patient will linger at the end of life, waiting for that special person to appear in their room. While words are not spoken, there may be a bond of love that remains unbroken by the decline of the physical body. That person's presence allows a silent goodbye to be said, as the patient's final chapter is written.

Another patient I know wrote a deep tragedy at the end of his life. His life was full of unresolved conflict and family bitterness. The tragedy was deep and profound, and full of pathos. Yet I respected the patient for the tragic story that he wrote.

One patient wrote a profound mystery story as her final days unfolded. She became very quiet and non-responsive. No one in her family had any clue about what she was thinking or feeling. She simply withdrew and slipped away quietly. Her story reminded me of the poem, *"Crossing the Bar,"* by Tennyson.

Crossing the Bar

Sunset and evening star,

And one clear call for me!

And may there be no moaning of the bar,

When I put out to sea,

But such a tide as moving seems asleep,

Too full for sound and foam,

When that which drew from out the boundless deep

Turns again home.[1]

Those who work with the dying find that patients may write what could be called "The Long Goodbye." There are patients who need time to put their life affairs in order and say "goodbye to family, friends, and loved ones. A patient may be close to death, but it seems that they are holding on for some unknown reason. Even if the patient is not responsive and is not taking any food or liquids, they seem to be waiting for something. It is often when a special friend or relative finally arrives that they feel they have received permission to come to the end of their life's journey on earth. Simple words of goodbye spoken to non-responsive patients often seem to have a deep and profound impact. There are many creative ways that the "long goodbye" may be written in the final days of a patient's life.

I remember Nancy had asked me to be with her when she died. I promised her that I would be her companion through the final days. Instructions were left with the hospice nurses who attended to Nancy to call me when it appeared the end was near. My phone rang on a Saturday night about midnight and I was asked to come over to the residential unit and be with Nancy. As I arrived, her family had gathered in her room. I helped the family members, including a little boy, get pillows and blankets as they settled in for the night. Hospitality came first. I began with quiet scripture readings and soft spoken prayers as I held Nancy's hand and wiped her forehead with a washcloth. A wonderful hospice nurse came in the room and dimmed the lights and kept checking on us. And so the long night vigil began.

Nancy's breathing was shallow and labored. The nurse said her pulse was "thready." Nancy seemed to be declining rapidly, as there were long pauses between each breath. I began silent contemplative prayer with Nancy, breathing in her final breaths and breathing out to her new life with hope and eternal peace. The vigil embraced the deep silence of the night on the quiet hospice residential unit. Three o'clock came and went, and the hours silently passed.

It was about five, when the family was asleep and it appeared to truly be the end that a miracle occurred. Just as the first rays of sunlight of a new day came into Nancy's room and touched her face everything changed. With the beams of light came new life and energy in Nancy. Her pulse suddenly became firm and steady, and her breathing regular and deep. I could sense the new flow of life in Nancy as I said a final prayer and slipped out of the room. I knew that I had witnessed part of the "long goodbye" of a soul that had come to the door at the edge of this life and yet was not ready to enter that passageway to what lies beyond. It was a beautiful and yet very mysterious moment that I could only honor with my presence, for there were no words to describe it.

It was about three days later that I had the feeling that Nancy was waiting for me to arrive as I walked down the hall of the residential unit to her room. As I stepped into her room in the middle of the afternoon, she had her head titled toward the door as she lay in bed. The moment I saw her, Nancy opened her eyes. She had a soft glow that was almost a radiance that enveloped her. She took her last breath, and her "long goodbye" was over.

Our role as those who practice the spiritual art of hospitality is not to write the final chapter of the patient's life for them. There is a temptation to want to "fix things" and guide the dying to write what we think is a proper ending for a life. We may get the notion that a Beautiful Death is coming to an acceptance and the resolving of all conflict and especially anger. But who are we to say that anger is a problem and cannot be part of a Beautiful Death? The art form we practice in companioning the dying is that of a gracious host or hostess who, while skilled as a clinician, walks with the dying and provides them with the incredible gift of spiritual presence. It is this gift that often allows the final chapter of the patient's life to unfold as a beautiful work of art.

I come back again and again in companioning the dying to how important it is to let the patient's final days unfold as their own creation. It is a mystery that we are letting unfold as we companion the dying. Hospitality can embrace both our holding on and our letting go. Through spiritual presence we come to know the right moments for each.

There is, as we have said, no particular order as to how the seven spiritual practices of the spiritual art of hospitality may unfold in the process of dying. They are explored here in a stated order simply for the sake of reflection. The patient is free to create the order and movement that expresses their life best. We are always their companion on this journey at the end of life, and they direct the journey as it unfolds. It is a beautiful and ancient spiritual art form that we practice in the hospice movement.

Conclusion. Being With the Dying in Body, Heart, and Soul.

I would like to paraphrase the words of Father Daniel Homan and Lonni Collins Pratt who wrote **Radical Hospitality, Benedict's Way of Love,** and apply their thoughts to the art form of hospice spirituality.[2]

As hospice caregivers, we don't have to have all the answers to give as we companion the dying. Our spiritual practice does not require that. In fact, it is the people who try to offer answers that end up not being of much value at the end of life. Do we really think there are simple answers to the great questions of life? Forget giving answers as the way to care for the dying. What we think and might have read are really of no use at the end of the day. What the dying yearn for is a person that is available to them. A living, breathing human soul that touches their life with a simple presence. A person with eyes and heart wide open, with room and space for them. A person who *lives* the spiritual art of hospitality of the ancient Hospice Way, who will make room in their lives for all the discomfort and messiness of dying. A person who is willing to be interrupted in their well-planned life. The dying yearn for a person who will be with them in body, heart, and soul as they embrace the great and awesome mystery of death and dying. Our companionship of the dying requires invites to be such a person.

This spiritual art of hospitality of this ancient Hospice Way is indeed mutual hospitality as an art form. Not only is it our being a caring presence in the world, but it transforms us as caregivers as well. It allows hospice workers to move past themselves and opens the door to transcending themselves. Hospice work as a true companionship gives you the opportunity to get yourself out of the way, as it were, and finally move beyond all the petty games of role and status and power that strangle the human spirit in our world. When we put aside our own pain and feel that pain of the dying, a beautiful power of compassion is released onto this planet earth. It is a power that has the ability to transform this world moment by moment. It can create a world where no terminally ill person is alone and uncared for.

The modern spiritual writer Henri Nouwen expresses so well what it means to be companioned in this life. While he was not writing about hospice, he does describes what the Hospice Way is all about as a companioning of the dying in body, heart and soul as one sacred indivisible whole. Nouwen writes: "When we honestly ask ourselves which people in our lives mean the most to us, we often find that it is those who, instead of giving advice, solutions, or cures, have chosen rather to share our pain and touch our wounds with a warm and tender hand. The[hospice companion] who can be silent with us in a moment of despair or confusion, who can stay with us in an hour of grief…who can tolerate not knowing, not curing, not healing, and face with us the reality of our powerlessness, this is a person who cares."   Such is the transforming power of the spiritual art of hospitality as an art form. Such is the ancient yet vibrantly alive companioning of the dying on the journey to the end of life that is the Hospice Way.

Chapter 4

Journey's End:
A Beautiful Death

The story of a Beautiful Death

In hospice care, a "Beautiful Death" naturally follows from a holistic companioning that walks down the ancient path of the spiritual art of hospitality in the Hospice Way. This companioning involves recognizing and responding to the complex and ever changing physical, emotional, and spiritual needs of the dying and their family. Each of these needs is seen as special and unique and respected as part of the journey of the Hospice Way. Above all, death is recognized as a wondrous and mysterious "next step" that follows from holistic companioning to the end of life.

What might a Beautiful Death actually be like in hospice care? What would take place on the journey to a Beautiful Death? How would it be experienced by a patient? How would a family walk this path with a loved one? If I could take the artistic liberty of creating a fictitious hospice patient and family using actual facts and situations from several patients and families I have companioned, a Beautiful Death might look something like this…..

"Granny" as she was known to the family, entered hospice care as a 99 year old Caucasian female who had lived most of her life on a picturesque farm that looked like something Norman Rockwell might have taken as the subject of one of his paintings. There was an old stone farm house that dated to the Civil War era. The farm's red barn could be seen as one drove down a country lane, and the VT painted on the side (for Virginia Tech) stood out. Although the farmhouse was modernized, it still had a wood stove in the kitchen and antique furniture. Even with running water inside, there was a spring house and the outhouse. It was almost like stepping back in time to a far simpler era to be on the farm.

Granny had a deep and abiding Christian faith that was founded on her life long love of scripture, hymns, and prayer. Her admitting diagnosis was "debility." She needed no assistance with ambulation or with transfers. Granny was able to tolerate a regulate diet most of the time, although she also took the dietary supplement Ensure. She was becoming incontinent of both bowl and bladder, although her proud, stubborn nature made it difficult for her to admit this to anyone, including her doctor. She suffered from hearing loss, and would at times be disoriented to herself and where she was. Still, she always seemed to be able to recognize the people around her. There were periods when she could become agitated and for a little while be sad and withdrawn, although this usually did not last long.

Granny had been married for fifty-eight years to a man who was, she said, the "love of her life." She described her husband (granddad as everyone in the family called him) as if he were her soulmate. He had died two months earlier of a heart attack. (Granny told her dearest friends that granddad did come back to see her many nights at the farmhouse. He laid in the sheets in bed just the way he had all these years). Granny was struggling to live out her final days on the farm. She had community nursing care, and the grandchildren took turns staying with her. Granny and granddad had raised their five grandchildren on the farm after the parents both died in an automobile accident when the children were young.

Her physical and emotional decline had taken place slowly over many years, although the family noticed that in the past few months she had "started to really lose it" according to one grandson. After being in hospice care for about two months, Granny had a serious fall at home that required hospitalization. Her medical doctor consulted with the family, and it was decided that the best care possible would be a placement on the residential unit of the local hospice. Granny was a proud and stubborn person, and very private. She did not want the grandchildren having to provide, or even know about, such things as changing her diapers, or other aspects of her personal care. The hospice social worker made all the necessary arrangements. Granny had been on the waiting list for a bed on the unit, and one became available within a few days.

Granny settled nicely into her bright and colorful room on the hospice unit. She enjoyed the attention she received from the nursing staff and volunteers. The visits from the golden retriever that came to see hospice patients became a favorite time for Granny. She always hid a little treat for the dog on the table beside her bed. Granny also enjoyed the hospice music therapist, who brought her guitar and sang old Gospel songs. Although her sight was failing, Granny knew the words by heart, and the singing brought her real peace and comfort. It took her mind off her failing health and carried her back to happier times as a child when she sang these same songs with her grandmother.

Granny was living at the hospice unit for about two weeks, when things began to take a turn for the worse. She began to refuse to eat, although she had enjoyed food all her life. She then started to give up on taking any liquids. Granny slept most of the time, was seldom awake and never out of bed. Her body became more and more emaciated and her face took on a shrunken, skeletal look. Her skin began to have a few small sores, although the hospice staff did all they could with medication and the dressing of wounds.

As Granny's respiration became more labored, she was given morphine by mouth to relax her chest muscles and help her breathing. The grandchildren began to keep a vigil with Granny, with soft religious music playing in her room (especially old Gospel songs). The hospice chaplain dropped by almost every day, and would talk with the family and have a prayer with Granny. He often read a passage of scripture. Although Granny did not respond, it was comforting to the family to know that Granny was being cared for this way.

About five o'clock one evening Granny died peacefully. At the request of the family, the hospice chaplain was called. The family gathered around Granny and they all held hands. Everyone said "goodbye" to Granny in their own way. One grandchild spoke a few words out loud, another kissed her on the cheek, and others just held her hand and cried. The chaplain read a scripture, said a prayer, and offered a blessing for Granny. All the family then went to the nearby kitchen on the hospice unit. They enjoyed a great meal that one of the grandchildren (a chef in a local restaurant) had made for everyone. As they ate, they shared stories about Granny and granddad, and how much they enjoyed growing up with them and living on the farm. It was a hard life, but a good life. There were stories about playing hide and seek in the barn, building a tree house in the old apple tree using scrap lumber granddad gave them, and of course the great story of the favorite "perfect" grandson. One summer day he drove grand-dad's tractor through the woodshed when the rusty brakes on the old machine went out. No one was hurt, and the tractor actually ended up in the pond and the grandson in the mud. Everyone laughed till they cried. Things then became very quiet and one grandson said, "We really had great grandparents, didn't we? God couldn't have done any better. I'm really going to miss them."

The hospice chaplain attended the viewing of Granny at the local funeral home a few days later. The family shared what they wanted for the funeral service.

Granny's service was the next day. The chaplain had earlier encouraged the family to put old photographs of Granny, the farm, and the grandchildren on a DVD disk, along with recordings of some of Granny's favorite. One of the grandchildren was taking a multi-media course at the local community college, and enjoyed putting this together. At the funeral, the photos and music were shared using a projector and laptop borrowed from hospice. It seemed that Granny was really there. The chaplain also invited any of the family to speak that felt like they could share what was in their heart. One of the grandchildren read a favorite poem of Granny, that she kept in her Bible beside the bed. As the hospice music therapist sang "Amazing Grace: and played her guitar, it brought back memories of Granny and her final days at the hospice.

After the funeral service, there was a brief grave side committal at the family cemetery on the farm. There followed a country dinner at the farmhouse, with ladies from the local United Methodist church where Granny and granddad had attended bringing most of the food. There were ham biscuits piled high on plates, potato salad, and great vegetable dishes. Just about every kind of pie and cake you could imagine was on a side table. The grandchildren and folks from the church stayed around and talked about the "good old days." It seemed a fitting way to remember and honor Granny and the long life of love that she had lived. It was truly a Beautiful Death.

The Essence of a Beautiful Death

So what do we learn from Granny's death? What stands out as beautiful about this path that Granny took as she journeyed to the end of her life? Most of all we see that her death was ***appropriate for her.*** There is no single kind of death that is a Beautiful Death for everyone. However, her death reflected all the loves of her life. Granny stayed in the farmhouse as long as possible, she had the grandchildren around her. She was provided privacy and dignity on the hospice unit. Then too, the hospice music therapist shared the music Granny sang with her grandmother, while the hospice chaplain read the scriptures Granny knew by heart and said prayers that brought her real comfort. In a word, her journey to the end of life led to a death that was appropriate for Granny. Even more, the celebration of her death at her funeral service also brought together the many loves of Granny and it provided a deep sense of closure for family as well as the community.

As Edwin Shneidman says of what we are calling a Beautiful Death, "It is a death in which the hand of the way of dying slips easily into the glove of the act itself. It is in character. It, the death, fits the person. It is a death that one might choose if it were realistically possible for one to choose one's own death."[1] Granny's death fit her life.

If we take Granny and her death as our teacher, are there more specific lessons we can learn about how we journey to the end of life and experience a Beautiful Death? What are some of the essential dimensions that need to be a part of our experience of dying for a Beautiful Death to unfold naturally?

First, we see the importance of a time for companioning and preparing for a Beautiful Death to occur. In hospice care, the cause of death is usually natural, as was the case with Granny, but companioning can also be from a death due to an accident, a failed suicide, or a homicide. The important criteria is that a medical doctor certifies that death is likely to occur within the next six months. A Beautiful Death is an expected death where we have the opportunity to journey our final days with companions in this life.

We also see with Granny the importance of death with dignity and privacy. Granny was a proud person, and did not want the grandchildren to be involved in personal and intimate care such as changing her diapers. Other people will have other issues that they wish to keep private with caregivers. Dignity and privacy are essential to a Beautiful Death.

Granny's life journey also reveals that control over pain, and the relief of physical symptoms, is fundamental to a Beautiful Death. Granny was kept comfortable on the hospice unit, and morphine not only helped control pain but also made her respiration less difficult. A Beautiful Death provides for as much control over pain as medical science can make possible.

This leads naturally to the understanding that Granny wanted as much control as possible over all the events and circumstances of her dying. She wanted to choose where she was going to spend her final days and who was going to be with her. Granny was outspoken about what support and comfort she wanted on this final journey. She asked for the dog that visited the hospice unit, she wanted to be allowed to hide a treat beside her bed, she asked for the hospice music therapist and said what songs she wanted to be played. She asked for the hospice chaplain and had long conversations about scripture and her faith; she requested prayer as the chaplain held her hand. Granny walked a path where she had as much control as possible over how her final days unfolded, and what brought comfort to her. Such is the way of a Beautiful Death. Granny's physical, emotional, and spiritual needs were recognized as she was companioned, and Granny had a real say about how these needs were being met.

We also learn from Granny that she was able to leave when it was time to go, and her life was not prolonged pointlessly. She was very comfortable at the hospice unit, and the emphasis was always on care, and not cure. There were no heroic measures to prolong her life when her body failed and could no longer sustain her. Her stay on the Unit was brief.

Finally, a Beautiful Death incorporates "spiritual presence." This is something that is easier to actually experience than to put into words. For patients and families, caregivers who offer spiritual presence truly offer a deep sense of comfort. Even beyond that, a person who "shows up" and is truly present provides the opportunity for allowing the dying and their loved ones to say goodbye, and move toward closure. As we have seen, the spiritual nature of hospitality creates a space where the person can be free to be themselves. Spiritually, hospitality is a gracious invitation to enter into a sacred space that is safe and secure, where emotions that are perhaps scary and frightening can be expressed and faced. Hospitality allows for the mask of pretending that everything is all right to slip away, and for the pain and heartaches of life to be seen for what they are.

Spiritual presence comes in many shapes and sizes in hospice care as patients and their families make the journey to the end of life. It shows up in the golden retriever and her owner that visits on the hospice unit. How natural it is to want to hug a friendly animal that showers you with love and affection. Spiritual presence comes in the hospice night nurse who notices you wince with pain and asks how your pain is on a scale of one to ten. It comes with the music therapist who really wants to know what music you enjoy, and loves to sing those songs with you. It comes with a hospice social worker who makes the arrangements for a bed on the unit so you can receive the care you need as the physical body declines. Spiritual presence comes with the hospice chaplain who holds your hand and allows you to talk about how it is when you find yourself "walking through the valley and the shadow of death." Spiritual presence truly opens the door to a Beautiful Death.

Granny is a great teacher to all of us. Her death shows so clearly what a Beautiful Death is like in our world today. As was said at the opening of this chapter: "In hospice care, a Beautiful Death naturally follows from a holistic companioning that walks down the ancient path of the spiritual art of hospitality."

Table three on the next page summarizes how a Beautiful Death flows from hospice companioning.

Table Three

"A Beautiful Death" In Hospice Care
Expressed Through the Spiritual Art of Hospitality
In Companioning the Dying

1. Observe the Dignity of the Patient above all else.

In a Beautiful Death patients are treated with dignity by those who are their caregivers. They are respected for being the person that they are, regardless of race, religion, beliefs, gender, sexual orientation, nationality or social status.

2. Provide Sacred Palliative Care, with a Focus on Pain Management and Symptom Control.

In a Beautiful Death, a goal is for patients have as little pain as possible in the activities of daily life, and as much comfort as possible. Their body is cared for (not cured) to the best of medical science's practical ability. Physical symptoms are controlled as allowed by medical science.

3. Offer Compassionate Care for the Family of the dying.

A Beautiful Death provides the opportunity for patients to be surrounded and companioned by those they love in life, and who love them. This may be whoever and whatever speaks to their heart, be it their family, friends, pets, or whatever they hold dear.

4. Provide Care Ideally in the Home of the Patient or a Home-Like Residential Facility.

In a Beautiful Death patients have the opportunity to live out their final days in a place that feels familiar and comfortable. The patient may die in a place that speaks of warmth and safety to them.

Table Three Continued

5. Let all Care Be Determined By the Needs of the Patient, as much as Possible.

In a Beautiful Death patients are given as much control as possible over how the final days unfold. They truly have a genuine say about their pain medicine and all their medical care, who are their caregivers, and how all the care that they want and desire is provided, as is practical.

6. Provide Holistic Care Through a Health Care Team.

In a Beautiful Death patients are companioned in their final days as one indivisible whole in body, heart, and soul. Their whole being is companioned as Sacred by members of a health care team.

7. Foster Sacred Presence Through Nature and All Creation.

In a Beautiful Death the patient and family are companioned in a holistic way. Pets and other animals are welcomed as companions, if the patient and family desire. There is the opportunity to see and enjoy nature.

Be Spiritually Present as a Companion on the Journey

to the End of Life Through Each Spiritual Practice.

In a Beautiful Death as patients come to their final days there are caregivers who are spiritually present with them. They truly care about the patient and are willing to be a companion. Caregivers know and practice the ancient spiritual wisdom of the spiritual art of hospitality.

Can we see how all of the many physical, emotional and spiritual needs of the dying and their family can be met by companioning through the spiritual art of hospitality? Table three summarizes how a Beautiful Death unfolds from this Hospice Way.

Here we see the nature of a Beautiful Death as described in terms of the spiritual art of hospitality. It follows all that Granny teaches us. This art is profoundly holistic, and sets out the deep spiritual nature of hospice work. It may or may not involve all the grief qualities illuminated by Kubler-Ross, but it does describe basic qualities of life that are to be a part of the companioning as the patient journeys to the end of life.

In a Beautiful Death, each of these seven qualities of companioning the dying, expressed through spiritual presence by caregivers, comprise an essential dimension of this ancient Hospice Way. Some of the spiritual practices of hospitality will usually be more in the foreground of the companioning, and some will be seen as in the background.[2] For example, in companioning a patient who has severe dementia at the end of life and is at times hostile and combative, there may be an emphasis on sacred palliative care, in providing for the patient to be as pain free and comfortable as possible. The dignity of the patient is also in the foreground, as the patient may not be able to feed themselves or perform any of the other normal activities for daily living. In the background may be the role of the family in companioning, as an elderly patient may have no recognition of their loved ones. The hospice health care team may, however, be very involved in the background with the family in terms of providing for care of the patient. This is often seen when care is no longer possible at home and requires placement of the patient in a specialized nursing home facility .Care for the patient's family and their needs is still an important part of the journey to the end of life, but not in the direct way that we might see if the patient were being cared for at home.

I have been amazed at how important spiritual presence can be in companioning patients that seem to be un-responsive at the end of life. I recently visited a patient that was admitted to hospice care, who did not speak at the time of his admission. As I saw the patient in a private home facility, he had his eyes closed and seemed to grimace as if in pain. After introducing myself as a hospice chaplain, I asked the patient if I could hold his hand and simply spend some time with him.

After about five minutes or so of quiet, he opened his eyes and said "I am suffering in silence." It was a startling statement. I asked him how he was suffering and he pointed to a bandage on his knee. He closed his eyes and had nothing more to say the rest of the visit. I called his hospice nurse after the visit, and told her what the patient said. Her first response to me was "he spoke to you?" The patient died shortly after my visit.

It is no coincidence or lucky chance that the Hospice Way teaches us about a Beautiful Death. The spiritual art of hospitality is an ancient art, and it contains within its sacred practices the great wisdom of Western civilization regarding how to make a Beautiful Death come true for the dying. It teaches us the spiritual path of hospitality, and sets clear road signs, in the form of seven practices, each expressed through spiritual presence, that guide us along the way. This wisdom, as we have seen, was known by monks and nuns from the time of the early middle ages, and it comes to us today in a highly medicalized modern form that we call the hospice movement. While science and technology may radically change the physical world that we live in, our heart and soul still make the same journey today to the end of life as our brothers and sisters did in past ages. The Hospice Way embraces the body, heart, and soul of the dying and their family, and stands today as a spiritual teacher of this path to a Beautiful Death.

This nature of a Beautiful Death in the hospice tradition is at odds with much of our modern society. Death is seen as something that is "out of sight and out of mind." We would rather send the dying away to some nursing home or hospital where we can visit them when it fits our schedule, rather than go through all the difficulties we may face at home with one who is coming to the end of their earthly days. And yet we miss an incredible opportunity for emotional and spiritual awakening in hiding away the dying.

In caring for the dying, families have the opportunity to come together and heal old wounds. The needs of the dying family member can bring out the best in us. Companioning the dying can be a powerful experience that forever changes your life and your family. Spiritually, the dying present us with an opportunity to know what real compassion is. Their needs can speak to our heart and soul in a way that we find ourselves changed and transformed through the giving process. Perhaps for the first time we truly know spiritual presence in ourselves, as we give from a deeper level than we thought possible. Companioning the dying can open us to true spiritual awakening.

We will now consider how a Beautiful Death can become a natural part of our society. What can make the spiritual beauty and power of this Way a path available for us and our loved ones as the natural end of life?

Chapter 5

A Vision For the Journey to a Beautiful Death in America

There are pathways that can open us to a Beautiful Death at home in our time. The real depth and life transforming power of this ancient Hospice Way of companioning can become a part of American society today. We can vision what a new Medicare Family Companioning Benefit might actually look like in our society as we companion on the journey to the end of life in our own communities.

Perhaps one might consider remodeling or building an addition to your house or the house of an elderly parent to allow a terminally ill mother or father to die a natural death in peace and with dignity. A bright, comfortable suite fully accessible by a wheelchair or walker, and designed with a bathroom and kitchenette as well as a view outdoors, could be much less expensive than quality care for even a few years in many nursing or assisted living homes. Small, affordable 'green" cottages using the latest in modern technology and equipped for the handicapped, are also now being designed as alternative housing that could be used by hospice patients. Whether a home addition for companioning the dying, or a small cottage, such "hospitality houses" could stand forever in the heart as a living memorial to a parent or other loved ones.[1] If those approaching the end of life could enter hospitality houses at home at a time when they are not dependent on care for all daily functioning such as bathing, dressing, etc., then this dwelling may prove an attractive alternative. A hospice residential unit could supplement this way of life, and provide care at the very end of life's journey when more specialized skilled care is needed.

The cost of a "green" hospitality house with modern technology may actually prove to be very feasible for many families. This is especially true if a primary residence is sold and the funds derived from the sale are used for an end of life dwelling to be added onto the home of a family member. The hospitality house could also be used in the future as a beautiful way to extend hospitality to others in the family, such as a young adult out of work and seeking employment. This dwelling may also potentially offer hospitality in the form of a private office or studio for those self-employed and working at home.

For the baby boomer generation, the great social question on this journey to the end of life again becomes: Can the face of dying be changed in America? I believe the ancient Hospice Way provides the path to make this change possible. Families need to be politically and financially empowered by the federal government to build an addition or make other alterations to allow the dying to be companioned at home their final days. Federal income tax credits or direct grants for home changes to companion the dying need to become available. There needs to be made available to families' nationwide simple and functional architectural plans for home additions that provide handicap accessible bedrooms, baths, and small kitchens.

Much of the groundwork for building functional living spaces for those who have limited mobility as they make the journey to the end of life is provided by ABLEDATE, a part of the U.S. Department of Education. The publication, *"An Informed Consumers Guide to Accessible Housing"*, contains a wealth of information for adapting housing to the needs of the handicapped.[2] There is also an extensive list of resources provided on handicap design and construction. All of this information needs to be adapted to hospice care today.

It is interesting to reflect that, in creating places of hospitality for the dying in our homes today, the hospice movement is embracing the way of the first hospices in the middle ages as extending hospitality to those on a spiritual journey. The spiritual journey today is to the end of life. We follow the ancient wisdom of first creating a place in our heart and soul for the dying through the spiritual art of hospitality, expressed through spiritual presence, and then actually build a small hospice addition to our house. This ancient tradition calls for "home hospices" or "hospitality houses" to become a normal part of the American landscape.

The vast technological resources of America can be employed in developing creative ways that the elderly can be safely companioned at home. The Quality of Life Technology Center is a National Science Foundation Research Center that is a joint venture of the University of Pittsburgh and the Carnegie Mellon Foundation . They aim to develop all aspects of modern technology to enable those with disabilities to live full and productive lives. They express their vision in these terms: Recent advancements of technologies, including computation, robotics, machine learning, communication, and miniaturization technologies, have brought us closer to futuristic visions of compassionate intelligent devices and technology-embedded environments. While many intelligent systems have been developed, most of them are for manufacturing, military, space exploration, and entertainment. Their use for improving health-related quality of life has been treated as a specialized and minor area. Assistive technology, for example, has fallen in the cracks between medical and intelligent-system technologies. The missing element is a basic understanding of how to relate human functions (physiological, physical, and cognitive) to the design of intelligent devices and systems that aid and interact with people.

The [Quality of Life Technology Center] directly addresses this core problem--human-centered, holistic design--by bringing together robotics and information technology engineers with biomedical and rehabilitation engineers, healthcare professionals working in assistive technology research and clinical practice, and experts in aging. The biggest research challenges are dealing with the complex environments encountered in daily life and with the unpredictably of people. The key to our success is studying real people in the real world in order to learn and fully understand their needs before building systems. Our research focuses on compensating or augmenting all aspects of human functions, including participation in the community. It is a platform for integrative research in which engineers of multiple disciplines, specialists in disabilities and aging and other non-technological experts collaborate to alleviate human impairments.[4]

As Cicely Saunders brought modern practices of medical palliative care into the modern hospice movement, so today we need to bring the advances of 'quality of life technology' into the ancient Hospice Way.

The research efforts of the quality of life technology relate directly to the idea of a "home hospice", which we can call a "hospitality house". Their research has resulted in the next step beyond the "smart house which is the "active home." Another cutting edge firm, Blueroof Solutions, in coordination with Blueroof Technologies, has designed and developed a new type of cottage for senior citizens. These smart cottages are state-of-the-art facilities that are designed using universal design concepts.

Design Qualities of Smart Cottages As Residences For Companioning the Dying.

• Easily Manufactured

• Energy efficient - Energy Star rated

• Wired for 'smart' technology

• Affordable (less than $100,000)

• Low maintenance

• Environmental friendly

• Compliant to ADA standards

• Safe[5]

It is interesting to review the "smart technology" that is employed in the "active home." This technology would be of great benefit to hospice patients and those who companion them at the end of life. The "active cottage" uses technology in the following manner: "Home Automation is a combination of hardware and software that enables a home to be more convenient, efficient, entertaining, and secure. Appliances, lighting, security systems, ventilation, as well as a myriad of other devices can be controlled through the use of Home Automation technologies. These devices are generally controlled locally, through the use of infrared, radio frequency, X-10, or emerging technologies such as Bluetooth, Z-Wave or ZigBee. In addition, home automation technologies also allow these devices to be controlled remotely via the World Wide Web"[6] The "active cottage" also makes use of network cameras. This would be of great value to caregivers to monitor patients and provide for their safety. The state of the art cameras are employed in this manner: "Network Cameras are digital motion cameras that can be viewed from anywhere via the World Wide Web. Unlike traditional webcams which must connect to a standalone personal computer, Network Cameras contain a built-in Ethernet server which allows the devices to connect directly to a local network. This allows Network Cameras to be much more flexible and independent than traditional webcams."[7] This allows easier monitoring of patients at their home anywhere that the world wide web is available, such as on a personal cell phone.

Quality of Life Center Credo

The research does not happen in a vacuum. All Quality of Life Technology systems need to:

• Enable people, whenever and wherever:

• Be safe and reliable.

• Protect people's privacy

• Respect people's privacy and modesty.[8]

As a hospice chaplain, I see the need for smart technologies to be developed for the elderly and handicapped terminally ill. Their needs include a computerized bed alarm that could actually speak to a patient in a soft voice if they got up at night, warning them of the danger of a fall. A bedside lamp could be automatically triggered, so that a patient never gets out of bed in the dark.

All caregivers with the elderly know the risk of falls and the danger of falls to the health and wellbeing of patients. Smart technology that can be of enormous value to the elderly, and could include the development of robotic walkers that have "arms" to catch a patient who might be in danger of falling. They could, perhaps, actually assist a patient in and out of bed.

New technologies for hospitality homes could include making one's favorite music, books, television programs and movies of the patient could be available by simple voice or touch pads. Entertainment, linked to the internet, offers limitless and the possibilities for enjoying "favorite oldies." The Kendall reading device is a step in this direction, but needs to incorporate video as well. Technology could be developed to allow the elderly to easily film and record by speaking their life stories as memoirs, and simply insert what is their favorite music at different times in their life. What a wonderful way to remember a loved one! The possibilities of technology are simply endless in the ability to improve the quality of everyday life for those who journey near the end of life.

A whole new industry could be developed in this country to provide 'Green' house plans of room additions and small homes that conserve energy and employ computerized technology for companioning the dying. These hospitality houses could serve as a wonderful family space used for generations to come. New homes could be built with this technology already in place. As such technology is developed on a nationwide scale, it could become affordable and accepted as a gracious gift to those at the end of life.

The time has arrived for baby boomers to be socially and politically engaged in developing a technological shift in America.   The American technology employed in building smart bombs and high tech weapons of war used in the recent Gulf War needs to literally "come home." The ancient Hospice Way can bring a change in spiritual consciousness in our land that allows for compassionate care for those who journey to the end of life with terminal illness. We need to employ the use of high tech in ways of peace rather than war. Perhaps this is the final and great peace march for aging baby boomers.

The federal and state governments need to empower the family to enable a loved one to be companioned at home on the journey to the end of a natural life. As we stated in the introduction, suppose that a child or grandchild or other relative is willing to take an extended leave of absence from a job to be a hospice companion at home. Such a leave could be available as a federal mandate. Also, a sliding scale tax credit provided the family for home care would be of great value in making the companioning of a loved one at home a practical, affordable, reality.   According to a recent study conducted by Met Life, the average cost of nursing home care in 2007 in the U.S. is $213 per day.[9] This amount does vary by region and types of care required. At $213 per day, a one year stay in a nursing home will cost $77,745. Companioning at home would save the federal government the direct Medicare cost, which could be provided as a benefit to the family who is companioning in the form of a tax credit. Given the typical nursing home stay of almost three years (the average length of   admission is 876 days), that's over $230,000 at current costs that could be saved by Medicare per patient companioned at home. For seventy eight million baby boomers, the Medicare savings are in the billions of dollars. Also, these amounts for nursing home care are expected to rise significantly in the future.

The same Met Life study concluded that in 2007, the national average cost for providing assisted living for private pay for a one bedroom apartment with a private bath is $2,969 per month, or $35,628 annually.[10] Over a three year period, this amounts to $106, 884. Assisted living are those communities that provide appropriate housing for individuals who need help in day to day living, but who do not need the round-the-clock skilled care found in nursing homes.

The Met Life study also reveals that for 2007, the national average daily cost of a room for Alzheimer's services is $197 or $71,905 annually. Over a three year period, that is $215,715.

Finally, consider that according to The National Caregivers Library, about one half of all persons in residential care in the U.S. pay for the cost of this care out of personal resources.[11] This is a result of the federal government's share of care for those at the end of life coming with strict guidelines and regulations

Can this considerable sum of money for long term care, provided in part by Medicare (Part A), Medicaid, Medigap insurance, private insurance, and very largely the patient's personal funds, be put to better use in providing a Beautiful Death at home?

For the baby boomer generation, the great social question is simply: Can the way we die be changed in America? I believe the ancient Hospice Way provides the path to make this change possible. It has the practical face of Family Companioning.

Current hospice professionals are well suited to train and certify family members so that they can provide safe, high quality end of life care. This could be done through mandatory workshops and seminars required for eligibility for a federal and state tax credit. Also, hospice caregivers could offer required supervision of Hospice Home Companioning, to ensure that the end of life companioning is quality care. Hospices could be reimbursed for these additional services under a new Home Companioning benefit of Medicare.

Acute care hospice residential units need to be widely available as a short-term resource for families who choose to companion a loved one at home. Hospice units are the ideal setting for short term stays when there are patient symptoms that need to be controlled by intensive nursing care. Also, at the end of life, the family may find the setting of the hospice residential unit a preferable place for final care.

Patients in hospice care who improve as a result of this care need to be governed under new guidelines and new standards in the Medicare hospice benefit that allows them to remain eligible for hospice care. Currently, they are discharged if they improve significantly. and no longer meet the strict criteria for hospice eligibility. I observe many patients who then decline because holistic care is not available, medically "crash" at the end of their life and then briefly re-enter hospice care before dying. Care for the elderly at the end of life needs to become more humane and compassionate in the United States. We need as a nation to shift our care for the terminally ill dying away from hospitals and nursing homes and re-focus it on hospice care provided as companioning at home. The ancient Hospice Way is our guide along this path.

As a Christian parish minister of many years, as well as a hospice chaplain, I have seen over and over how much a physical building can mean to people. Religious sanctuaries, whether they be large or small, are often places of the heart. Here within the walls of a sanctuary are found deep and powerful memories of a baptism or wedding, or a funeral. The heart returns again and again with fondness to such places, regardless of the twists and turns life takes. I wonder if we have the courage to create places of the heart in our homes for our mothers and fathers, our husbands and wives, our companions and life partners and other loved ones. Can we add a small addition on to our homes so that we can companion those at the end of life? Perhaps we may want to simply add doors to our seldom used dining room, and make it a bedroom on the first floor. Can we give of our heart and soul as companions who know the boundless wisdom of the spiritual art of hospitality? Can we let the often messy way of death touch our very busy and scheduled way of life? The hospice way of a Beautiful Death presents a great challenge and yet an incredible opportunity to us today. Hospitality houses need to be part of our American lifestyle. The dying call us to courageously create sacred places in our home for them, places which remain forever sanctuaries of the heart as we remember their presence.

Can we hear this call and respond to the dying in ways that myste-riously transform us and the dying? The spiritual art of hospitality is a powerful spiritual tradition that can change our lives as we journey with our loved ones to the end of their life. It holds out the eons old way of a Beautiful Death. Can we companion those at the end of life with a courageous heart that is willing to venture into the spiritual depths of hospitality? Can we allow a Beautiful Death to touch our lives and those we love? I find as a hospice chaplain that those who do this companioning are forever changed in their heart and soul.

Summary: A New Vision of Dying in America.

So how is it that this ancient wisdom calls us to change the face of dying in America? , We find that a compassionate approach to dying a Beautiful Death at home requires first and foremost a discovery of the ancient Hospice Way as a *spiritual tradition*, one rich in wisdom and teachings. This tradition can empower the family as caregivers and companions on the journey to the end of life with a loved one. What is essential for over 70 million boomers to die at home in safety and comfort is to expand the modern hospice movement into a more "bot-tom up" approach to companioning. The family needs to be seen as central to the task of companioning those on the journey to the end of life. Ending the journey of life at home safely and with compassion-ate companioning requires what we have reflected on as a three fold empowering of the family in America.

This new vision calls on American industry and technology to make available the practical place and means of companioning at home a loved one on the journey to the end of life place means. The hospitality house, incorporating modern technology and built as either a free standing "Green" cottage or as an addition to an existing home, offers the *place* where extended end of life companioning can occur in our country. Hospice residential units also need to be available to families who are companioning as a place of brief respite care, and as short-term places of care where life's journey can end with dignity and compassion.

The application of modern technology to caring for those on the journey to the end of life offers a *means* of companioning. Technology can be of great value in providing for safety of a loved one at home, as well as opening new doors for entertainment and communication.

This new vision of death and dying challenges our nation to provide the practical financial resources for a family member to companion a loved one at home. This empowering can be through the federal and state government offering, as a new hospice Home Companioning Medicare benefit, extended leave of absence from work and a tax credit for those who choose to not work and serve instead as end of life companions. Direct Medicare payment to very low income families who serve as certified hospice caregivers would extend home companioning along the entire economic spectrum. Current hospice professionals are well suited to provide the necessary training and supervision of family members in companioning a loved one at home. Families need access to hospice professionals on an "as needed" basis, (prn) and for extended periods.

Our vision of death and dying is a prophetic call to the faith communities all across America to become partners in providing the emotional and spiritual support for those who companion at home a loved one on the journey to the end of life. The constant companioning of a loved one at home can be emotionally demanding and spiritually exhausting. The resources of faith communities in America to provide support for those companioning are immense. Hospitality, as we have seen, is a central belief of every major world religion.[12] Local faith communities are called to partner with families who are companioning on the journey to the end of life.

Part Two

Stories of Companioning
On The Journey

Chapter 6

Stories From the Path

Thus far, the spiritual story of hospice work has unfolded as the story of a tale of hospitality. Hospitality offered to weary, sick travelers who most needed care and comfort on their spiritual pilgrimage is the rich heritage of the hospice movement. We have shown how this hospitality provides the spiritual foundation for hospice care in our own time.

In this chapter, we will use actual stories from hospice companioning to further illustrate the practices which form the spiritual art of hospitality as it is observed by hospice workers today. Here we find the living tradition of hospice work in our midst Stories are a wonderful way to share the spiritual truth patients bring to us. As the spiritual author Anthony De Mello writes: "the shortest distance between a human being and truth is a story."

First Practice

In Offering Hospitality, Observe the Dignity of the Patient Above All Else.

The foundation of all spiritual practice in hospice is a fundamental respect for the dignity of the patient. Death is seen as a natural process, and it is to be accepted as a part of the process of life.

I remember a visit with an elderly lady patient in the residential unit of Blue Ridge Hospice. As we talked, she said to me, "You know all my secrets, don't you?" "Well, I may know a few that you have shared with me," I replied. "The nurses here have been pressing me to take a shower, and I keep saying no to them. Do you know why?" "I have no idea," I answered. ""Well, I am a country girl brought to the city. In all my 92 years, I've only taken one shower when I went swimming at the local Y. I don't like getting undressed in front of others. But I

guess now it's about time to give in and let them give me a shower."
The dignity of the patient is basic to the spiritual art of hospitality. It
appears in so many ways and forms, in a moment's conversation.

For many men, dignity can be a powerful issue at the end of life, as
they loose control of bodily functions and sense their "manhood" slipping away. The practice of dignity as a spiritual art is sensitivity to
dignity in the dying person, and allows them to control as many areas
of their life as possible.

Recently, a member of our family had a serious injury that required
surgery and involved a painful recovery in the hospital. It was difficult to see him suffer because of a struggle with hospital staff over pain
medication. The medical attitude that prevailed in the course of the
treatment was that physicians dispersed medicine when they thought
it was best for the patient and in the prescribed dosage they felt was
proper for the patient. It almost became a begging for relief from pain.
The needs of our family member seemed like an afterthought.

I was struck by how radically different is the attitude of care with
the dying at Blue Ridge Hospice. A skilled nurse provides a comfort
kit in the home of the hospice patient that offers the medicine needed
for the patient's comfort at the end of life. As the patient needs pain
relief it is the family, with the guidance of the hospice nurse, which
can administer the needed medication. The dignity of the patient, in
not having physical relief withheld, comes first in hospice.

> ## Second Practice
>
> Hospitality is Offered through Palliative Care, with the Focus on Pain
> Management and Symptom Control.

In practicing the spiritual art of hospitality in hospice we provide
palliative care for the patient which is quite distinct from medical cure
offered in a hospital setting. The spiritual practice is to allow for the
highest possible quality of life and to value the sacredness of each moment of life. The monastic orders of the West have recognized since at
least the time of St. Benedict that manual work can so deeply be a part
of the spiritual life. The physical care for the dying can be a beautiful
spiritual art if practiced with awareness and compassion.

I was once asked to visit a fairly young man who was the near the end of his life with a painful illness. Although he was a church member, the hospice social worker said he didn't have "much use for the church or religion." As I made an appointment for the visit, his sister said on the phone to "not be surprised if he asked me to leave after a short visit." I expected to be kicked out shortly after the visit started, but was glad to be available if I could provide any comfort.

As we sat alone in the living room, he shared with me his painful journey in the last few days. It seemed that no pain medication had given him much relief and he had not slept for a while. I asked him if we could try something together. "Could I share a form of contemplative Centering Prayer," I asked. I thought it might bring some relief. "Okay", he said, "What have I got to lose?" So in the quiet living room, I began to share a relaxation exercise and then Centering Prayer. Then a strange thing happened. The patient began to snore! I was glad he could relax and get some relief through the prayer. In palliative care we find an emotional and spiritual dimension to pain.

Music therapists also have their stories to share with us as they companion those at the end of life. Carol Joy Loeb, a former opera singer, is a certified music practitioner and a registered nurse.[1] She realizes that approaching death can be a long descent into anxiety and fear. She finds music therapy brings many patients a sense of peace.

"I use the music to bring calmness to them," Loeb says. "It helps with pain and agitation. And in the case of those who are actively dying, it helps them to go peacefully."[2]

Dr. Deborah Wertheimer, the medical director of Seasons Hospice in Baltimore, was startled by the powerful effect of music therapy brought with one dying patient. She relates that "This (patient) who had been so agitated and just all over the bed and on the floor, occasionally, because we just couldn't keep her comfortable, and quieted down."[3] Wertheimer continued that the patient was "obviously attentive to the music, even though I would have thought that it would have made somebody who was so afraid of dying more afraid to hear harp music coming at her"[4]

She observed that "This lady remained peaceful for some period of time. It was just a pleasure to see, because we clearly had not been able with traditional medicines to achieve that kind of comfort for her."[5]

Music-thanatology also has stories of palliative care as the dying are companioned at the end of life. I would like to share at length Theresa Schroeder-Sheker's remarkable story of how she began this spiritual work. She writes:

"The work began for me almost thirty years ago in experiences with two dissimilar but essential figures: a priest and a patient. The priest was a brilliant thinker, and had a particular commitment to young adults, making himself available to grapple with the issues of the day.

Essentially, he taught me a master-class in commitment. He listened and played back the scenario to me as I had presented it. I was a rookie; he on the other hand had life experience, a strong formation, vigilant purpose, and intelligence of the heart. I saw a problem and he saw a spiritual opportunity. He said with rather burning focus and solemnity, "Don't leave them. Protect them." He described the possibility of a protective zone of interiorized stillness and holiness, and asked me what would really happen if I entered a room, found a resident newly deceased, and did not immediately ring the buzzer as we had been taught. What would really happen if an employee took a moment to stand there quietly and say a prayer, giving the soul the possibility to leave the tabernacle of the body gradually? He also told me (among other things) that my understanding of the words "religious" and "spiritual" were narrow and undifferentiated, that I should deepen my own spirituality and religious commitment and expand these dimensions in order to serve more freely and cleanly. He even suggested that I familiarize myself with the world's sacred scriptures, not only the New Testament, and learn to love these other sources, to be able to pray them silently from memory, to be open to the diverse religious and spiritual differences and needs in human beings.

His assignment was a tall order. He never reduced the critical distinctions between religions or even denominations, nor was he syncretic. Rather, he asked me to broaden my own dimensions and deepen them into a far richer and more conscious sacramental life. I was in my early twenties, and this counsel was nothing short of comprehensive.

96

Then I met a second person in this story: an elderly man in the geriatric home who was dying of emphysema. He was a combative resident, often verbally and physically abusive, so it was hard to love him. Whoever was daily assigned to his room to bathe and feed him or to pass the meds used to take a deep breath and grit their teeth. When I came on duty that particular day, I was informed that he was expected to die very soon, perhaps on our shift or the next, and I was assigned to his care. Every medical intervention had, in fact, been exhausted; his lungs were simply disintegrating. He was imminent.

When I entered the room, the death rattle was very loud, and he was thrashing. In retrospect, I understand now that it was alarming for both of us, but in such different ways. There was an immediacy to the situation that is difficult to describe. Everything fell away and just two human beings were left in the same room, facing a moment that would become very large. The notions of revenue streams and sanitation protocols did not exist.

*Acoustically, his death rattle filled the room, like a kind of sound ocean saying "anxiety – anguish," and these affected my own heart instantaneously. I closed the door to give him privacy and hold his hand, calling his name. He was suffering, frightened, gasping and crying out. This is what the literature of monastic medicine calls an agonal death. To my surprise, unlike the year in which he avoided contact, as soon as he heard his name, he held on to me, and met my eyes through his spoken terror. Before I knew it, I had simply gotten into bed and propped myself up behind him in a midwifery position, the way a Lamaze partner will help a mother with a gravity position in an unmedicated labor. With my head and heart lined up behind his and my legs folded near his waist, it was possible to bolster his diminished body. Before I had time to think, I found myself singing quietly to him, holding him. I made my way through the entire **Mass of the Angels**, the **Adoro te devote of Thomas Aquinas**, the **Ubi Caritas**, the **Salve Regina**, and the **Mass of the Blessed Virgin Mary**. These came out simply because they are beautiful, and were as much parts of me as are my hands and feet. I never learned the details of his life or his religious* *identity, if he had one. I only knew that he was dying, his lungs were filling up with liquid, and he was unable to breathe. That moment of combined song and prayer now seems crucial – the music was not a form of distraction therapy. This delicate, permeable event was a real vigil, and the music, sung prayer, inseparable from intention, had become a genuine medicine.*

*Although no cure was possible, a death-bed healing occurred, interiorly. He shifted. The desperate thrashing stopped. The rattle quieted; we might have been together for as much as forty-five minutes. This man who had a history of pushing everyone away actually trusted me, rested into me, and slowly, because of the quiet singing, we began to breathe together. Although ignorant then about chronobiology, synchronization, or systems of entrainment, I knew of them unconsciously, in an inward body-wisdom, because I am musical. But I was young and a young musician too, lacking the language of phenomenology and the physiological lexicon to describe what happened in medical terms, but I did know what happened in terms of grace. Because our two bodies were linked, heart to heart, breastbone to spine, there is no doubt in my mind now that he must have experienced the bone conduction from the singing even if it was new to him and neither of us knew the term. In singing flesh-to-flesh, in a life and death situation where everything is amplified and time stops, some of his fear dissolved. Long after his heart had ceased to beat, I was allowed to hold him. The other three women on the shift covered for me discreetly. A palpable and luminous substance seemed to either fill the room or fill my eyes, and though admitting it in print might make me less credible to some, it might also corroborate for others what they too already know and sense. When I walked home that night, after he died, I understood his passage as a kind of birth, and what had happened to him and between us and an invisible choir of presences was something I could only call, at the time, **musical-sacramental-midwifery.***"

Thus, the ancient Hospice Way has power to touch the lives of the dying through the beauty of music shared from the heart and the soul.

Third Practice

Hospitality Provides Care for the Family of the Patient.

The family is intentionally included in the sphere of the hospice spiritual practice of hospitality. I remember that in the course of the treatment of our family member in the hospital, a nurse "cleared the room" when she felt that too many visitors were present. By contrast, at the residential unit of Blue Ridge Hospice, I have seen what looked like a family reunion as family and friends gathered around the bed-side of a dying patient. If the patient wanted them there, loved ones were not simply tolerated but welcomed. Everyone in the patient's room seemed to enjoy the occasion, and the happy gathering spilled over into the hallway outside the room. A nurse at the nurse's station was annoyed with the noise and confusion and asked me as chaplain to "break up" the gathering. However, I felt that practicing the spiritual art of hospitality should come first in hospice care, so I went into the room and welcomed everyone and told them how great it was to have them here. I asked them to 'hang around' as much as they wanted. Hospice care is family focused, and as hospice workers it is sometimes necessary to live with the confusion and messiness families bring into our organized plan of care.

I recall being asked about dinner time to be with a family who had a loved one dying on our residential unit. After the patient died peace-fully following a long illness, the family members all got together in the kitchen to share a wonderful homemade Mexican meal. Gathering around the table as they ate, each person shared what memories were in their heart about this loved one. Some reflections were funny, and some were sad. It was a wonderful way for a family to experience death together.

As a chaplain, I remember being contacted by a hospice family a month or so after a patient's death. The patient was a young person, who was full of life and vitality almost up to death. The family re-quested that I help them with the scattering of the ashes. So on a beautiful Saturday morning we gathered together in a country cemetery. The sky was a brilliant blue, with a few clouds like balls of cotton. The family had brought the urn containing the ashes and we gathered in a circle on a hilltop. I shared a simple blessing and dedication of the ashes. Without any direction from me, the lid was gently taken off the urn. One family member slowly poured out a handful of ashes and gracefully sprinkled them out on the ground. The urn was silently passed around the circle, and the ashes scattered. When everyone in the circle had taken part, each family member seemed at once to look at their hands. On each person's hands were a few remaining ashes, and they spoke so loudly of the person they had just honored. The ashes called back memories of joy and despair in this young man's life, of the hope and hopelessness he had known. It was one of those "ah-ha" moments in life, when the shortness of life on Earth really strikes home, and you realize down deep how valuable and precious is the gift of life. It was a moment of grace, and a family shared it together through the Hospice Way.

Fourth Practice

Offer Hospitality Ideally in the Home or a Home-Like Facility.

Hospice practices the spiritual art of hospitality in the most natural of all settings; the home of the dying person. When home care is no longer possible for the dying patient, hospice tries to do the next best thing and duplicate as closely as possible the setting of home in a residential unit. The hospice residential unit of Blue Ridge Hospice in Winchester, Virginia has a very comfortable home-like setting. It seems like a place far removed from a sterile hospital room or an institutional nursing home room. It is a place decorated for comfort and peace, with all kinds of personal touches.

Spending time in a patient's home can speak so deeply of where they have been and where they are now in their spiritual walk. The home speaks to us as we take in the pictures on the walls of loved ones or the holes in the wall from the last fight with a spouse, the soft classical music or the blaring television with the soaps, the beautiful antique furniture or the clutter of beer bottles on the floor, the exquisite wall paper or the stinging smell of years of cigarette smoke that has left dirty, stained streaks. All this offers windows into the life of the dying person. Where could you find a more perfect place to practice the spiritual art of hospitality and companion someone in their last days?

What an incredible spiritual work in offering hospitality at a home! In hospice work we are challenged to leave our judgments and opinions at the door, and simply companion another fellow human being in need of comfort and care.

I have found as a chaplain that the photos and personal collections of mementos in the home are such powerful doorways to the depths of the patient's life. In companioning the dying, the things that matter most and speak most profoundly in the patient's life are all around you as you enter the home of the patient. Simply noticing the collection of military medals, carefully preserved in a wooden display case, can be the opportunity to hear almost endless stories of the patient's military service.

I remember visiting Mary in her nursing home room. It was as close to her room at home as she could make it. The thing that seemed to matter most to her in her nineties now were the birds and the squirrels outside her window. The animals were her friends and her companions at the end of life. Feeders kept them coming all the time. "They come to my window and look in to see how I'm doing", she told me once. She knew that they really weren't looking for her, but it was still comforting to have them as friends. I brought by a book on birds one afternoon and we spent a delightful time finding all the creatures outside her window illustrated in the book. Sharing her love of the birds outside her nursing room window was a way to companion Mary in her home. This kind of companioning would not have been possible in a hospital room. The home is a natural place to practice the spiritual art of hospitality.

Fifth Practice

In Offering Hospitality let the Patient direct the Care, as Much as Possible.

The needs of the patient provide the direction for how the spiritual practice of hospitality is to unfold in hospice care.

As a hospice chaplain, I love to find out what it is that brings a sparkle in the patient's eyes and a smile to their face. What do they find interesting, and want to talk about?

I remember one patient whose life centered on World War II. He could talk on and on about war memories, in a very quiet and gentle way. I checked out of local library the book, **The Band of Brothers**, a book about World War II. He had been in many of the battles described in the book. It was a powerful experience to have him share his own account of combat and how it had changed his life. The sharing seemed to bring closure to his life, and a sense of peace.

Another patient of mine was a former college professor now in her nineties. The computer and the world wide web did not exist while she was teaching. As we shared reflections on her teaching career, she could only remember bits and pieces of her favorite poems. This bothered her a great deal, for literature had meant so much to her through the years. I jotted down the verses she could remember from memory, and would find the entire poem on the web and bring it to her on the next visit. Over time, we formed a book called "Recollections" and she kept it by her bedside. It seemed to mean a great deal to her. She then became curious about how the computer worked and how you can find poetry on a web site. One afternoon, I took her in her wheelchair to the library in her nursing home. I introduced her to the desktop computer. She delighted in finding with me all kinds of information that she could only vaguely remember from teaching and from her early days. She literally discovered a whole new world that fascinated her. The Hospice Way is about true spirituality; it is connecting with the body, heart and soul of patient's and families as they experience this companioning in the final days. Perhaps the sign of true spirituality is that glow in the patient's eyes that deep connecting brings to them.

This was brought home to me by one patient who loved dogs. He enjoyed so much having the hospice golden retriever visit in his room and climb into bed with him. With a sparkle in his eyes he told the volunteer who brought the dog, "Just let the dog in the room with me. You stay out in the hall". Hospice care is patient driven care.

Sixth Practice

Hospitality is offered as Holistic Care. Through a Health Care Team.

The hospice spiritual practice of hospitality includes the care of the body, heart, and soul. Many modalities of care are included in hospice, as a respect for this holistic view of the patient.

I remember so well visiting a hospice patient in the hospital with a hospice social worker and music therapist. The patient had built a bond of trust and affection with her hospice companions. I noticed that she acted cold and unresponsive with hospital staff and nurses. However, when the hospice workers entered her room the patient's eyes opened bright and wide, she lifted herself up a little in the bed, and held out her arms for a hug.

The music therapist had such a calming, soothing effect on her. The patient's eyes remained bright and alert throughout the songs that were shared. You could see the patient's body physically relax, and her breathing become calm and peaceful as she enjoyed the presence of the therapist and her playing.

The scripture I shared with June also seemed to touch her soul. As someone raised in the Episcopal Church, she was at home with the sacred spiritual dimension of scripture. She asked me to read on and on, passage after passage. The patient seemed to take in the words of my prayer at a deep level. The hospice social worker remarked afterwards on how the team visit seemed to have such a profound calming effect on the patient who was struggling with many difficult issues. The spiritual art of hospitality, extended through the practice of holistic care, was what June's soul truly needed and this is what she responded to.

Seventh Practice

Foster Sacred Practice through Nature and all Creation.

All my life, I have enjoyed nature and the outdoors. In 1987, I had the opportunity to hike the Appalachian Trail solo over 2,000 miles to help raise funds to open a day shelter for the homeless in he Shenandoah Valley. I have found in working with patients that a simple presence with nature and the outdoors is a very powerful dimension in companioning the dying.

I remember visiting an elderly man on our residential unit. As I talked with him, he seemed rather unhappy and depressed. I asked him what was upsetting him. He was dressed in bib overalls and reminded me of a farmer. Sure enough, he lived on a farm most of his life and was miserable at being cooped up in a residential unit room.

In talking with the nurses on the unit, he was able to move to a room across the hall that was brighter and sunnier, and had a better exposure most of the day. That seemed to cheer him up. Also, a new hospice nurse Brian was visiting patients with me. Brian also had a small farm, and he had a picture of his cows on his cell phone. The patient's eyes light up as Brian shared his cow photos. That really made the patient's day.

Another patient I see regularly loves to sit outside on a large swing on the patio of the nursing home facility. She is not allowed to sit out by herself. Whenever I go to see her, she always grabs my hand and says, "Let's get out of here" and pulls me down the hall to the door outside. I know to dress warmly for the visits, because no matter what the weather, she will sit and swing for happy hours, just talking away about her early life in Germany.

Just the simple presence of sunshine in a swing, after days in a dreary nursing home, can bring so much joy to a patient. We often do not appreciate the comfort and care that nature can bring to those at the end of life.

> As Hospitality is shared, we are called to Be Spiritually Present as Caregivers.

In practicing the spiritual art of hospitality, the hospice caregiver is called to be present with the patient and family as a courageous act of hospitality. As a hospice chaplain, I was asked by a staff social worker to help a family plan a Quaker/Baptist memorial service for a hospice patient. As I visited with the family, I found that the husband was Baptist and the patient was Quaker. I suggested that perhaps we could focus the service on the theme of light. We could use scripture to talk of Christ as the light of the world and then have a time in silence to reflect on how the light of this patient was known by family and friends. The service was one of the powerful memorials that I have ever experienced as a minister. As we sat in silence, an elderly gentle-man rose at the back of the congregation. With tears in his eyes and a sobbing voice, he spoke of how much he had loved the patient back in the 1940's. However, another man had "beaten him to the punch" and married her. And so he stood today to say how much he still loved her. He sat back down and the silence continued. Another older lady stood up and said "Nobody here knows me. But many years ago, this lady helped me out in a difficult time in my life. I have always appreciated that. I just wanted you to know now how much she has meant to me." She sat back down. It is remarkable what happens when we allow opportunities for spiritual presence in life. Hospice care fosters the practice of being spiritually present.

The practices of hospice spirituality that have been presented here together form the foundation of hospice care called the art of spiritual hospitality. No single practice is sufficient by itself in hospice care. However one aspect of hospice spirituality may predominate in the care of a particular patient.

A simple home comfort kit for medication illustrates in an eloquent way all the practices of hospice spirituality. The respect for the dignity of the patient in hospice in seen in having a plan of intervention for meeting the patient's physical needs for pain relief and discomfort. The kit also demonstrates the practice of sacred palliative care as physical care is provided by a nurse. The family practice of hospice spirituality is their role in giving medicine and other care. We see this medicine being dispensed in the home of the patient, and not in an E. R. or hospital room. The patient is allowed to have a say in pain management, and the practice of patient driven care unfolds naturally. The family provides medical care with the supervision of a hospice nurse and physician, and so the practice of a holistic team is available to the patient. Finally, the many needs of the patient for pain relief and care in their home calls all companions of the dying to be truly present in the patient's life. This practice of being present is fundamental to hospice care. The family may ask, "Is it time yet for her medicine?" "Can we call the hospice nurse and see if we can give her more to help with her breathing?" "Does she want some ice chips in her mouth? " All companions of the dying are called to "show up" in being present to the needs of the patient, perhaps for the first time. So it is that a simple thing like a medication kit in a patient's home can show us so beautifully the practices of hospice spirituality that together very naturally form the spiritual art of hospitality.

Conclusion

As a chaplain at Blue Ridge Hospice, I love the honesty and "realness" of companioning the dying at the end of life. I was asked a few days ago by a hospice nurse to visit a patient that was about to die. I had never met the patient. The family had requested a prayer at the end. As I went into the home of the patient, I saw a small, frail very elderly lady curled up in a tight knot in her bed in the living room. She had her eyes closed and seemed to be in some distress, although I did not know why. I told her who I was and why I was there. As is my custom, I asked her if I could have a prayer with her since that was the desire of the family. I don't force prayers on people. She opened her eyes, looked at me with a stare of disgust, and said, "Okay chaplain. But make it quick, because I really have to pee!"

That response of the patient allowed the whole spiritual art of hospitality to be unfolded in the present moment. As a spiritual practice, can I treat this patient with respect and dignity? I went out of the room to find out from her caregivers how she could do what she needed to do with dignity. And then too, sacred palliative care was essential. Did she use a bedpan, or perhaps a catheter, or maybe pull-ups? I asked the lady caregivers with her about how we could respond to her physical need. The family needs were addressed through my brief prayer that they had requested. The needs of the patient were obvious and easy to respond to. The health care team was involved in this care, as it was a hospice nurse that called me to the home. Spiritual presence was responding to the need for a brief prayer, as there were other things going on for the patient in the present moment. As hospice caregivers, we have unlimited opportunities to practice the spiritual art of hospitality with patients and their families. It also helps to have a sense of humor in doing this work and not take yours

Chapter 7

The Dying Speak to Us
as Our Companions

Remember the story of the Wizard of Oz?[1]

It is the tale of a little girl Dorothy who suddenly finds herself lost in a storm in life and she cannot find her way home. It is the story of her journey to her home place. Even though she is lost she has great courage. Along the way on her path she meets many colorful folk. One is the Tin Man who is searching for a heart. Then there is the Scarecrow who wants a brain, and finally, the Cowardly Lion who seeks courage. Here is a story of the search for courage; to find out who they really are. Courage is hard to come by in the tough times. Finally, as they stand before the hall of mirrors with its smoke and loud voices, they lack the courage to reveal who they are to the Wizard- all expect Dorothy that is. The little girl has walked the Yellow Brick Road with courage, and it is courage that will take her home.

What follows in this chapter are interviews with hospice patients who have the courage to reveal themselves to us in their deeply personal death and dying. Like Dorothy, it is courage that has brought them this far in life, and courage that will bring them home. They share what is called in hospice terms a spiritual life review which is simply opening up your spiritual journey in this life to another person. It is a sharing of your story of faith and discouragement; of what matters most, and what counts least at the end of the day. The interviews all center on the theme of hospitality, and patients were asked to describe important moments of hospitality in their life. The interviews are presented simply to reflect the spiritual art of hospitality of the Hospice Way in a real and concrete form. As you read these spiritual stories, consider what is said and done regarding the dignity of the patient. Look carefully at the role of sacred palliative care. Notice the importance of the family and the home to the person. Consider how the patient is allowed to speak in the interview; observe what the patient has to say regarding care for their body, heart and soul through a team approach in hospice care. Then too, see how there is a place for nature and all of creation in their companioning. And most importantly, notice if the hospice caregiver comes across as being spiritually present to the patient. Ask yourself, "Is the patient treated with dignity and respect, and how does their spiritual story unfold? Is there a real, genuine human response made to the patient? Do I see the spiritual art of hospitality practiced here?" Does the ancient Hospice Way seem to take on flesh and bones in these interviews?

All of the interviews are with patients I had the honor of knowing as a chaplain at Blue Ridge Hospice, in Winchester, Virginia. The patients gave both oral and written permission for the interviews to be used as research material. Some of the interviews took place in the hospice residential unit, some in a nursing home, and others in patient's own homes.

The interviews reveal the needs and concerns of the interviewer but, hopefully, the soul of the patient still shines through in these responses. While not all of these patients are now living, their spirit lives on in the hospice movement. I give thanks to each person for sharing with me the courageous gift of your spiritual life story. It has been a beautiful experience for us to share together in the ancient Hospice Way.

Life Review of Reuben H. Hulver
June 6, 2007
Assisted by Ken Patrick, Chaplain, Blue Ridge Hospice

Introduction

Mr. Hulver is a 96 year old patient who lives alone in a small detached house in a urban setting. He has done hard manual labor most of his life, and has many recollections of his days logging and working in a saw mill. He grew up in an isolated, rural community, of southwest Virginia, where people had little opportunity for formal education, and life was a difficult struggle. He quit school while very young, and worked hard to support his family. Mr. Hulver has a deep Christian faith and loves to read the Bible. He requested Bible study by the chaplain and enjoys discussing religion.

Brackets[ ] indicate places where the tape was difficult to understand, and corrections have been added.

Ken: Can you tell me, Reuben, what are the sort of things that people do for you when you live here now?

Reuben: Just say that again.

Ken: What are the things that people do to help you live here in the house? Like maybe your meals or do some cleaning. What are the things people help you with?

Reuben: People comes here to take care of everything. They ask me what I need, and I give them a list. And part of the time, I don't know for sure, but [those] that come now to take care of me know what I need. They get it in their mind what to do and they take over. They ask me how I feel in the morning, and that's about it as far as that goes. And then they take it from there on to see what condition I'm in and I talk to them back. So I talk to them and say exactly what's wrong with me, and anything that happens over the night, or whatever. That's how we do it. As soon as they get [here] they find out if I had any trouble. So I report that to them and they know about [it] and then they [do] it themselves.

Ken: Okay.

Reuben: I don't do it. I'm not rational enough to do that. I tell them and they turn it in. And they know more about me than I know about myself. I get confused on these things. It's just like [I think of it] now, but in five minutes I've kind of [forgotten].

Ken: Okay. Now do they do things like take care of your meals and your medicine?

Reuben: The medicine. They take care of all my medicine. I'd forget to take my medicine if it was up to me. I can't get to it. They fill up the box and they come to see if the medicine is there at the right place and where it belongs. They take care of all that themselves and it's hid.

I don't know where it is.

Ken: Mm-hmm (Indicating affirmatively.)

Reuben: They don't allow me to know where it is. They come in and they put new tablets in and everything. I don't see it until somebody says if I need it, and they give it to me. But I don't have anything to do with that. They said I wouldn't need extra, or nothing, and want me to take my right medicine. So I don't do that. I wait for somebody to come, and they take over.

Ken: Okay. Tell me about your meals. They bring everything in for you?

Reuben: Yeah. All of it's taken care of and everything. I have these ladies that come in every morning and take care of my breakfast. Part of the time, I get up myself in the morning and fix a cup of coffee and toast, and that's what I eat until they get here in the morning because they come later than I do. So I get up in the morning and eat that on my own.

Ken: Mm-hmm. (Indicating affirmatively.)

Reuben: But they get it as soon as they get there and they fix me a breakfast or whatever I need. But I don't fix any eggs or anything like that. I just do little things that I get myself.

Ken: Mm-hmm. (Indicating affirmatively.)

Reuben: I drink hot coffee and I cook toast, a slice of toast, and that's what I make my breakfast on. That's early breakfast. And then when they come, they fix me whatever I want for breakfast, like a regular meal if I need a regular meal, which I don't eat that much anymore.

Ken: Mm-hmm. (Indicating affirmatively.) You said all these people that come in are kind of like your family?

Reuben: Yeah.

Ken: They look after you?

Reuben: Yeah. They know exactly what I have to do and they start on their own. If my medicine is not in its place where it belongs why they see that it's there. Of course, now, it's that little green box over there setting. But [just] overnight medicine is in it. The other medicine I don't know where it is.

Ken: Okay.

Reuben: They don't allow me to know where it is. Part of the time I'm not too rational.

Ken: I brought you some CD's, some tapes of the New Testament. You said you enjoyed listening to those?

Reuben: Yes. Yes. I've enjoyed them. They put tags on the [CD player] now so I can do it myself. I turn it on and get the preaching there. And the other side over there, I've never used that. I don't know exactly what that thing is for, but they got the main tag here.

Ken: Uh-huh. (Indicating affirmatively.)

Reuben: I'm not used to all [those] gizmos, you know. All this old stuff I got here is these things I fixed up myself. I got plenty. All kinds of musical things and everything, you know, that I fixed up on my own because I used to tinker with all that stuff...

Ken: Now you've had the music therapist- I think Kristen comes in and plays music for you. Have you enjoyed that?

Reuben: Yeah. Oh, yeah. I love her. She comes in to sing for me. Once she gets here, we sing together. I can't sing, but she sings and I follow. Now she used to come with a great big book, but now she memorizes it, so she can sing without the book anymore. I sing along with her. We get along fine. She loves to do [it], and for me to hear it.

Ken: Good. How do you feel about everybody doing all these things for you?

Reuben: I just can't praise them enough for it. They just do so much for me. I don't think I deserve it.

Ken: Mmm.

Reuben: I feel like I'm taking advantage of them, you know, because I never had to do that [before now].

Ken: Mm-hmm. (Indicating affirmatively.)

Reuben: I just had responsibility that I had to do it.

Ken: Right.

Reuben: Because I was able to take care of myself, and if I didn't, somebody was taking care of me.

Ken: Mm-hmm. (Indicating affirmatively.)

Reuben: I've had a good life. God has taken care of me my whole life, so He's helped me a lot. I couldn't have made [it] alone.

Ken: Mm-hmm (Indicating affirmatively.) So you appreciate everything done for you, but you're trying to do as much as you can yourself?

Reuben: I'll do what He wants me to do and I ask Him. He helps me. Because He's the one I have to call on. I don't have anybody else to talk to.

Ken: Mm-hmm. (Indicating affirmatively.)

Reuben: I can talk to Him. And I appreciate being able to do that. [some unclear conversation].

Ken: Right. Has hospice been a help to you to?

Reuben: Oh, they've been great to me-ever since they've been with me.

Ken: Mm-hmm. (Indicating affirmatively.)

Reuben: And I get things confused, and I know I say things lots of times. I actually don't mean it, but I've already said it, or something. It gets me out of track and I kind of—because I'm like an old man-many people notices it, but I don't seem to catch it any more.

Ken: Mm-hmm. (Indicating affirmatively.)

Reuben: I got to wait to see if it soaks in; and I try to say the right thing at all times.

Ken: You've really had to depend on all these people taking care of you, and that's hard to do, but that's the way it's worked out.

Reuben: But I got to do it, and I know I need them. Just like these neighbors across the street. I couldn't do without that lady across the street. She's right there. She comes every [day] to see me- that I've taken care of every day. [Some unclear tape conversations]

Ken: Okay. Is there anything else you want to say about hospice and people who have care for you?

Reuben: No. They're just so great, I can't say a thing. They're just perfect. They do everything they're supposed to do, and I have no complaints whatsoever. They're just so great to me that I'd just like to say - **I'm just with them like I am with my family.** I love every one of them and they all seem to be doing exactly what they're supposed to do and that's as far as you can go. (My italics). They never put anything on me that I can't handle.

Ken: Okay.

Reuben: We get along great. And I know, at times, I don't think I said the right thing to some of them, but they've learned me that you got to explain yourself. That they don't understand you sometimes.

Ken: Okay. Thank you for talking with me. I appreciate it.

Reuben: Thank you.

**Life Review of Eleanor H. Talbert
June 14, 2007.
Assisted by Ken Patrick, Chaplain, Blue Ridge Hospice**

Introduction

The patient is an 84 year old female, who lives alone in a rural area. She has been in hospice for close to a year. She used to be a cook at Holy Cross Abbey, a Trappist monastery on 1,200 acres of farmland that is nearby. The monks follow a life of strict prayer, discipline and physical labor. The monastery has a guest house for those on retreat. The Blue Ridge Hospice nurse Dorie Kastanek suggested the patient for an interview.

Ken: Maybe if you could start out by telling me about hospitality in the monastery. What did you do in the monastery? How did you provide hospitality for people?

Eleanor: Well, the monastery practices hospitality-always. It's offering it to me now. And as a cook in the old guest house, they all congregated in the kitchen.

Ken. Okay.

113

Eleanor: Which makes for a kind memory. In the new retreat house, it was silent, but still with the spirit moving and they're all there for the same purpose. I'm there for the same purpose as well. It works out well.

Ken. Good. If you could tell me about your experience in hospice and how hospitality has helped you. How has hospice offered you help and provided the healing that you have now in your life? What of the story about the herbs and how hospice [offered] that kind of hospitality for healing for you?

Eleanor: In the first place, they were so nice. And the difference with this hospice, is most doctors don't call hospice until the patient has about one or two months to live. My doctor called right away.

Ken: Mm-hmm (Indicating affirmatively.)

Eleanor: And so they came right away and offered; they took the strain out of the prognosis just by being friendly. They sent me to the Wellness Center where I received not medicine but food [herbs] in the form of capsules, which my body was deficient in.

Ken: Mm.

Eleanor: And the fact that [hospice] comes every week, and we have tea.

Ken: Mm.

Eleanor: And sometimes they stay an hour, two or three hours. And we're just talking, but all the time the nurse is, and I saw this at first and it constrained me somewhat, but she's checking all the physical[s] you known, even through a normal conversation.

Ken: Okay.

Eleanor: She's making a diagnosis. So I don't think I would have gotten to this point with [out] them because I knew nothing about cancer; nothing at all. And living alone and my friends don't have it, what friends are left.

Ken: Mm-hmm. (Indicating affirmatively.).

Eleanor: I would have, my imagination could have conjured up, a whole lot of things.

Ken: Mm-hmm-(Indicating affirmatively.)

Eleanor: Which they put to rest.

Ken: Good. I appreciate that. So hospice has allowed you to [stay] in this home and be here?

Eleanor: Oh, yes.

Ken: And that's been important to you?

Eleanor: Oh, yes. It is very important to me to say at this home because I love it. And my eldest son promised me that I would never be put into a nursing home. He said he'd shoot me first.

Ken: (Laughs). Okay.

Eleanor: And the other boys are great too.

Ken: Uh-huh. (Indicating affirmatively.)

Eleanor: In fact, they come here two to three times a year. One is in Georgia, one's in Chicago, and one's in Wisconsin.

Ken: Okay.

Eleanor. So. But I just go on with my life as I always have. There doesn't seem to be any change once I climbed over that hurdle.

Ken: Mm-hmm. (Indicating affirmatively.)

Eleanor: Because at this last stage of life, you know [you reflect about death].

Ken: Sure.

Eleanor: I'm not mulling yet, but close to it.

Ken: Uh-huh. (Indicating affirmatively.) Tell me a little bit about your relationship with your hospice nurse- with Dorie. How does she treat you? Does she have respect for you? How have you all gotten along in Hospice?

Eleanor: Well, we hit it off right away. And when my two younger sons' came- one of the sons has a nurse for a wife

Ken: Mm-hmm. (Indicating affirmatively.)

Eleanor: And Dorie wanted to meet her, so we had a party with the neighbors and everybody. [my italics]. And then I have-this doesn't

115

have anything to do with hospice, but it has a lot to do with my attitude: I have this friend. She is the first person I met when I came down here, she sold me this property. And she's back and she comes twice a week. Now my eldest son is coming in August, and his wife is connected with hospice in Chicago.

Ken: Okay.

Eleanor: So we'll have another party. So I think by telling you this, you more or less know that it's turning into a family affair with hospice. [my italics].

Ken: Uh-huh. (Indicating affirmatively.) Great.

Eleanor: I mean that's the way I feel.

Ken: Uh-huh (Indicating affirmatively.)

Eleanor: I could go to them for anything.

Ken: Good.

Eleanor: Even when I call in people on the phone, the nurse on duty. If I can't get a hold of Dorie, it's not that I call very often, I've only called once. But she answered my questions perfectly without ever having seen me and was so nice about it.

Ken: Mm-hmm. (Indicating affirmatively.) Okay.

Eleanor: I just can't praise [them] enough.

Ken: So the hospitality of hospice has kept you going?

Eleanor: What do you mean by hospitality?

Ken: Well, I think hospitality is opening your heart and making a place for another person. It is bringing them in and welcoming them as if they are part of your family.

Eleanor: They do that. They certainly do that. And with my experience at the monastery, and my job experience before, I've always worked with the public. It's very easy.

Ken: Mm-hmm. (Indicating affirmatively.)

Eleanor: For that to happen.

Ken: Okay.

Eleanor: I mean to occur just almost spontaneously.

Ken: Okay. Good. It seems like that hospitality came at a time when you really needed it in your life. It seems like it has really helped you get over that big bump and keep going.

Eleanor: You mean after the prognosis?

Ken: Yes.

Eleanor: Yes. I don't know what I would have done without [hospice] because they answer my pertinent questions about the disease.

Ken: Mm-hmm. (Indicating affirmatively.)

Eleanor: As well as my pertinent questions about what's going on in the world.

Ken: Mm-hmm. (Indicating affirmatively.)

Eleanor: I mean it's an all inclusive thing.

Ken: Okay.

Eleanor: And I do have questions every week to ask her about. They couldn't have done more for me. And, of course, they send medicines out here that I have to take. I'm not taking any treatment for this.

Ken: Right.

Eleanor: Because of my age, I do have things that I need to take just like any old octogenarian.

Ken: Anything else you want to say about Hospice care?

Eleanor: I think I've praised it to the sky.

Ken: Okay. What of your experience of how hospice care changes people's lives?

Eleanor: It has changed my life. It's opened up [so much]. There's a music therapist that comes [from hospice]. I have two granddaughters, who are both 13 years old, and the music therapist is 26, working on her Masters in music. And I want her to come to the party when they come too because she's a perfect role model.

Ken: Good.

Eleanor: It would be good for them to see her.

Ken: Uh-huh. (Indicating affirmatively.) Hospice has sort of become your extended family.

Eleanor: Yes. It has.

Ken: And hospice seems to have provided a home for you at this point in your life.

Eleanor: A home for me?

Ken: Well, in the sense of a [home] in their hearts- that there are people offering you a place in their hearts.

Eleanor: Yes.....And I'm sure that they do that for everybody....

Ken: That's great. Well, thank you. I really appreciate your sharing [with me].

Life Review of Mildred L. Brannock
May 21, 2007.
Assisted by Ken Patrick, Chaplain, Blue Ridge Hospice

Introduction

This is an interview with Mildred Brannock, who is a patient in the residential unit at Blue Ridge Hospice. We are reflecting on a spiritual life review of her life. I have corrected a few grammatical words in the verbatim transcript to have the English flow more in a written style. Corrections that were necessary because the tape was hard to hear or understand are shown with brackets [ ].

Ken: We are going to begin by talking about hospitality. About making room for those things that are important in our life. [Let's talk] about creating space and being able to say "Yes" to those things that are most important to us. During our earlier conversation this morning, Mildred, [you] were talking about hard it is to give up the beautiful room and bathroom, the pink bathroom, that you had with your daughter. So I thought we could talk a little bit about that. Tell me about that room you had with your daughter. What was it that you really liked in that room?

Mildred: Well, first of all I'd like to say that I am nearly 92 years

118

old. I went to live with my daughter due to my problems [of] getting around and so forth. I took a lot of the old furniture that I had in my home and the old furniture she had in her home. We made a lovely old bedroom out of that leftover furniture from her house and my house. I am still attached to my home in Richmond, Virginia. I lived there in the '20's, and at times I find myself very homesick for my old home and her old home. We lived right on a main thoroughfare into Richmond, Virginia. Lots of people who were looking for work or looking for a place to stay would come to our back door. [They would] come to our back door and beg for clothes or food or anything that was usable that we could pass on to them. We used to say, "Whoever had been to our doors weeks before evidently talked to the people that were riding the rails and told them where they could get a good meal." Or if they wanted clothes, to make their needs known. My mother and sister, who were getting old themselves, would collect [things] that anybody could use who came to our back door and say, "Do you know where I could get so and so?'

Ken: That's great. Tell me how you felt. Were those happy times for your family even though you were poor?

Mildred: [We] couldn't have been any happier anywhere in the world.

Ken: Okay.

Mildred: We were proudly happy.

Ken: So you created this place for these other people?

Mildred: Yes.

Ken: And they responded to you.

Mildred: Yes

Ken: And that makes you really happy, in a way that it doesn't when you just keep the [things] for yourself?

Mildred: If we hadn't said "Yes" to these people, how would they know if we [cared]?

Ken: Do you think coming into hospice was kind of saying "Yes" to life changing for you?

Mildred: Why yes. It has definitely changed [life] for me. But I look at the other side of it and think how thankful I and my family [are] that there is a place like hospice. That they could take this old lady in, and show her how to be comfortable even though things were not the way she might have liked to have them.

Ken: Okay. We were talking a little bit earlier about your nurse, and how she's willing to take you around to different places and really care for you. Did she show you hospitality? Did she show you how to be kind or gracious?

Mildred: I don't have any words that can possibly describe Theresa Gertson. When I moved up here to live with my daughter, I needed some transportation. For the times that I would need transportation to doctors appointments, [or] any kind of appointment for which I had no transportation. She was visiting me today and I told Theresa; I said,

"Theresa, you are my angel!" when she walked in the door.

Ken: That's great.

Mildred: Our friendship has continued even though my need does not continue for transportation.

Ken: Let's take this apart just a little bit. Part of it was that she responded to whatever need there was. Like a lot of nurses [that] might respond to you physically. [But] she would also respond to a need for transportation or [for] somebody to listen to you to – she was just kind of there whenever you needed her.

Mildred: That's right.

Ken: And that really makes her a special person in your life.

Mildred: Very much so.

Ken: Okay.

Mildred: Because, you know, we traveled up as far as-what is it, Berryville?

Ken: Mm-hmm (Indicating affirmatively.)

Mildred: And anywhere that I needed to go for help, physical help, Theresa was right there to make it possible for me to go.

Ken: And it seems like a big part of hospice care is that it's included your whole family. Like your family came here to visit, or like on

Easter, when we had the Easter [worship] Service, your whole family could also come here for a meal. So it's not just you, but it's your whole family as part of the [care].

Mildred. That is exactly right.

Ken: And that really makes it special, I think, that the whole family can be part of this.

Mildred: And, of course, the thing that I think about [is] that it's such a God's blessing to us to have a privilege to live in a place like this.

Ken: Mm.

Mildred: I can only hope in the future that I can return all of this somehow or the other.

Ken: So you feel really blessed?

Mildred: Yes.

Ken: That's great.

Mildred: One reason I feel so blessed is because [when] I lived in Richmond before I ever got married, somehow we always managed [even] in the Depression.

Ken: Mm-hmm. (Indicating affirmatively.)

Mildred: I guess one reason is most of the people who live around us helped in the Depression too.

Ken: Okay. Have you felt like hospice workers really respect you? Have you felt like there's a dignity with hospice?

Mildred: To respect me?

Ken: Un-huh. Have you felt respect for you in hospice?

Mildred: They couldn't help but have respect for me.

Ken: Okay. hospice has been a real blessing for you?

Mildred: It has.

Ken: Okay.

Mildred: The nurses are wonderful.

Ken: Let's talk a little bit about how you feel toward the end of life towards God. Has that changed any in hospice? Like you said you accepted cancer, and you're just waiting to go.

Mildred: Yes.

Ken: Is that okay?

Mildred: Well.

Ken: It can't be any other way, huh?

Mildred: Yes sir. It's the way.

Ken: Okay. Anything else you want to say about your time in hospice or where you are at in your life right now?

Mildred: Oh, I have thoroughly enjoyed my time at hospice. Sometimes I have been very homesick. At the same time, I am grateful that I have this home to go to.

Ken: That's great that hospice could give you a home.

Mildred: Yes

Ken: That you could have a place. So you're sort of traveling in between now, so you've given up this home that you've had in Richmond. You've given up this home that you've had here with your daughter, and you're waiting for God to take you home?

Mildred: Yes. And I understand He is waiting for me.

Ken: Everybody's kind of waiting. So you're sort of a traveler right now? You're kind of a pilgrim.

Mildred: Yeah.

Ken: And this is kind of where you are right now.

Mildred: I'm on a pilgrimage.

Ken: Is that okay?

Mildred: Well, the way I feel, it has to be okay.

Ken: Okay. So hospice is able to give you a home when you're kind of between homes?

Mildred: Yes.

Ken: Right now. And that's kind of what hospice has done for you.

Mildred: Mm-hmm. (Indicating affirmatively.)

Ken: I think you've come to a pretty good place here even though it's hard.

Mildred: Yeah. I hate to leave this place.

Ken: Uh-huh. (Indicating affirmatively.)

Mildred: But at the same time, all my life I have tried to live by the Bible. I know what the Bible says about our situation in life, and I think, "Well, I've got to believe that place of comfort and move on."

Ken: The Bible in a way is kind of your road map while you're traveling along.

Mildred: Yes. That's right.

Ken: Okay. And that's been a real comfort to you to have that.

Mildred: Yes. To be able to believe what the Bible says.

Ken: It seems like the Lord has really been with you in all these [times].

Mildred: He's been with me.

Ken: You've had God's promise with you.

Mildred: Yes.

Ken: Let's go back to a passage in the Bible we've talked about quite a bit, the 23rd Psalm. And we did it by putting your name in into it so it [says]:

"The Lord is Mildred's shepherd. Mildred shall not want."

Well, the sheep are always traveling from one pasture to another. So that's kind of where you are: It's like being the sheep right now. You're kind of moving from one pasture to another. And the amazing thing is you expect the sheep to be afraid or really not very happy. But the end of the passage is:

"I shall not want".

It's because the shepherd is with you.

Mildred: That's right.

Ken: So that's kind of where you are now-moving from one pasture to another like the sheep, but the shepherd's with you.

Mildred: And even though I don't particularly like where I'm headed, you know, I know it's the way that he has put out there and it's okay.

Ken: And it seems like that's a lot of comfort to know He's with you as you're moving from one pasture to another.

Mildred: It is.

Ken: Mm-hmm. (Indicating affirmatively.). So your faith has really been that big source of comfort for you. Good. Anything else you want to say about where your life has gone, or how you found the Shepherd with you?

Mildred: I have had some problems that I will not go into, but he has been with me.

Ken: Like the Shepherd kept showing up in your life?

Mildred: Yes. Any time I needed Him.

Ken: Okay. And that's a real comfort to find the Shepherd?

Mildred: It's very comforting.

Ken: Okay. [Sensing that patient was getting tired and wanted to end the interview].

Do you want to have a prayer together?

Mildred: Nodding her head yes.

Ken: Dear Lord, we do give you thanks for being the Good Shepherd in Mildred's life; for all the ways that You have comforted her through the years. We ask the blessing now of Your presence as the Good Shepherd. Be with Mildred in heart and soul and body and mind. May your loving presence as the Good Shepherd lead her and guide her and direct her all the days of her life. This we pray in the name of Christ our Lord, the True Shepherd." Amen

Mildred: Thank you. That's very nice.

Introduction

The patient is a retired university professor, with rich and diverse life experiences. She has a deep fondness of literature and especially poetry. The patient lives in a very attractive private room in a church related nursing home facility. The hospice chaplain has companioned her in hospice by finding complete poems when she can remember a verse or a phrase. The poems are then collected in a book of "Recollections" that the chaplain reads with her. The poems often form the basis of Lee's sharing stories about her life. She has a delightful sense of humor and is a great story teller. The interview has been edited to allow the stories to flow more smoothly, and editing is indicated with brackets [ ].

Ken: You shared with me some wonderful stories. Maybe they're stories about ways hospitality didn't happen in your life, but I was wondering if you could share those stories so I could record them. [How about] the rock and the pill?

Lee: I was eating my lunch, which was a blueberry tart, and I bit into a white rock. Now it was an odd looking rock. It had no shape to it whatsoever. But later on I put the rock by the table by my bed, and when the nurses [aide] came in and saw this rock, she thought it was a pill! I tried to tell her that it was a rock; that my noon pills were green and the shape of the pentagon and they don't look anything like this rock. But she wanted to be sure she covered all her bases, so she went to the head nurse and said I had one of my pills lying on the table. The head nurse came in and she decided it was a pill, and I thought that the two of them were going to make me take a rock!

Ken: What was the outcome of the story? Did you have to eat the rock?

Lee: No. I told her that I would take my medicine tomorrow.

Ken: Well, that was a good way out. How about the apple sauce story?

125

Lee: Oh, one of the head nurses that we had who served the pills thought she read some place that I liked my pills ground up. Well, I don't. It's a hideous mess when they're ground up, so I told her this time please just bring me some apple sauce and the whole pills and I'll take them. The next time she came and there were all the pills ground up making a purplish colored apple sauce. I told her again not to bring it to me again all ground up. I can swallow a pill very easily. And she came back the third time with the pills ground up and I said to her, "You take them."

Ken: Did she take them?

Lee: No. She never brought me a ground up pills again.

Ken: That was a good way to handle it. Can you tell me again about your hair? That people didn't really ask you and they just sort of did what they wanted to do.

Lee: Well, I had two hospice ladies come in to help me do my nails and my hair. I think one of the nurses here on the floor here (not a hospice lady) suggested they cut my hair. Well, the end of it was that one was that one was working on my nails and I didn't realize [the other] cut my hair. And [after] I took my bath, [I felt back] and I had hair that looked very much like- what's the Indian name?

Ken: A Mohawk?

Lee: Yes. Very much like a Mohawk.

Ken: How did you feel when that happened?

Lee: Well, I felt kind of out of control.

Ken: Okay.

Lee: I felt sort of helpless.

Ken: It seems that there wasn't a feeling of dignity there. -They didn't respect who you are as a person.

Lee: Well, if you had beautiful hair when you were young, you hate to lose it. You hate to have it cut even more.

Ken: So that's a hard thing to go through, the way they treated you.

Lee: Well, the hardest thing is every day for me [now] [with my hair].

Ken: Can you share any other stories about hospitality?

Lee: Well, the story that comes to my mind right now was that my parents loved to walk in the woods, and they tromped all over every inch of the ground that we owned. One day my father found a perfect tree. It was a maple tree and it was shaped exactly as if it were made by some automatic machine. Every limb came out the same way, and every branch was at the same distance. And the tree was so perfect that even the north side was not smaller than the rest. And that tree became an object almost of worship. We accepted the tree as God's gift to the countryside, and we were so afraid that somebody would find the tree and would carve [their] initials in it and let the insects in to kill the tree. Now maybe a tree doesn't seem important to everybody, but this tree changed with the season, and we would go make a pilgrimage there every season. In the spring, the tree was black with moisture and had red leaves; tiny little red buds coming out. The nicest time, which my mother like the best, was in the summer. The leaves were so perfectly formed and so perfectly spaced that many of the animals stayed there because they had protection. You couldn't see even a piece of blue through the tree if you were looking for the sky. And then in the fall, it was splendid, so pretty. The leaves turned yellow, and red and green in the center, and it looked as if it were a flame. It made the whole hillside seem to light up. In the winter, we used to go and sit on a rock and watch the tree fill up with snow.

Ken: Hmm.

Lee: Now I would like to go back and see that tree [again]. I know if do, somebody will have cut it down and there's probably a [row] of houses that look just alike or it's a three-lane highway now.

Ken: Mm-hmm. (Indicating affirmatively.)

Lee: Anyway, let's hope the street [there] is called "Grateful".

Ken: It seems like the tree offered hospitality. It offered a place for the animals and a place for you and your family in your heart.

Lee: That tree meant a lot to us, and we never told anybody. Nobody knew it but us.

Ken: It's nice to have secrets in your heart that you keep. What about that story that you shared yesterday about your father? Do you remember that? I like that.

Lee: Where we lived food was a problem. Some of [the people] didn't have [land enough] to plant [food] to last them through the winter. My father would plant two extra rows of potatoes. Now those were long rows and they would take a long time to get the potatoes [up]. He would [also] plant two extra rows of corn, and we would cut the corn off and dry it on top of the porch roof. When it turned into winter, and we needed some vegetables, we would soak the corn overnight and then cook it in milk. [When] it cooked down we would put a little butter in it and fry it a little bit, and we had fried corn. It's quite delicious and very wholesome.

Ken: What about your father being Santa Claus at Christmas time?

Lee: He always walked through the woods with my mother and he knew all of the [local] children. If it snowed on Christmas (and it usually did in those days), he would harness up the sled that he used for carrying hay and straw. My mother would have fixed stockings for all the children under twelve and my dad would go through the countryside with the bells ringing on the horses and throw a stocking on the front porch of all the little children. Now I think you need to know what was in the stocking. There were vegetables and oranges; a rare treat in those days. There were two apples from the man who had the apple orchards in the town. There were [also] two pieces of licorice, which I think every child hates.

Ken: Laughs.

Lee: There was a little sack of round candy, which I think is made from molasses. Anyway, it tastes awful. And [I remember] three candy canes. And on top of it all there would be nuts because we lived in a nut growing country. And then on top of all the nuts, there would always be a book. My mother would buy the books at the second hand store for a nickel or less. These were the depression days in the country.

Ken: That's a wonderful story of how much hospitality your father had for everybody, and how much he cared for those around you.

Lee: He was a principal of a school, and he loved wearing the Santa Claus suit. My father was the fun one in the family. My mother [however] was very serious about reading.

Ken. Mn-hmm. (Indicating affirmatively.) You seem to have a love of reading from her.

Lee: Well, I read anything that's in front of me. My boss would say, "Don't put anything down you don't want her to see. She has no manners when it comes to reading." I do love to read.

Ken: You made a statement to me. You said, "The Cadfael book saved my soul." Can you tell me how that book meant so much to you?

Lee: Well, I had a back problem. I had two operations, which left me with a bad case of sciatica, and that hurts about as much as anything can hurt. Pain is pain, and sciatica is a special pain. I had to stay in bed because I couldn't work and I couldn't sit. I was getting cabin fever of the worst kind. My neighbor brought me a book, which was one of the series of the Father Cadfael books. It was written about the 10th century. [The main character] was a priest. He uses herbs and ice and hot water to treat all the people that came to him with the worst of diseases- like leprosy. It's just a wonderful book. The cover of the book and the way faces were shown was marvelous. I think there are twenty-two books [in the series].

Ken: Okay.

Lee: The books had some young warrior and a beautiful lady. I could read those books and forget about myself. And that's half the fun of reading- when you forget about yourself.

Ken: Okay. What do you feel about being in hospice now as a far as people taking care of you and showing you hospitality? What has that meant to you now?

Lee: Well, I'm very pleased with the hospice group. **They seem to have an extra dimension in understanding what makes pain** (my italics). When some of the nurses that do not belong to hospice give me a bath, I swear they don't know which way the [elbow bends]. The hospice girls, nurses and nurse's aides, know exactly how to get the leverage that the human body needs to be moved. I'm very impressed with that and that might be because I have such a back condition. Any movement is excruciating. I think they are very trained.

Ken: Anything else you want to want to say about people caring for you?

Lee: Well, I didn't know what hospice was five years ago. A lady who lived behind [though] became ill and she had a long goodbye. Her family would sit with her and they were finally just about worn out, and hospice came to take over. And I had no idea what was going on. So I think [hospice] has managed to do marvelous things [for] a lot of people without feeling they [have to be praised].

Ken: Thank you for the interview. I appreciate all your stories. They are wonderful.

These four interviews hopefully reflect the power of the spiritual art of hospitality to deeply touch the lives of both patients and caregivers. Hearts and lives are forever changed from the spiritual presence known in the companioning.

So where did this courageous hospitality with the dying as a spiritual work come from? We have called the Hospice Way ancient, and so, precisely how old is it? What are its deep historical roots in society? Can we look back through the dusty history of past centuries and see how this spiritual companioning of the dying came to be? How are the seven practices of hospice spirituality part of a long, cherished tradition in the West? Can we see them centuries ago as hospice came into existence through the spiritual work of Christian monks and nuns in the urban centers of Byzantium in the first centuries, and later in the Middle Ages? Let's unfold the next chapter of this remarkable story of offering comfort and compassion to those at the end of their life's journey through the spiritual art of hospitality in this ancient tradition called the Hospice Way.

Part Three

Wisdom for the Journey
The Ancient Path Stretching From
the Middle Ages

Chapter 8

The Historical Roots of Hospice Companioning

Introduction

The hospice tradition of companioning the dying through the ancient art spiritual of hospitality began long ago in a time quite different from our modern world. The first dim, hazy memories of what was later to become the "Hospice Way" trace back to the pioneering work of Christian monks and bishops in the 300's. The usual place for treatment of illness was the home. However, the need arose for facilities to care for those who were homeless, lacked caring family members, or were traveling and needed care.

As the historian Guenter B. Risse relates in his book, ***Mending Bodies, Saving Souls. A History of Hospitals***, one of the first institutions providing medical care was established when Aetius, a sectarian Syrian with medical knowledge, and his followers began to treat the sick at a hospice in Antioch in the 304's.[1] The medical treatment of the time was palliative, offering good nursing, rest, and food.

The flowering of these early beginnings of the spiritual art of hospitality occurred in the Medieval period (476 A.D. to mid 1400's). Here we see the Hospice Way practiced in different forms by several social institutions that were emerging in the West: hospices, hospitals, leper houses, and monasteries with infirmaries. Often these early institutions expressed hospitality for the needy through Christian service offered by the Roman Catholic Church. Many of the medieval hospices and hospitals were founded and run by monks and nuns who followed the ***Rule of St. Augustine,*** while monasteries where needy guests might find palliative care often had infirmaries and practiced their own form of Christian hospitality commonly following the ***Rule of St. Benedict.***

133

What brought forth this remarkable expression of Christian hospitality, and how was it actually practiced? What was the prevailing spirit of these times and how did Christian hospitality become so completely woven into the very fabric of medieval society?

We could start with a snap shot of the times. There were several powerful social factors that brought hospitality to center stage in this period of Western history. With the fall of the Roman Empire in the fifth century, there were immense social problems facing Western culture. Where were the poor, the sick, the dying, and the destitute to turn for help? There was no national welfare state to offer assistance. Rich private benefactors, such as noblemen and Lords, provided some relief. But the major burden fell on the one remaining charitable institution in the West: the Roman Catholic Church.

It was also the church that inherited, by default, the learning of early classical age schools of medicine. The church preserved the ancient Greek and Roman medical knowledge. During the Dark Ages the church stood as the repository of Western learning.

The spirit of this time was also one in which hospitality became seen by the medieval church as a fundamental message of the teachings of Christ. As we find Christ's words recorded in the sacred scripture of the *Gospel of Matthew:* "Then the righteous will answer him, 'Lord, when did we see you hungry and feed you, or thirsty and give you something to drink? When did we see you a stranger and invite you in or needing clothes and clothe you? When did we see you sick or in prison and go to visit you?' "The King will reply, I tell you the truth, whatever you did for one of the least of these brothers of mine, you did for me."[2]

These words were taken into the heart and soul of monks and nuns in the Middle Ages. They embodied a living out of the Gospel that called for an embracing of the poor, the sick, the needy, the destitute and above all the dying, with a heart of compassion. *The church's care for the dying was seen as sacred care in the Middle Ages, for it was care that was offered in the name of Christ and to Christ. All care for the dying was firmly rooted in spiritual presence, for it was the very presence of Christ that was seen as with caregivers as they companioned the dying.*

Many centuries later this teaching would be echoed in the life of

Mother Teresa of Calcutta, who called her nuns to see Christ in His "horrible disguise" as they picked up the dying from the streets of Calcutta and offered them care at the end of life. From its very beginning over 1,500 years ago, the Hospice Way in the West has been grounded in a spiritual presence with the dying.

In the medieval monastic movement this concern for spiritual hospitality and spiritual presence developed as a part of their rich spiritual legacy. This is clearly seen in the ***Rule of St. Benedict*** (c530) which states: "All guests to the monastery should be welcomed as Christ."[3] This is one of the most familiar and quoted phrases of the Rule, one that emphasizes the preeminent position which hospitality occupies in every Benedictine monastery.

Finally, our snap shot of the early Middle Ages reveals that the need for care of the poor and dying was immense at that time. No established system of hospitals, hospices, and care for lepers or medical training as we know it today existed in the early medieval period.

If we could go back through the years of Western history to the fifth or sixth century, when the Hospice Way first began, what would it be like to walk down the street of a town or city in the ancient world? While no digital cameras existed that would have allowed us to film this period in history, we can paint a mental description of this era of the early Middle Ages from the historical accounts we have today. It might be an experience something like this:

The first thing we might notice is that except for a few buildings in public commons or wealthy houses and spas, there do not appear to be sewers underground as we know them. The stream that flows through the town seems dark and smelly, and we see people throwing the excrement from their chamber pots into the polluted water. The roadways are formed by narrow mud walks. As we step into a house, we see no flush toilets. Our modern bathtubs with hot and cold running water do not exist. There are no gleaming stainless steel refrigerators to keep food fresh. There is no air-conditioning that keeps the rooms comfortable. No plastic containers keep dust and insects off of food. What we know as soap is more like our grandmother's. It is lye soap that is caustic and harsh. All around the city are found plenty of rats, ticks, and flies. Dead animals are noticed as an everyday occurrence. Intestinal worms are common. We see that water for drinking comes from the same nearby stream where sewage and garbage are dumped. Even the water from a well smells bad, and we suspect that it may be contaminated by sewage seeping into the ground water from nearby latrines. It appears that some drinking water is kept in large jars or barrels which are put in one fairly central location. When we lift a lid to look at it, the water appears stagnant, and we wouldn't be surprised if there were germs breeding in it.

What strikes us is that groups of people keep coming into the town day after day. There is a lot of noise and confusion, almost like a parade. As we ask about all this, we are told these are pilgrims on a holy pilgrimage to Rome, as they pass in almost a carnival atmosphere. It seems like a page out of Chaucer's **Canterbury Tales**.

It is clear that there is no modern medicine in the form of strong antibiotics or clean, modern, hospitals. There is no way to stop the spread of plagues. We are told plagues happen on a regular basis, and as much as one-fifth of the local population would die. All the comforts and conveniences of our modern world, such as bright lights, indoor plumbing, central heating and air-conditioning, telephones, packaged food, computers with e-mail, and our microwaves lie many centuries ahead in the future.

In this medieval world we find disease, limited sanitation and cleanliness, and basic palliative medical care. Western society obviously faced immense social issues at this time in providing care for the poor, the sick, the needy, the destitute and the dying. As we saw, it was the collapse of the Roman Empire in the fifth century that was a major force in bringing the need for hospitality to the forefront of Western society. This medieval culture was the rich spiritual soil into which the Hospice Way of companioning the dying sank deep roots. From these roots would spring the flower of what we know today as the modern hospice movement.

The response of the Roman Catholic Church to the social needs of the time was truly remarkable. There emerged throughout Europe and Great Britain hospices, hospitals, leper houses, monasteries with infirmaries and guest houses, as well as military orders of hospitals during the crusades to care for the needs of sick and dying.

This outpouring of hospitality was grounded in what are known as the corporal and the spiritual works of mercy of the Roman Catholic

Church. The great Christian social activist Dorothy Day once said that everything a baptized Christian does should be directly or indirectly related to these acts.[4] The corporal acts of mercy, which focus on care for the physical body of the needy, include feeding the hungry, giving drink to the thirsty, clothing the naked, harbouring (sheltering) the homeless, visiting the sick, ransoming the captive, and burying the dead. The spiritual works of mercy, which focus on care of the heart and soul of the needy, include instructing the ignorant, counseling the doubtful, admonishing sinners, bearing wrongs patiently, forgiving offences willingly, comforting the afflicted, and praying for the living and the dead. Dorothy Day understands Christianity not as primarily personal beliefs or feelings, but above all as a spiritual practice extending the hospitality of Christ to those in need. The Christian faith is a living out of the Gospel message that as we care for the least among us, so we care for Christ.

The modern scholar, Heinrich Pompey, has reflected on the corporal and spiritual works of mercy. He explains that *colligo*, or sheltering the homeless, is giving hospitality to strangers. *Condo*, burying the dead, is a concern for death and dying that is reflected in hospice today. He writes about the corporal works of mercy saying: "The new worldwide hospice movement assumes the commitment of caring for the dying and the grieving."[5] The Spiritual Works of Mercy include *sola*, comforting the afflicted. He explains that "Comforting the grieving can mean enabling the irreversibly or terminally ill patient to realize that in spite of everything he/she is loved and esteemed. Someone suffering needs to experience comfort and warmth."[6]

Pompcy makes clear the spiritual power behind the beginning of the spiritual art of hospitality in the Middle Ages. For our early brothers and sisters, the "…redemptive presence of Christ characterizes Christian Charity and provides the foundation of its liberating help. Nowhere can the Christian encounter God more concretely and experience Him in more humanly real form that in the suffering human being."[7]

The reason for founding the hospices, hospitals, monastic infirmaries and leper houses has been well expressed by Pompey: "Ever since Jesus Christ, God no longer hovers over the suffering world: he is present in the midst of the suffering world."[8] From this comes the spiritual desire to be in service through acts of hospitality.

This hospitality is, from the beginning, a spiritual force that transforms both the host and the hostess. As Pompey explains, "In the ministry of Caritas the individual Christian does not only encounter and accompany his suffering neighbor: at the same time the individual helper becomes a helping Christ for the suffering person, i.e. the helper acts 'in persona Christ' and through His service Christ is salvifically made present to the suffering. The two-fold sacramental presence of Christ in the suffering and in the helper represents a spiritual power."[9] In non-theological language, we could simply say that the journey to the end of life by the Way of the spiritual art of hospitality transforms all who walk this path including both those who give care and those who receive it.

The corporal and spiritual acts of mercy of the Roman Catholic Church, tracing from the Middle Ages, form the beginnings of the spiritual art of hospitality.[10] In companioning the sick and dying, there emerges sacred palliative care extended in hospitality. This is known as "monastic medicine." It is from this palliative care practice in the Middle Ages that the Hospice Way develops. A striking characteristic of this care is its holistic nature. It was truly a companioning of the sick and dying in body, heart, and soul. Above all else, it was a sacred companioning.

Monastic medical practice recognized that natural causes could lead to illness and disease, and so simple palliative care was offered for those in need. This natural healing included techniques such as general cleanliness and proper diet in care for the sick, as well as bloodletting and herbalism. Behind this natural care stood a firm spiritual belief that God had ultimate authority in the health and healing of the person. This is seen, for example in the monk's view that it is the divine origin of herbs that is the main reason for their healing powers. Citing the prevailing spirit of the Middle Ages, D. W. Amundsen writes: "A dependence on the power of herbs…without reference to their Creator [God] was regarded as improper for a Christian."[11]

It was God who was seen as the spiritual source of the growth of plants. This divine origin made natural herbs a spiritual means of healing in those times. Many plants were also used by Christians in sacred rituals and ceremonies, and this further developed the spiritual nature of herbal care offered in monastic medicine.

The architectural design of the monastic infirmaries and hospitals also expressed the spiritual nature of palliative care in the medieval world. The buildings themselves were for care of the heart and soul as well as care of the body. A "chapel for the sick" was often found in the monasteries and hospitals of this period. The poor, sick, and dying lay people would be cared for in a separate house for pilgrims and paupers, which was often a shelter for those in need in the local community.

In the Middle Ages, the practice of monastic medicine was a balance between natural palliative care and spiritual presence expressed in the unquestioned authority of God.[12] It was in the early period of the Middle Ages that we find in the monastic hospitals the belief in the authority of God over palliative medicine, while a more delicate balance of spirituality and palliative care developed in the late Middle Ages with the cathedral hospitals. It has been noted that throughout the medieval times, "Monks were permitted and encouraged to practice natural medicine, but only with the knowledge that the Lord created it and ultimately reigns over a patient's health and survival."[13]

The basic spiritual principle that formed the practice of sacred palliative care in monastic medicine was that "the material world was created by God for man's use."[14] The natural forms of palliative care were created by God to assist mankind in dealing with sickness. All palliative care, while it does treat the body, is sacred and spiritual because it has a divine source. The great church father Augustine expressed this sacred nature of all palliative care when he wrote:

> For as the medicines which men apply to the bodies of their fellow-men are of no avail except God gives them virtue (who can heal without their aid, though they can not without His), and yet they are applied; and if it be done from a sense of duty, it is esteemed a work of mercy or benevolence; so the aids of teaching [medicine], applied through the instrumentality of man, are of advantage to the soul only when God works to make them of advantage.[15]

For Augustine, natural palliative care requires God's will to be effective. While God may be able to bring healing without natural medicine and physicians, the physicians have no ability to offer healing without the divine assistance of God. For monastic medicine, all

139

care of the body, heart, and soul is spiritual, for it is a gift of divine origin.

Monastic medicine was practiced in many different places and forms. The hospices of this time were residences for people who were traveling, especially pilgrims on a journey to a holy site such as Rome or Jerusalem. Their primary purpose was to offer hospitality through a place of shelter and provide food for those far away from home. Some hospices offered basic medical care for the sick or injured traveler.

The *early medieval hospital* offered palliative medical care and basic hospitality in the form of shelter for the poor and destitute. The focus of medical treatment in monastic medicine was on *care* and *not cure* for the sick and the dying. The number of hospitals increased throughout Europe over the period of the Middle Ages. It was finally in the 15th century that the term "hospital" came to refer to a medical facility rather than a residence for travelers or the poor, the destitute, and the dying. Hospitals were usually staffed and managed by religious orders, especially those of the tradition of St. Augustine. Many of the hospitals of this period were adjuncts to monasteries and other religious institutions.

Leper houses were places where care could be found for those ostracized from society. It was here that dignity was offered for what was considered a disease without dignity. Lepers in the Middle Ages were seen as dead to the world."

The *Benedictine monasteries* of the time offered hospitality as prescribed by the Rule of St. Benedict. Hospitality was offered in the name of Christ to those in need. Many monasteries had an infirmary for the care of their monks or nuns. Over time, this care was extended to strangers in the name of hospitality.

The *military order of hospitals* developed as an outgrowth of the crusades. As sick, wounded, and dying "soldiers of Christ" returned from their pilgrimages to far away lands, the church needed to provide medical care. One of the most remarkable of these orders was one solely for soldiers who were themselves lepers.

The common thread of care and compassion offered by the medieval monks and nuns in all these various ways was the spiritual art of hospitality. The spiritual roots of the Hospice Way today are found in the tradition of Western hospitality expressed in the Middle Ages as monastic medicine.

A modern example of this ancient expression of hospitality through monastic medicine may be seen in the work of the late Mother Teresa of Calcutta. As a Roman Catholic nun, she experienced in her life a powerful spiritual calling to care for the sick and dying who were neglected and abandoned in this life. On October 7, 1950, Mother Teresa received permission from the Holy See to start her own order, The Missionaries of Charity, whose primary task was to love and care for those persons nobody was prepared to look after.[16]

In 1952 Mother Teresa opened the first Home for the Dying in space that was made available by the city of Calcutta. With the help of Indian officials she converted an abandoned Hindu temple into the Kalighat Home for the Dying, a free hospice for the poor. She renamed it Kalighat or "the Home of the Pure Heart. "Those brought to the home received medical attention and were afforded the opportunity to die with dignity, according to the rituals of their faith. It was here that Muslims were read the Quran, Hindus received water from the Ganges, and Catholics received the Last Rites.

Mother Teresa of Calcutta

"A beautiful death is for people who lived like animals to die like angels-loved and cared for."

~*Mother Teresa*[17]

Behind Mother Teresa's care for the dying stands a powerful spiritual dimension. Reflecting on her life, Pope John Paul II asked: "Where did Mother Teresa find the strength and perseverance to place herself completely at the service of others? She found it in prayer and in the silent contemplation of Jesus Christ, his Holy Face, his Sacred Heart."[18] Mother Teresa reminded the nuns of her order that in the face of each dying person they are to find the suffering face of Christ. Her work was not for a social cause, but for a person: the person of Christ. She understands being unwanted as the worst disease.[19]

This was much the same situation as in the Middle Ages. Monks and nuns simply made themselves available to care for the poor, the sick and the dying in their midst as their response to the living presence of Christ. We see in both monastic medicine and its modern expression in the work of Mother Teresa a deeply spiritual model of companioning the dying.

From an historical point of view, the companioning of the dying by Mother Teresa and her nuns may be called an expression of the *pure form* of the ancient Hospice Way of companioning of those at the end of life. The pure form of hospice companioning is distinguished by its embracing all that are suffering and by a fundamental holistic nature. Our modern hospice companioning of the dying is a *medicalized comfort and care* that has been developed from this pure form of the deeply spiritual Hospice Way. The great contribution of modern hospice pioneers such as Cicely Saunders and Kubler-Ross was their shaping hospice into a focused form of companioning of the dying that is based on Western medicine and supported by the resources of the national government. The modern hospice movement, as they have redirected it, has become a movement focused on death as a physical event, with all emotional and spiritual needs of the patient filtered through some medical symptom or problem. This contrasts sharply with the approach of both Mother Teresa and religious caregivers in the Middle Ages, who began with a distinctively spiritual basis of palliative care for all who are sick and needy, and then incorporated medical palliative care as one expression of their spirituality. What we know today as hospice is thus a creative reshaping of this ancient pure form of the Hospice Way that began so long ago.

The spiritual art of hospitality serves as a bridge, as it were, between the ancient pure form of hospice companioning of the dying and the modern form of the hospice movement. It brings together the medieval spiritual tradition of a holistic companioning of those in need with our modern medical palliative care for those at the end of life. As a bridge, it connects ancient sacred wisdom with modern medical care.

The seven practices of the spiritual art of hospitality form a connecting span to our heritage and tradition as we practice hospice work today. The practice of spiritual presence in hospice companioning of the dying anchors us firmly in the ancient sacred wisdom of times past. The practice of the very best palliative care of medicine today anchors us firmly in the modern world with all its technology. The other spiritual practices serve as planks that complete this bridge of hospice work with those at the end of life. Hospice as a tradition of companioning the dying is ancient and yet ever new as the medical technology of palliative care advances. In the spiritual Way called hospice, a very ancient spiritual wisdom embraces the latest developments in medical palliative care. This embrace is the heart and soul of what we know today as the Hospice Way.

Let us now "take a tour" of the institutions in the Middle Ages that were founded by monks and nuns who offered a remarkable response of hospitality in this ancient time of great social need. What was the Hospice Way like in its early form? We will start with the hospitals of this era.

Medieval Hospitals

If we walked into a hospital of the early Middle Ages, we would be surprised to find the institutions that were referred to as "hospitals" were not necessarily "hospitals" in terms of what we would recognize today.[20] All around us are the poor, the sick, the needy and the dying. We are struck by how destitute all the patients are. There were some medieval hospitals that were actually almshouses for the poor, and also some that were hospices for sick and weary travelers. The almshouses offered hospitality through residences for people who were poor and destitute, but not sick. The upkeep for these residences and their occupants was paid by charitable donations or alms. The occupants were expected to offer in return prayers for the souls of the donors.

It was not until the 16th century that the term "hospital" took on its modern meaning as "an institution where sick or injured are given medical or surgical care."[21]

What would seem most unusual about this medieval hospital was not only was it a place where the poor, the destitute, and the dying could receive help, but there were also few physicians offering sacred palliative care. Here we would find the practice of clerical medicine, often called monastic medicine, which was provided as part of a religious duty, with payments and income made via a church rather than directly. Almost one half of the hospitals in medieval Europe were directly affiliated with monasteries, priories or other religious institutions. Many of the rest followed the pattern of religious communities. They would have precise rules of conduct, require a uniform type of dress, and worship services for patients and staff would be a normal part of their daily routine. As one author writes about this early practice of monastic medicine:

> "...the traditional spiritual context of the hospital enhanced, but did not overshadow, their genuine therapeutic achievements. Adopting a religious model was not only the tradition of the times; it was also an eminently successful therapeutic device. Through prayer, patients were supposed to help each other and, indeed, to assist their relatives and friends and people everywhere. Many hospitals had definite local community responsibilities - education and housing students, feeding paupers, maintaining bridges, and sponsoring commercial fairs. All this was both good theology and good psychology." [22]

What would a hospital be like in the Middle Ages? What would Augustinian monks and nuns do for the sick and dying? How would they practice the spiritual art of hospitality?

The focus of comfort was sacred palliative care. This normally consisted of regular meals, regular cleaning, and rest in an airy and sunny setting .[23] Hospitals did offer medication, as their budgets allowed. We find the widespread use of herbs and other natural remedies to treat the sick and dying. The use of herbs dovetailed naturally with this system, the success of herbal remedies being ascribed to their action upon the humours within the body. The use of herbs also drew upon the medieval Christian doctrine of signatures which stated that God had provided some form of alleviation for every ill, and that these things, be they animal, vegetable or mineral, carried a mark or a signature upon them that gave an indication of their usefulness. For example, the seeds of skullcap (used as a headache remedy) can appear to look like miniature skulls; and the white spotted leaves of lungwort (used for tuberculosis) bear a similarity to the lungs of a diseased patient. A large number of such resemblances are believed to exist. Most monasteries developed herb gardens for use in the production of herbal cures, and these remained a part of folk medicine, as well as being used by some physicians. Books of herbal remedies were produced, one of the most famous being the Welsh tome, **Red Book of Hergest**, dating from around 1400.[24]

While many of the drugs that were available to monastic medicine were from plants and developed from folk remedies, mineral and animal substances were also used. Some drugs proved effective, especially as laxatives or pain-killers. While many drugs were simply harmless, others were downright disgusting, such as pig manure thought to be an effective cure for nosebleeds!

Recent archeological discoveries have shown we need to reconsider the "primitive" nature of monastic medicine in the Middle Ages. It appears that the first use of anesthetics was not in modern times, as widely thought, but in the medieval period. As is reported:

> *"Scientists in Scotland have now found evidence that medieval monks used crude anesthetic and antiseptic agents. According to a Reuter story, on August 31, 1997, the discovery was made in digging at Soutra Hill some 20 miles (32 kilometers) south of Edinburgh where a large hospital was founded in 1165 and run by Augustinian monks for nearly 400 years until the dissolution of the monasteries. The monks there ministered to casualties from more than 80 armies that fought in the area. The new excavations have uncovered two surgical wards where amputations were done on warriors 'anesthetized with opium and hemlock' and where 'traces of an analgesic ointment made of opium and lard and a disinfectant ointment laced with arsenic' were also discovered. Our view of general anesthesia as a 19th-century creation now needs to be revised. We need to push 'rapid reverse' to go back to medieval times and credit the monks with some major medical advances, including anesthesia."* [25]

Excavations from medieval hospitals at St. Mary Spital and Soutra in the British Isles have found seeds of many medical plants. [26] Pipkins that could be used to prep medicines were found at St. Mary Spital and a jar was excavated at Soutra that contained residues of hemp, opium poppy, rose, cedar and pine. Herbal remedies were the mainstay of hospital palliative medicine.

Surprisingly, these early hospitals appear to have rarely employed physicians to examine and treat their patients. Most of the care and treatment was done by the monks and especially by the nuns who staffed the facilities. Their training and experience in the practice of patient care came from practical experience and by reading medical texts in their order's library.

A distinctive feature of this period is the variety of healers. Unlike other professions there was no controlling elite, indeed, almost no profession. As there was no consensus regarding standards or methods, many practitioners proved part-time care and all integrated a number of roles into their work-lives rather than that of just 'doctor'. Those offering healing encompassed both sexes, all religions, and people at every level of society from serf to the most educated and wealthy academics. For many practitioners, such as nurses, dentists (***dubbedent*** or ***adubedent***), apothecaries, and midwives, their work was considered to be a trade.[27] Not until the 16th century did various regulatory bodies begin to be granted a legally enforced dominance over medical practices.

It is attractive to categorize these early medical practitioners into two rough categories, noting the vague and porous nature of the boundaries. The major split is between the clerical and elite university-educated personnel ("physicians") and trades people. The ordinary practitioner sold medical assistance and potions. They worked either as guild members with a license from local authorities, or were attached to a major household, or perhaps, a monastery. They were paid either for their services on a case-by-case basis or with an annuity and payments were often in kind—food or clothing—rather than cash. As previously noted, clerical medicine, often called monastic medicine, was provided as part of a religious duty, with payments and income made via a local church rather than directly.

Medieval hospitals were small by modern standards.[28] The largest hospital was in Florence and provided care for two hundred to three hundred patients. Most were far smaller and probably accommodated fifty patients at the most. The normal building was a large residential structure that resembled a dormitory in the monastery or the convent. The hospital would consist of these wards for housing the patients along with a chapel, kitchen, laundry facility, and living quarters for the staff. Descriptions of these early hospitals depict them as long, open halls with rows of beds along the walls. It is interesting that in many hospitals the patients shared beds, usually with two patients per bed. One account mentions up to a dozen children sharing a single hospital bed. The sharing of beds was the common practice in the Middle Ages. It was the norm both in homes and in public places such as inns.

The hospital was a charitable institution, and as such most patients had no choice in their accommodations. Care was provided as an act of hospitality by the monks and nuns. Those who could afford medical care were usually treated in their homes, or else went home to recover after treatment by the physician at their office. The major source of charity in the Middle Ages remained the church. Churchmen building hospitals had a model ready to hand, since monastic houses dispensed charity as a sacred duty. They gave alms to the poor, often from a special almory (place where alms were dispersed) by the gate. They had guest houses for travelers and infirmaries for their own sick. What was more natural than to create hospitals along monastic lines? Most medieval hospitals were run by a community following a religious rule and headed by a prior or master.

The core elements were a chapel and an infirmary. The architecture reflected the care of the soul and the care of the body in extending the spiritual art of hospitality to the poor, the sick, and the dying. The chapel was central to the whole medieval concept of charity. Charity is linked with faith and hope as a Christian virtue. Hospitals cared for the soul as much as the body. "Where suffering is constant and death close at hand, faith can be a powerful comfort."[29]

Roman Catholic bishops of the Middle Ages were bound by their vows to give alms to the poor and many built hospitals or almshouses. An example of a medieval hospital was that founded around 1180 by Bishop Reginald Fitz Jocelin. He established the Hospital of St John the Baptist for the poor of Bath, England. It was run by a master and brethren, with the help of "two or three women, not noble but suitable ... who are willing and able to serve the infirm poor."[30] Early deeds of the Bath hospital refer to the master, the brethren and sisters serving God there, and the poor and infirm. St. John's was built by the aptly named Cross Bath. No doubt bathing soothed the aches of arthritis then as now. The standard plan of a medieval hospital was an open hall with beds either side, like a modern hospital ward. This was called the infirmary. At one end was a chapel, so that those facing the end of this life could contemplate the next. Ancient deeds of St John's mention the chapel and infirmary.[31] As with other early hospitals, the sisters were expected to sleep in a room in the infirmary and "be watchful and ready, night and day, to help the infirm." There was also a kitchen and a house for the master.

147

Community was designed into the very nature of the hospitals in the Middle Ages. From the start, we often see a courtyard plan. A gatehouse would lead the patient into a quadrangle. This plan would form a sheltered area that was an enclosed community where patients would not be disturbed.

The communal nature of the hospital was to form a large family unit where patients would eat meals together, pray together, and share a common dormitory together. As the monastery formed its own community in the world, so the hospital was a community following the monastic model. The hospitals of this medieval period also had many similarities to the family. They would be much like a manor house, with the hall, chapel, and outbuildings all arranged around a central courtyard. The lord of the manor would live with his household, and eat and pray with them daily. The inherent lack of privacy reflected the life of the times. The plan of St. Giles in Norwich shows the principal elements of a medieval hospital. The infirmary hall is at one end of the hospital, attached by the nave of St. Helen's Chapel to a chancel. Patients could take part in both the palliative medical care of herbal medicine, food, and shelter, and also observe religious services in the Chancel. There was holistic blending of care for the body, heart, and soul in the monastic model of medicine. Faith and hope were central virtues to care of the poor and dying.

The Middle Ages saw the founding of some one and a half thousand hospitals in the British Isles alone. About one fourth were leper houses. A good 10% were set aside for the care of pilgrims and wayfarers as hostels. Only about 8% were for the sick and dying.[32] The primary concern was palliative care of the poor and needy. While it was hard to distinguish the poor from the infirm or the dying, the main function of these hospitals was palliative care through offering a home, food, and clothing.

Many medieval hospitals were established and run by Augustinian canons. The Rule of St. Augustine was a common choice for hospitals, as it allowed for an adaptable rule. In Scotland, for example, we have the House of the Hold Trinity Soutra. One courtyard held the chapel and staff quarters, while the kitchen and bakehouse were in a second courtyard. At St. Leonard's in England, there was one courtyard for the hospital buildings and another for the church and clergy. Large hospitals could offer some separation of the clergy. The endowed

Soutra was the largest hospital in Scotland, while St. Leonard's was of similar importance in England. The great hospital in York had more staff and patients than any other English hospital of its time.

As we tour a medieval hospital, we find bread and ale the staple of the diet. The typical dishes available depended on how well endowed the hospital might be. The wealthy St. Leonard York offered meat three times a week, with fish, eggs or cheese provided on the other days. The hospital of St. Mark Bristol in England was founded to provide food and shelter for the poor. The food consisted of one meal a day of pottage made from oat-flour and bread made from wheat, beans, and barley or rye. Beans were a valuable source of protein.

There are few accounts of vegetables mentioned in hospital records and no mention of fruit. However, the latrine drains at St. Mary Spiral reveal that its patients enjoyed apples, blackberries, raspberries, and figs. Hospital records from the fourteenth century onwards suggest that a more varied diet was served in hospitals, including leeks, onions, pears, and apples.

All these accounts paint for us a picture of palliative care for the sick, the poor, the needy and the dying in the hospitals of the Middle Ages. The hospital was a place to care for the body and the soul. Hospitals took seriously the provision of spiritual comfort for the dying. Care focused on providing a warm, clean place with herbal medicines available. A good diet, a place of shelter as a home, nursing care, and the presence of spiritual care were the core of the medieval hospital. This is the essence of monastic medicine.

The Leper Houses

In her essay *"Unclean! Unclean!"*, Maureen Miller gives an interesting description of lepers in medieval times. She writes: "You are walking along the dirt road outside your village in England, and see a decrepit figure stumbling toward you. This 'human' creature is dressed in rags and a dirty brown coat, holds a bell that he rings from time to time, and extends a cup distantly from his body. As you come closer, you notice a horrible stench and disfiguring lesions on the man's face and hands. What do you do?

If you are a resident of that village in Medieval times, you know immediately that this horrifying creature should be reviled and avoided at all costs: he is a leper. If you are a particularly compassionate person of the times (and have some wherewithal) you might drop a coin in the man's cup, never meeting his eyes, then escape from his presence as quickly as possible. If you are a nun, monk or priest who is benevolent, you might direct this man who is 'dead' to the church and society, to the closest lazar house..."[33]

The lepers of the Middle Ages were the terminally ill of that society. Their disease was understood as contagious and a danger to the social welfare of everyone. They were viewed much as AIDS patients are in our modern world. It is important to review the care of the lepers in those days for here we have a clear picture of how the dying were companioned by Christian monks and nuns. A whole host of people with differing needs might be in the hospices or hospitals, such as the destitute, the sick, the blind and the homeless. Yet in the leper houses, or the lazar houses, all the patients were terminally ill. Here we see a focused hospice care for the dying in ancient times.

We can begin with the radical attitude taken toward lepers in the Middle Ages by St. Francis of Assisi. Luke Eggleston, in the **Catholic Sun**, writes: "One of the earliest stories in St. Francis of Assisi's life tells of his embracing the lepers.

St. Francis

"St. Francis famously embraced a leper, a transforming experience that led to his belief that the divine exists in all humanity, no matter how lowly or scorned."[34]

At first Francis was overwhelmed with disgust when confronted with the diseased unfortunates. But one day, while riding, he spotted a leper and rather than obey his impulses and steer his horse clear, Francis leapt from the saddle, embraced him and pressed some coins into his pocket. Overwhelmed with joy after the event, St. Francis rode to a lepers' dwelling near Assisi. Because he had so often considered the lepers as lowly, Francis asked for their forgiveness. He remained in the leper community for some time, distributing money among them. By the time he left, he had kissed each one on the mouth."[35]

Very little was know about the true biological causes of leprosy in ancient times, although it was thought to be very contagious. There was little distinction between the specific disease we know as Hansen's disease and other skin aliments, such as smallpox or skin disorders. Anyone who showed the signs of leprosy, such as sores or ulcers of the skin, could be called a leper. The Old Testament **Book of Leviticus** gives clear guidelines for how to diagnose and deal with infectious skin diseases.

"The Lord said to Moses and Aaron, "When anyone has a swelling or a rash or a bright spot on his skin that may become an infectious skin disease, he must be brought to Aaron the priest or to one of his sons, who is a priest. The priest is to examine the sore on his skin, and if the hair in the sore has turned white and the sore appears to be more than skin deep, it is a 'plague of leprosy' ... The person with such an infectious disease must wear torn clothes, let his hair be unkempt, cover the lower part of his face and cry out, Unclean! Unclean!" As long as he has the infection he remains unclean. He must live alone: he must live outside the camp."   **Leviticus** *13*

Most of the houses for leprosy were built in the twelfth and thirteen centuries so there is the assumption that the disease was most widespread then. The urban development of towns and villages would help to spread leprosy. As the disease was thought to thrive on human contact, the church acted to separate leprosy from the general public. In 1175 the English Church Council ordered that lepers should not live among the healthy. The Lateran Council at Rome decreed in 1179 that leper communities should have their own priests, churches, and cemeteries .

The leper of the Middle Ages brought forth many emotions. There was deep sense of pity and a revulsion and horror. Not only was there a fear of infection, but also the disfigurement of the disease. At first it was thought that leprosy was a punishment from God. However, when holy Christian crusaders returned from the Hold Land Crusades with leprosy, it was clear that the disease could not be God's punishment. The Christian view shifted to seeing the disease as a form of suffering that would bring the person closer to God. Those with courage to care for lepers were revered.

What was life like in the leper houses of the time? At St. Mary Magdalene leper hospital in Gloucester, England, the rules decreed that the lepers should observe basic disciplines.[38] These included obedience, patience, and charity. All the property of the lepers was held in common, in the monastic way of life. Meat was allowed on three days of the week, and on feast days, but not allowed on other days. There was a strict segregation of men and women both inside and outside the leper house. At the leper house at Exeter, England, the lepers were expected to live chaste and honest lives. They were not to enter the city without the permission of the warden. This may have been the general rule of life for many other leper houses.

Hospitality and Benedictine Monasteries

As we have seen from our review of the middle ages, it was with the fall of the Roman Empire that the Roman Catholic Church emerged in the swirling social chaos of the times as the primary institution of learning and education in Western culture. In a pre-scientific age, learned monks and nuns responded to sickness, leprosy, plagues, and the need to companion the dying through the remarkably holistic palliative care know as monastic medicine. The monasteries collected ancient Greek and Roman medical texts, and so Western medicine developed for about the next one thousand years in this way of a balanced ancient wisdom and palliative care.

A leading figure in this way of sacred palliative care was St. Benedict of Nursia (480-543), the father of the Western monastic way of life. It was with his founding of the monastery on Monte Casino in Italy in 529 that a deep interest in medicine awoke in the far flung cloisters of the Roman Church. St. Benedict had a deep interest in medicine and care of the sick and dying. Not only was the monastery at Monte Casino a place where medical teaching and practice were developed, but it was also a center in the West for the collecting, copying, and preserving of ancient medical manuscripts.[39]

It was through the influence of St. Benedict that the Benedictines cared for the sick and dying through Christendom. In England, the order established schools at Oxford, Cambridge, and Winchester.

From the very beginning, this Benedictine interest in medicine was welded to hospitality. A key component of the Benedictine life style has been hospitality. It has been said that "There is no Benedic

152

> ## "Let Everyone that Comes Be Received As Christ"
> ## Rule of St. Benedict
>
> " Infirmorum cura ante omnia et super omnia adhibenda est"
>
> "Care of the sick must rank above and before all else...
>   be extremely careful they suffer no neglect."

tine Spirituality without the welcoming of guests." In his **Rule**, Saint Benedict says "Let all guests that come to the monastery be received as Christ. For, one day, he will say: I was a stranger and you welcomed me." In other words, monastic hospitality is essentially rooted in the Gospel values.

"Let everyone that comes be received as Christ" is one of the most familiar and oft-quoted phrases of the **Rule**. As has been said of this expression of hospitality, "It emphasizes the preeminent position which hospitality occupies in every Benedictine monastery. Benedictine hospitality goes beyond the exercise of the expected social graces—the superficial smile or the warm reception of expected guests. Hospitality for Benedict meant that everyone who comes—the poor, the traveler, the curious, those not of our religion, or social standing, or education—should be received with genuine acceptance. With characteristic moderation, though, he cautions against 'lingering with guests,' realizing that the peace and silence of the monastery must be protected."[42]

Benedictine hospitality in the Middle Ages has a character very distinct from that of the Augustinian canons that founded hospitals, hospices and leper houses. For the Benedictine community hospitality was offered within the monastic community as an expression of the faith of the community in Christian compassion. As the infirmary of the Benedictine monasteries cared for the sick members of the community, care could be extended to the sick and needy that arrived as guests at the guest houses of the monastery. However, Benedictine hospitality was generally focused within the monastic community as an expression of a community's life of faith seeking God, and did not extend widely beyond the physical bounds of community life. For this reason, we find the **Rule of St. Augustine** to be the main Rule in the founding of other institutions of monastic medicine. This concern for community life is seen in the mission statement of a modern Benedictine community.

Mission Statement of a Benedictine Community

"We, the Sisters of St. Benedict of Ferdinand, Indiana, are monastic women seeking God through the Benedictine tradition of community life, prayer, hospitality, and service to others."[43]

One profound expression of monastic medicine was through the infirmaries of the Benedictine monasteries of the Middle Ages. In the monasteries, an infirmary would be maintained for the care of the sick that were received as guests at the monastery. The plan of a medieval monastery shows the central place of the infirmary.

Infirmary Music

Music was used in the care of those dying in the monastery infirmary in Cluny, France, starting in the 11th century.[44] This use of music was an intimate expression of French monastic medicine.

Today, this sharing of music with those at the end of life continues as music-thanatology. Thanatos is the Greek term for death and as such the goal of this palliative care is to bring a blessed death and the gift that conscious dying can bring to the fullness of life.[45]

Therese Schroeder-Sheker continues this use of music with the dying in modern times. Music thanatolgy interns seek to integrate spiritual and clinical values in the use of music for the dying, as we see for example .at the Chalice of Repose Project which began in Missoula, Montana.[46]

As has been noted, Benedictine monasticism provided for the needs of the sick and the aged as prescribed in the *Rule of St. Benedict*. At Cluny there developed a series of infirmary practices concerning the care of the dying that formed a foundation for sacred palliative care. A central concern of the monastic infirmaries was what later came to be called "total pain" by Cicely Saunders in the modern hospice movement. In the medieval infirmary, palliative care was offered that sought to offer relief from any physical, emotional, mental and spiritual pain that might impede or prevent a person from a blessed death. At the monastic infirmary at Cluny there are detailed accounts of the use of music as a form of palliative care for the dying. The monastery infirmary was both "a sanctuary to complete the last stage of life and a gateway to a conscious death."[47]

The ancient practice of music thanatology is not the same thing as modern music therapy, but is a close relative. Music therapy as a therapeutic application engages interaction, participation, or response from an attentive patient. The patient is involved in singing or playing of an instrument, or in responding to the listening environment.

Music thanatology, rooted in monastic medicine, is a palliative medical modality. The focus is on the patient receiving, rather than responding to, the use of music. The music thanatologist sees "the entire surface of the skin as an extension of the ear."[48] The dying patient is viewed as a chalice and is anointed with the healing presence of sacred music. The spiritual well-being of the patient is an integral part of music thanatology. The current practice of music thanatology involves only live prescriptive music for the patient rather than any recorded music. It is specifically singing and harp playing.

Music hematology is seen as both an art and a science. As a science, it is a form of palliative medicine that reduces physical pain, as well as emotional and spiritual suffering. An accomplished musician-clinician can decrease a patient's pulse and heart rate, stabilize breathing and change body temperature, according to Schroeder-Sheker.[49] These calming effects of musical palliative care can help a patient fall into a deep, restorative sleep. Music thanatology, as an expression of the medieval wisdom of monastic medicine, does not seek to cure, entertain, or distract, but to "heal and to ease the interior suffering that can attend the end of life-both for the dying and their loved ones."[50] It is a deathbed healing but not curative. Music thanatology is a profound expression of ancient sacred palliative care offered in the medieval monastic infirmary for those at the end of life.

Reflections on Monastic Medicine and the Hospice Way

The Dutch theologian, J. C. Hoekendijk has a helpful understanding of the distinct ways Christian faith may be expressed in our world.[51]

His model may be of use in presenting the ancient roots of hospice spirituality. He distinguished between what we can call the dynamic 'Go Structure' and the established 'Come Structure' of the church. The Go Structure is built on three directional words: self-emptying, service, and solidarity with the people. In terms of this structure, Hoekendijk states: "If someone asks where the church is, then we ought to be able to answer: there, where people are emptying themselves, making themselves as nothing; there, where people serve, not just a little, but in the total service which has been initiated from the Messiah-Service and in which the cross comes into view; and there where the solidarity with the fellowman is not merely preached about but is actually demonstrated."[53] Those early monks and nuns who followed the *Rule of St. Augustine* in establishing hospices, hospitals, and leper houses as they practiced the spiritual art of hospitality were following this Go Structure of expressing the Christian faith. To loosely paraphrase Hoekdiik, if someone asks where do we find the hospice movement in our world today, we ought to be able to answer in Augustinian terms, "Hospice is where caregivers companion the dying and their families in body, heart and soul in a spirit of hospitality. Hospice lives where caregivers are truly making themselves available, where caregivers are being spiritually present with the dying"

On the other hand, the monks and nuns who followed the *Rule of St. Benedict* in offering hospitality to the needy were, in the model of Hoekendijk, using a Come Structure in their practice of the spiritual art of hospitality. Those of the Benedictine order saw it as their spiritual work to have an established monastery infirmary and guest house that was available for the needy pilgrims. The focus was on those 'outside' coming 'inside' to receive companionship. The Come Structure is seen in terms of the image of the cathedral. It is "symbolic of a stable society, a permanent resting point..."[54] The Go Structure is revealed in the image of the chapel. It is understood as a "moveable house...It can easily be dismantled and moved, so that it can be where the people are."[55]

It was to be that much of the early work of the followers of the *Rule of St. Augustine* would be swept away with the changing tides of society, beginning in the early 1600's. From within medicine, the end of the Middle Ages saw the decline of monastic medicine and the rise of medicine as a separate secular profession. The Protestant

Reformation and the reign of Henry VIII in England ended much of the financial support for religious hospitals, hospices, and leper houses throughout Europe and England. And yet we can still learn from, and draw upon, these ancient Augustinian spiritual roots for how to companion the dying.

The medieval model of how to companion the dying following the *Rule of St. Benedict* can be depicted in this manner:

Table Four
Benedictine Come Structure of Hospitality

Spiritual Life	Monastery	Pilgrim/Family
Ancient Spiritual →	Monastic Medicine	← Physical Needs (body)
Wisdom of St. Benedict	Monastic Guest House	Emotional Needs (heart)
	Infirmary	Spiritual Needs (soul)

Here we see the central place of the Rule of St. Benedict in establishing the monastery as a spiritual community. It was at the monastery that a guest house and an infirmary would be established. The needy stranger would come to the monastery to find help with spiritual and physical needs. The community would practice monastic medicine in the infirmary. This would tend to be short term care.

The medieval model of how to companion the dying following the *Rule of St. Augustine* can be depicted like this:

Table Five
Augustinian Go Structure of Hospitality

Spiritual Life	Pilgrim/Family	Places of Care
Ancient Spiritual →	Physical Needs (body) →	Monastic medicine
Wisdom of St. Augustine	Emotional Needs (heart)	Hospices
		Hospitals
	Spiritual Needs (soul)	Leper Houses

In the Augustinian Go Structure there is first the concern with meeting the needs of the pilgrim as a direct expression of the spiritual life established by the Augustinian Rule. From this spiritual work comes the establishment of wide variety of expressions of monastic medicine, such the hospices, hospitals and leper houses of the Middle Ages. Hospices, for example, were often established at key crossroads or mountain passes where weary and sick pilgrims would travel to and from their pilgrimages to religious sites. The Augustinian cannons would go out to where the people were in need and offer them the spiritual art of hospitality.

It is interesting to reflect on how these ancient spiritual ways of companioning the dying have made their way into modern hospice work in our day. The impact of both has been profound, for they are the very foundation of how hospice in modern times cares for those at the end of life's journey.

We might depict the modern hospice hospitality extended through the *Rule of St. Benedict* as follows:

Table Six		
Benedictine Spiritual Heritage in Modern Hospice Work		
Come Structure	**Hospice Residential Unit**	**Patient/Family**
Ancient Spiritual →	Sacred Palliative Care ←	Physical Needs (body)
Wisdom of St. Benedict	Concern for Family	Emotional Needs (heart)
	Spiritual Presence	Spiritual Needs (soul)
	(Other practices of Spiritual Art of Hospitality)	
Expression of Hospitality: Patient's come to the hospice home (residential unit) to be companioned.		

In this Benedictine way of companioning the dying, the patient and their family come to the modern hospice residential unit to be companioned in their final days. There is an emphasis on the sacred palliative care of the patient, for physical needs often predominate in the plan of care. For this reason, the physical needs of the patient/ family are shown first, followed by the spiritual needs and finally the emotional needs.

There is an ancient spiritual understanding that the needs of the patient and the family are one indivisible whole. Companioning the dying is a companioning of the body, heart, and soul, although certain needs may be more present than others in the spiritual art of hospitality. As I visit on the residential unit of Blue Ridge Hospice, I personally reflect on the spirit of St. Benedict who made this modern hospice work possible.

We might depict the Augustinian way of companioning the dying in modern hospice work as is depicted in table seven below:

Table Seven		
Augustinian Spiritual Heritage in Modern Hospice Work		
Go Structure	**Hospice Caregiver**	**Patient/Family Home**
Ancient Spiritual →	Sacred Palliative Care →	Physical Needs (body)
Wisdom of St .Augustine	Concern for Family	Emotional Needs (heart)
	Spiritual Presence	Spiritual Needs (soul)
	(Other Practices of Spiritual Art of Hospitality)	
Expression of hospitality: Hospice caregivers Go to the homes of patients to companion the dying.		

In this way of caring for those at the end of life, the modern hospice caregiver goes out to the patient and family home to companion the dying. It is the same Go Structure as followed in medieval times, with the caregiver "going out" to the home and the patient receiving the care. In the Middle Ages, much of the needy population did not have a physical home for the caregiver to visit, and so a place for a home would first have to be established. Thus, hospitals, hospices and leper houses were above all else a place of home for those who did not have a home. This makes them so very different from our modern institution of the hospital. While the lepers might be set apart from the rest of society in medieval Europe, they were given a home by the Augustinian monks and nuns in leper houses. It is amazing to reflect that every time a hospice caregiver today makes a visit to a hospice patient in their home they are following in the ancient tradition of companioning the dying that was founded as far back as the fifth century by our Augustinian brothers and sisters who did this same spiritual work.

St. Augustine had a deep vision of this life on earth as a journey to our true spiritual home. We are pilgrims on the move, and this earth is our hospice. It was his view of life as a great pilgrimage that spiritually under girded those who followed his rule and offered hospitality for the dying. As St. Augustine wrote in a commentary on ***Psalm*** 60:

We live here for a few days and then must move on. In this life we are no more than temporary borders; only in heaven will we dwell in our own home. A sign that we are only visitors here is that someday we will hear the voice of the Lord commanding us: "Move On!" No one will tell us to "move on" once we are in our eternal home in heaven. Just now we can be nothing but wanderers...

As long as we live on earth our lodgings will not be permanent. Only when we get to that great land beyond death will the Lord give us dwelling places that abide. That is what he promised when he said: "There are many permanent abodes in my Father's house" (John 14:2).

Such eternal dwellings obviously cannot be reserved for mere lodgers but only for those who deserve to live there forever."[56]

It was this Augustinian view of life on earth as an inn for travelers that made hospitality so central to the life and work of those who followed in his spiritual tradition.

We need the comfort and support of others on this journey to our true home. As the scholar Donald X. Burt remarks, regarding St. Augustine, "We are in the midst of a truly *dying life*. Whether we are young or old, we are all travelers on the same road, a road that leads ultimately through the door of death to life without death. We are in the midst of a life that is rushing towards that death-door that is the entrance to eternal life."[57] In this spiritual tradition, we are to be companions of those who are traveling to their true home.

A Medieval Hospice

The best known of all hospices of the Middle Ages was the St. Bernard Hospice. It dates back to 962, when it was founded by Augustinian canons. The hospice was located on the "roof of Europe," high in the western Alps between Switzerland and Italy. At an elevation of over 8.000 feet is found the desolate Great St. Bernard Pass. It is here that we find the main route across the Alps leading to Rome. Many devoted French and German pilgrims would use this oldest of the Alpine pass routes to go to Rome on pilgrimage. The pass has been in use since the Bronze Ages, dating to about 800 B.C. Tribes and armies have tramped their way to and fro through this mountain pass for millennia. According to legend, the great general Hannibal made his famous crossing of the Alps in 217 BC with elephants through the Grand St. Bernard, although there remains little historical evidence. In Roman times, Julius Caesar crossed the Summa Poenina, as the pass was then known, to conquer the pagan people of Martigny, who worshipped the Celtic god Poenn. It was soon after this that Emperor Augustus built a road across the pass. On the top of this desolate mountain crossing was left a temple to Jupiter, and so the surrounding area came to be called Mons Iovis or Mont Joux. The temple was sacked with the fall of Rome, but a refuge may have remained on the pass to aid those traveling this route.[58]

After many years of tumultuous history, with the Huns and Saracens sweeping through the region, raping, pillaging and destroying churches, order was restored by local monarchs. On the scene came Bernard of Menthon, who had spent years providing aid and comfort to travelers coming down from the pass.

The traditional route of the Alps crossing is covered with perpetual snow, from seven to eight feet deep, and drifts sometimes accumulate to the height of forty feet. Although this route was extremely dangerous, especially in the springtime on account of avalanches, pilgrims found this a favorite route on their way to Rome. As an act of courageous hospitality, St. Bernard founded a monastery and hospice for the convenience and protection of travelers in the year 962 (or 1050 by some accounts), and over time the pass came to bear his name. A few years later he established another hospice on the Little St. Bernard Pass which is a mountain saddle in the Graian Alps. These religious foundations were placed in charge of the Augustinian monks after Bernard traveled to Rome where he received the pope's blessing for the hospices.

Well into the twentieth century, these hospices were renowned for their generous hospitality extended to all travelers over the Great and Little St. Bernard passes, named in honor of the founder of these caring institutions. All seasons of the year, and especially after heavy snowstorms, the brave monks would venture forth with their well-trained dogs, the common herding dogs of the Valais St. Bernards (as they are called from the 1600's), searching for victims lost in the storms. The monks would offer food, clothing, and shelter to the needy pilgrims, and take care of the dead and dying. The order depended on gifts and collections for their acts of hospitality.[59] In 1913, the order consisted of about forty members, the majority of whom lived at the hospice while some served local parishes.

From medieval times, hospices like St. Bernard were established at major crossroads or passes where sick or dying pilgrims might find comfort and care on their spiritual pilgrimage to and from holy places. These Christian hospices were places of extraordinary hospitality, which extended hope to those who needed care and comfort in their lives. Hospitality was the reason for their very existence.

How might care be offered to suffering pilgrims at the St. Bernard Hospice and other hospices established throughout Europe? In the world of the Middle Ages, hospices came to be remembered as a community for sojourners along the way, a place of replenishment, refreshment and care. As we have seen, the reigning moral theme at the time of the medieval hospice was the statement of Christ, "as long as you do it for the least of my brothers that you do unto me." Hospice care was seen as an expression of Christian compassion through the spiritual art of hospitality.

We also see at the St. Bernard Hospice an early use of animals in caring for the sick, the weary, and the dying. The dogs came from the valley below the pass, and were likely descended from Molossus dogs left behind by the Romans.[60] The monks from the hospice traveled to

---

Barry, an Ancient Hospice Dog of Hospitality

Barry is indisputably the most famous Saint Bernard dog in history. He was born at the Hospice in 1800, the year Napoleon crossed the Alps with his army of 40,000. The legendary Barry is credited with saving 40 lives and for years afterward, when tales of great dogs are told, the story of Barry ranks at the top of the list.

The story goes that in March 1806 Anna Maria Vincenti, a young Italian widow was trying to return home with her infant son over a pass high in the Alps. The young woman and child were caught in an avalanche. Near the St. Bernard Hospice, Barry and his handler, Brother Lvigi, were out for a walk. The monk wanted to return to the hospice. Barry disobeyed-something he had never done before. He ran off alone. That night Barry returned with a child. Before the boy's mother died, she'd wrapped the child in her shawl and tied him to the back of the big dog. After returning to the hospice with this nearly frozen bundle, Barry then reportedly led the rescuers back to the now dead woman. Barry is a shinning model for all hospice dogs today as they provide hospitality in companioning the dying.[63]

---

the valley and likely brought back the big dogs as companions and guardians for the long winters. For awhile, the great dogs were known as Hospice Dogs or Barry Hounds; the breed name St. Bernard was not established until later in the 1800's.[61] Their thick coats protected them against the snow and ice, and their keen sense of smell aided in finding victims buried in snow banks or avalanches.[62]

As we explore life in the middle ages we may consider what was the hospice attitude toward those who were brought to the hospice and then died? How is it that a traveler on a spiritual pilgrimage might experience death and dying in a medieval hospice such as St. Bernard?? To these fascinating questions we now turn.

Death in a Medieval Hospice

While we do not have an historical account from 962 of a death at the St .Bernard hospice, we do know the customs of death at this time in Europe. We can create from research a narrative description of how death was likely to occur in this era. A death in a hospice may have unfolded like the following story.[64]

A weary pilgrim on the way to Rome, and perhaps lost in a snowstorm and suffering from exposure in the deep snows of the high St. Bernard mountain pass, would be brought into the hospice. The pilgrim may have also suffered at the hands of thieves and robbers, who preyed on known travel routes. The traveler sensed that he was dying. He shared this knowledge with the people who were closest to him, and then he went to the place where he slept. In preparation for death, the pilgrim laid down upon his back on the bed, spreading his arms in the shape of a cross, as was the custom. He remembered to lie in such a way that his head faced east, toward Jerusalem. Soon people started entering into his room in the hospice.

His family, relatives, children, friends and even people he didn't know who were also in the hospice, crowded into the small space. The people had seen a priest carrying the viaticum to the room. The viaticum was understood by all as the term the Catholic Church uses for the Eucharist or Communion given to a dying person.[65] It was not the same as the sacrament of the Anointing of the Sick, but rather it was the Eucharist administered in special circumstances. The word viaticum is a Latin word meaning "provisions for a journey," and stems from via, or "way." The Eucharist is seen by the church as the ideal food to strengthen a dying person for the journey from this world to life after death. (Originally the Eucharistic bread was placed in the mouth of the dead person. This provided food for what the early Christians believed was a three day journey between this world and the next).[66]

As mourners saw the procession with the priest, they felt a responsibility to attend the ritual that would follow and dropped what they were doing to be a part of this observance. Death was a community event in the Middle Ages.

As the people gathered in the room, the windows and doors were shut and candles lit. The pilgrim who was dying now was the one to start the ritual in the room and decide on the timing of all that took place. The dying person began by expressing his sorrow over the end of life. This was a sad, moving recollection. Some in the room could be heard weeping and sighing.

After the expression about the sadness of dying came the pardoning of the many companions and helpers who surrounded the deathbed. Ritual words were expressed, such as "I pardon you here and before God," and with these words the forgiven would bow to the dying. The dying would speak the ritual words that they had learned from attending the same ritual many times before when they had witnessed the death of others.

Then the dying pilgrim began to commend all who were dear to him to God, saying "May God bless my dear wife. Lord, may you remember my poor son, who is orphaned so young, for you alone can sustain the fatherless."

After his farewell to the world, the dying pilgrim commended his soul to God. In the Song of '**Chanson de Roland**', where the last prayer is given, it has two parts. First, is the confession, or the *cupla*. "God, forgive me by your grace for my sins, the great and the small, which I have committed from the hour I was born until this day that have faced death." The prayer was made with hands clasped together and lifted to heaven, and a petition that he be granted paradise.

The second part of the last prayer is the '*Commendation Animae*' This is a very ancient prayer of the early church, which was handed down through the ages. It is a paraphrase borrowed from the Jewish synagogue. A brief form of the prayer which may have been prayed would be, "My true Father, you who never lied, you who raised Lazarus from the dead, you who saved Daniel from the lions, save my soul from all dangers and from the sins I have committed in my life." In this ritual there is no extreme unction, or sacramental anointing of the dying, for that was reserved for the clergy.

At this point absolution was granted, the great act of the Roman Church. The priest would bend over the dying man and sprinkle him with holy water. After the dying pilgrim had finished all the social customs, they would lay waiting for death to come.

There would be a ceremonial, ritual quality to the dying of the pilgrim in the St. Bernard hospice. If death was slow in coming, the dying pilgrim waited in silence. At the moment of death our pilgrim may have spoken the words, "I cannot hold on to my life any longer." The priest would then repeat the absolution over the dead body in the hospice. In the society of the Middle Ages, the greatest fear was not death itself, but a sudden and unexpected death that would rob them of being able to take part in their final ritual. There was a deep sense of pride in being able to anticipate the time of one's own death. This was not difficult in medieval society, for any serious injury or sickness would likely foretell of death, because medicine had not developed sufficiently to greatly prolong human life. Death itself was a natural event and the accepted conclusion of life on earth. And so in 1050, the weary pilgrim in the hospice would most likely face and accept death as the natural end of the human cycle of life. With the rituals of society satisfied, it was possible to say "Yes" to death.

It is important to see how the extent to which the dying themselves controlled their own death in the hospice. Death was a ritual organized by the weary pilgrim, who presided over it and knew all the proper customs. As we find in the modern hospice movement, patients and families are involved in control of patient's care.

There was a profound public aspect to death in the Middle Ages, and this was to last until the end of the nineteenth century. The dying person was to be the center of a group of people. The great fear was not death itself but of dying alone. There was then a more public character to death in medieval times. This ancient model of death and dying, which involves the family and the faith community, serves well as a model for the proposed Family Companioning Medicare Benefit.

Hospitals and Hospices in The Crusades

Another remarkable place where we see the practice of monastic medicine extended through the spiritual art of hospitality in the Middle Ages was in the military order called the Hospitallers. Their very name in medieval Latin means "giver of hospitality." As has been written of the Hospitallers:

> *"Hospitality holds the highest rank among all works of piety and humanity. All Christian peoples agree with that because hospitality includes all other virtues. It must be practiced and respected by all men of good will - especially by those who carry the honorable name of a Knight Hospitaller. Therefore we must not devote ourselves to any other task with more dedication than to this very task the Order has got its name from."*[67]

The Crusades

The Crusades saw the creation of a new kind of religious institution in the form of the military orders that allowed the laity to show their religious zeal. The Hospitallers, who followed the Rule of St. Augustine, were the most resilient of the military orders,[68] although they had not started out as a fighting force at all. The many names by which the Hospitable were known throughout their history reflects their long tradition. At first they cared for poor and sick pilgrims in the holy land. They were called from their founding in the 1100's until the 1300's the Hospitallers of St. John of Jerusalem.

The Origin of the Hospitallers

The origins of the Hospitallers are obscure and many versions exist.[69] They may trace back to a mid-11th century Benedictine abbey which was established in Jerusalem by merchants from Amalfi, Italy. About 30 years later, a hospital was founded next to the abbey to care for sick and poor pilgrims. After the success of the First Crusade in 1099, Brother Gerard (or Gerald), the hospital's superior, expanded the hospital and set up additional hospitals along the route used by pilgrims to the Holy Land.

Hospitaller Knights

In 1120, Raymond de Puy succeeded Gerard as leader of the order. He replaced the Benedictine Rule with the Augustinian Rule and actively began to build up the order's power base, helping the organization to acquire lands and wealth. Possibly inspired by the Templars, the Hospitallers began to take up arms in order to protect pilgrims as well as to tend to their illnesses and injuries. Hospitaller Knights were still monks, and continued to follow their vows of personal poverty, obedience, and celibacy. The order also included chaplains and brothers who did not take up arms.

Spiritual Life

The spiritual roots of the Hospital Order of St. John of Jerusalem reflect the importance of hospitality in companioning the sick and dying. Grandmasters of the Order called themselves, "servant of the poor of our Lord Jesus Christ" or "Servant of the poor Sick" They saw the care and concern for the needy as a service of hospitality to Christ. The order was founded on the words of Christ, "Whatsoever you do for the least of my brothers, that you do unto me!" As has been said of the Order:

> *The practical connection between the spiritual and the physical service to the poor shows that the Brethern of .St. John did not restrict service to the physical welfare of the sick, but that they were also concerned about their spiritual well being. Therefore they used to have an altar for saying Holy Mass right in the wards. Later on, St. John's Hospitals were often built as double story churches, where the sick lay on the first floor and could look down from their beds to the ground floor and thus have audio-visual contact with the events on the altar of the church.*[71]

Sacred Palliative Care in Monastic Medicine

The Brethren of St. John expressed the practical connection between the spiritual service to the poor and the sick in the way they designed and built hospitals. They would have an altar for saying holy mass in the wards. This custom has continued in modern times in the hospital San Giacome in Agusta of the order.

The connection of physical and spiritual companioning of the sick is also seen in the oldest seal of the order, which symbolizes the interior of a hospital. The seal depicts a sick person who lies in a bed with his face turned to one side. The "Eternal Light" is hanging down from a dome in the background, and this is to remind the sick of Christ's presence in the Sacrament of the Altar. The swinging censer in the seal is a symbol of the prayers of the Brethren for the healing of the sick.[72]

We have a remarkable detailed account of monastic medicine and care for the sick and dying at St. John's Hospital in Jerusalem. Berthold Court of Waldstein discovered the report of an unknown German monk John of Wurzburg or Theodericus in the Bavarian State Library of Munich, Germany in 1988. He published this account in the book, *"Die Vasallen Christi" (The Servants of Christ)*. The narrative left by the monk shares with us a powerful first-hand account of sacred palliative care in the Middle Ages.[73]

According to this priest, the hospital in Jerusalem admitted anyone who was sick, regardless of their nationality, sex, religion or gender. If a people were in need, they were considered a "neighbor of Christ."

As soon as the sick would arrive in the hospital the porter had to receive and treat them like lords. The first person they met in the hospital was the priest, to whom they could confess their sins and receive as the first food, "the remedy of heavenly medicine," which was the Holy Communion of the Roman Catholic Church.

The sick person was then brought to the ward. The hospital was divided into eleven wards with each ward specializing in a particular type of sickness or injury. One ward had between ninety and one hundred and eighty beds. There was a special nursing team for each ward that consisted of twelve nurses and a master nurse. The womens' ward, which was mainly a maternity ward, was in a separate building. It was near St. Magdalene's Convent.

The beds in the hospital were big and covered with a bedspread and a linen sheet and feather cushions. The comfort of the patients was important, so that the sick did not "have to suffer from the roughness of the shaggy blankets nor through the hardness of the bed." The personal clothing of the sick was put in sealed bags. The patients were issued coats, furs, and shoes. This not only kept their feet clean, but protected them from the "coldness of the marble floor."

The nursing care was to prepare the beds, to straighten the blankets and to loosen the cushions. They were to be available to the sick to cover them and set them up and to support them in walking. Their hands were washed and dried with a towel as often as necessary.

When it was time for meals a "tablecloth" was put on top of their beds. Bread was given out in special baskets. Every sick person got his own loaf of bread so that all would have the same portion. The type of bread was changed often, so that the sick would have a good appetite. The food for the sick was prepared in the monastery kitchen. The menu included beef and mutton on Tuesdays and Thursdays, with flummery the other days. (Flummery from the Welsh llymru is a sweet soft pudding that is made from stewed fruit and thickened with cornstarch. Traditional British flummeries were like porridge as they were often oatmeal based and cooked to achieve a smooth and gelatinous texture. Often sugar and milk was added, and occasionally, orange flower water. The dish is typically bland in nature).[74]

The members of the order, knights, and serving brothers and sisters served the food to the sick and afterwards ate the same meal. The nurses were responsible to see that the food was well prepared and that the sick ate regularly. When the food was poor or the sick did not eat, the patients were given additional food such as chicken, dove, partridge or lamb. Eggs or fish were also available at times. The nursing staff had to buy food for the patients and this included fruits and vegetables such as dried figs and lettuce. The doctors of the hospital decided which patients were to have a special diet. Certain foods were not served in the hospital such as meat from mother pigs and smoked meat.

There were certain Brethren of the hospital that had the special task of washing the head and trimming the beard of every patient. They had to wash the feet and clean the soles of the feet with a pumice stone every Monday and Thursday. These brethren had to go though all the wards during food distribution and sprinkle everybody with water and apply incense. This was done by burning thyrus wood, the so-called oriental tree of life. The oriental custom was to disinfect the wards, but "chased away the insects in any case."

Doctors were given responsibility for the healing of patients. "Because doctors have learnt a lot and have practical knowledge," we are told, "the community of the Order entrusts the practical healing to the experience of science, that the sick may not be deprived from what is possible to man." Since there were few trained European doctors in Jerusalem, Jews, Arabs, Armenians and Syrians were recruited as doctors. The doctors visited the wards every morning and evening. They were accompanied by two nurses. One of them had to get the medicines, and the other had to hold the urinal and write down the prescriptions. (urine analysis by a physician was a basic part of medical examination in monastic medicine).

The hospital also employed barbers, who were recommended by the doctors. It was their task to bleed the patients according to the prescriptions of the doctors.

At dusk, the day shift ended and two brothers per ward took over the night shift. The brothers had to light three or four lamps in the ward "in order to prevent the sick from illusions, errors, and dubiousness." One of the brothers had to go round with a candle in the left hand and a wine jar in the right hand and call out clearly to the patients: "You Lords, wine from God." Another brother did the same with a jug of water calling out: "You Lord, water from God." When all the patients had quenched their thirst, both brethren came with a copper full of warm water calling" warm water, in God's name." It was their task to wash the sick and they used to do it "without force, but mild persuasion." Afterwards they had to walk around in the ward continuously to watch even those sick that were asleep. Those who were uncovered had to be covered. Those who were lying uncomfortably had to be repositioned. If a patient were dying, the priest had to be called and the body removed after death.

Other accounts state that the priests in the hospital had to pray daily after dark with the patients. The sick were also asked to pray because they were believed to be closer to Christ and their prayers were more effective. After the brothers had prayed the nocturne, all brothers on night duty met to form a procession by candlelight. Together they proceeded through all the wards and could notice, "if one of the wardens was careless or disorderly or even antagonistic to this task." Afterwards they choose a brother from among themselves who was the night supervisor. This brother continuously walked through the wards and kept an eye on the guards. He made sure nobody feel asleep and that the sick were properly cared for. If the sick were mistreated by word or deed the punishment was flagellation. If there were repeated cases of mistreating the sick the person was removed immediately from service and replaced by another brother. The punishment could be imprisonment of 40 days with only bread and water for nourishment.

The hospital for women is also mentioned in the eyewitness account of the hospital. This was in a separate building. There were nurses who were called "Mothers of St. John" and nuns. The main function of the hospital was to serve as a maternity ward. The delivering mothers got warm baths and everything that was needed for their bodily hygiene. The commissioner of the hospital provided napkins for the newly born children who were laid in a cradle next to their mother. When a mother was ill or neglected her child, the child was passed on to a wet nurse. As soon as the mother's condition had improved, the child was returned not later than two weeks after birth. If the mother was not able to raise her child because of poverty, the master of the hospital visited her and arranged the transfer of the child to a foster mother. This was a common occurrence, and it was reported that up to one thousand children a year had to be supported by the hospital.

Conclusion

So what are we to make of this remarkable outpouring of hospitality for the poor, the sick, the needy and the dying in the Middle Ages by monks and nuns of the Roman Catholic Church? Above all else, it is clear that hospitality is not an incidental spiritual practice in this time. Medieval society had many profound needs, such as poor sanitation, limited medical care, poverty, disease, starvation and war. It was the Christian religious orders, and especially those who followed the ***Rule of St. Augustine*** and that of St. Benedict, who sought to offer hospitality as a true expression of Christ's compassion for a broken world.

A recent historical conference stated that people living in Europe during medieval times actually had a progressive view of illness due to the fact that disease was so common and "out in the open" in society. Instead of being isolated in hospitals or nursing homes as is the case today, the sick and dying were integrated into society and taken care of by the community, the evidence suggests. "Parents, neighbors, and friends all tried to get each other to a place of healing; it was a community affair."[75]

Hospitality for those at the end of life was woven into the very fabric of medieval society by Christian orders that founded and ran large numbers of hospices, hospitals, leper houses and monastery guest houses and infirmaries. This created, as it were, a tapestry of great beauty. The spiritual practice of hospitality would remain in the weave of Western society down through the centuries. The modern hospice movement emerges not as something new in the 1960's and 1970's, but as another golden thread in this rich pattern of caring for those in need at the end of life through the practice of an ancient spiritual art.

How is it that this our spiritual practice of hospitality in hospice work today relates to this ancient spiritual art? In summary, we may lift up each of the seven spiritual practices that form the art of spiritual hospitality and see how their roots sink deep in the life of medieval times. Table Eight below provides this account.

Table Eight

The Historical Roots of the Ancient Hospice Way.

The Medieval Beginnings of the Spiritual Art of Hospitality in Hospice Companioning of the Dying

1. Observe the dignity of the Patient above all else.

   Medieval hospitals and hospices provided comfort an care for the sick and dying. The "outcast" lepers were offered care in leper houses.

2. Provide Palliative Care, Focusing on Pain Management and Symptom Control.

   Palliative care in Medieval times is sacred care for all

Table Eight Continued

healing is seen as from God. Monastic medicine provided a wide range of sacred palliative care including herbal medication and anesthetic agents. Palliative care also included shelter, food, and clothing. "Infirmary Music" was offered as palliative care at the Cluny monastery in the Middle Ages.

3. Offer Compassionate Care for the Family of the Dying and Empower the Family to Companion the Patient.

   The family was included in the care of medieval hospitals and leper houses. The family was included throughout a patient's death and dying.

4. Provide Care Ideally in the Home of the Patient or a Home-Like Facility.

   The Medieval hospices, hospitals, and leper houses were places of shelter. They offered a "home for the homeless" in the Middle Ages.

   The Augustinian monks and nuns were especially active in going into the world to offer shelter for those in need.

5. Let all Care Be Determined by the Needs of the Patient as Much as possible.

   The palliative care of monastic medicine allowed patients to remain in care as long as necessary. There were no certification periods for hospice care.

6. Provide Holistic Care Through a Health Care Team.

   Monastic medicine cared for the body, heart, and soul of patients as one sacred indivisible whole. It was truly holistic in nature, as seen by an infirmary and a chapel included in

Table Eight Continued

the design of early hospitals. The priest is seen as both priest and counselor.

7.Foster Sacred Presence Through Nature and all of Creation.

Monastic medicine utilized natural herbs and the healing presence of gardens. Hospices were situated in natural settings, such as mountain passes, to assist stranded pilgrims. Dogs were introduced at the St. Bernard Hospice as rescuers of the dying in the harsh environment.

Be Spiritually Present as a Companion on the Journey to the End of Life through each Spiritual Practice.

The Medieval Rule of St. Benedict calls for the stranger to be treated as the living presence of Christ.

It has been the view of certain historians that the medieval companioning of the dying was so different from what occurs in the modern day hospice that we cannot forge a connecting link between the two. From this perspective, hospice work should be seen as only a contemporary movement, dating to the late 20th century. For example, in the article, "***Hospice In Historical Perspective***," the author writes:

"Some commentaries on hospice history, particularly from inside the hospice movement, are inclined to seek ancient roots for what is actually a modern phenomenon. ... These connections between the past and the present contain a powerful symbolic message. They suggest that modern hospices are rooted in deep and ancient traditions of compassionate care that go back to earliest civilizations. Yet they tend to lack historical veracity. It is inaccurate, for example, to draw too close a parallel between places called hospices in early times and those carrying that name in the twenty and twenty-first centuries. The

former contained a broad spread of the diseased, the poor and the downtrodden, cared for over the longer term. The latter have tended to focus on the relatively short-term care of those close to the end of life and especially those dying from malignancies. No doubt in human societies going back over two millennia or more there have existed individuals...who patronized and nursed the sick and dying, but scholars should be cautious in seeing [them] as [prefiguring] the charismatic leaders of the modern hospice approach, developed in the second half of the twentieth century." [76]

In reply, we can say that indeed we have come far in palliative medical care from the pre-scientific times of the Middle Ages. Today we have knowledge of pharmacology, health, and sanitation that could only be dreamed about in medieval times. Only a fool would cast aside our modern medical care for the dying. And yet, is the medical model of death and dying able to encompass the "wholeness" of the dying experience? Can it embrace the full emotional and spiritual nature of death?

What we inherit from companioning the dying in the Middle Ages is an amazingly holistic spiritual work that is fully compatible with modern palliative medicine. This ancient model of sacred palliative care understands that all patient care is to be holistic in the deepest sense: a care of the body, heart and soul as one indivisible sacred whole. This palliative care is sacred care for it connects the patient to what gives meaning and value to life.

This sacred care connects the dying to the physical relief of pain and suffering in the body. It connects those at the end of life to emotional healing as they are surrounded by those they love and those who love them in return. It connects the dying to spiritual peace as they are given the opportunity to embrace and affirm the eternal values that guide and shape their destiny on earth. This is the deep understanding of sacred palliative care in companioning the dying that is our hospice legacy of ancient spiritual wisdom from medieval times. It is a beautiful model of care for how we can be with those at the end of life.

As Faye Getz says in **Medicine in the English Middle Ages**, monastic medicine contains the shinning ideal of the physician who companions us as a physician, counselor and a priest. She writes, "The human need for a wise and kindly adviser..., who had the learned judgment to determine that death was near and the courage to let the suffer know it, is with us still. Medieval English medicine may have been a patchwork of foreign imports-texts, institutions and people-but it also left us with an ideal: the physician as priest and counselor."[77] This ideal speaks to us today the profound message that hospice companions not only the patient's body in the process of dying but also their heart and soul as one indivisible and sacred whole. Such is the depth of the ancient spiritual art of hospitality from medieval times.

This holistic nature of the physician-counselor-priest in the Middle Ages impacts the modern hospice movement in an important way. Here are found the historical roots of the healthcare team we have in hospice today As we saw, hospitals in these early times were more like homeless shelters that offered palliative care, rather than the modern specialized hospital for the sick and dying we have today. It was the specialization of health care and the development of the health care professions, which led to the need for the modern hospice health care team. This specialization began in the 1500's and has continued into modern times. We come back to this early holistic care today through the modern health care team, as patients and families are companioned through the spiritual art of hospitality. The modern nature of health care is so complex, and knowledge of palliative care is expanding so rapidly, that no one health care worker in hospice could ever hope by themselves to offer a companioning of the dying and their family that embraces the physical, emotional, and spiritual nature of life. However, the modern hospice health care team is simply an expression of what existed so long ago: the shinning ideal of the physician, counselor, and priest in one person.

Hospice teams today may employ medical doctors, nurses, social workers, chaplains, music therapists and volunteers in providing patient care. But didn't the medieval caregivers go even beyond this in their caring for the body and soul of patients in their early companioning of the dying? They offered the best palliative care available in their society, and that truly was *sacred* palliative care. It was care given out of a deep spirituality and not the secular, medicalized care that we offer today. The palliative care of the Middle Ages, while primitive in technology, was holistic beyond our one dimensional medical care in modern hospices. The health care team of hospice work today only truly has value if we are companioning the patients and their families in body, heart and soul as one indivisible whole. In our secular, medical model today we are companioning the dying through the management of physical symptoms in the dying process. While we pay lip service to a health care team, it is actually excluded from hospice work by our medical model for there is no true place for the heart and soul in this model. Monastic medicine teaches us a true holistic companioning of the dying.

In order to appreciate the deep spiritual roots of hospice work of companioning the dying in medieval Europe, it is important to see beyond the specific ways that sacred palliative care was offered for the dying, not only in hospices but also in early hospitals, leper houses and monastic guest houses. It is true, for example, that medical palliative care has made tremendous strides in the use of pharmacology in managing patient's pain. But when the founder of the modern hospice movement, Cicely Saunders, introduced the concept of "total pain," as this a new idea? She understood "total pain" in hospice care as addressing the patient's pain rooted in the emotional and spiritual as well as the physical dimension of life. It may well be that this concept was known in medieval times and was "repackaged" with modern pharmacology by Cicely Saunders. Early monks and nuns provided for the many needs of patients and dealt with their "total pain."

Further, as we have seen, the family was normally present at the time of death in the medieval period. These ancient caregivers knew and appreciated the importance of being with loved ones at the time of deepest need. Death was a social experience in the middle ages and seen as a natural part of life's journey on this earth. By comparison, how alone and isolated so many die today in modern hospitals and nursing homes.

Most of all, our brothers and sisters in the Western hospice work of companioning the dying that dates through the ages offered the spiritual art of hospitality to the poor and needy in truly astonishing ways. There was no mandated federal government standard of eligibility for gaining admittance to a hospice or hospital. The doors were wide open and almost anyone in need could move in and take up permanent residence. While we may be more comfortable with a modern focused care, this was hospitality of the heart. The Medicare requirement of having six months to live to be eligible for hospice care did not have an equivalent in the Middle Ages. There was nothing like a 90 or 60 day Medicare certification period, with continual re-certification imposed on the dying. Hospitality was truly practiced from the heart and soul of a deep spirituality by these early monks and nuns.

The hospitality we see in monastic medicine in medieval times reminds us of the radical hospitality of Maximilian Kolbe, "the saint of Auschwitz." In both we see a radical hospitality without bounds; a care and concern that does not count the cost. It has been written in a biography of St. Kolbe that this is "A story of the ordinary becoming the extraordinary story of faith in God's love, strength, and purpose."[78] We could say the same thing about our spiritual brothers and sisters who companioned the dying in the medieval era. Theirs is a story of the ordinary becoming the extraordinary as they practiced sacred palliative care. The willingness to meet a leper and bandage their wounds is a simple thing, and yet it is extraordinary that someone would touch the untouchable and love the unlovable in that time of deadly plague. In their spiritual work we see an unfolding of faith in what they understood as God's love, strength and purpose.

This ancient expression of the spiritual art of hospitality makes our modern attempts to share hospitality seem weak and frail in comparison. We have a tame hospitality in the modern hospice movement; a hospitality that has become meek and mild when seen in the light of this radical hospitality.

From a medieval perspective, our modern "bottom line" of financial gain and profit would be secondary to offering care for the dying. The dying were companioned for the duration of their life on earth regardless of how they fit into a government plan of hospice care. Yes, medical technology has made palliative care for the dying very different in a modern hospice. But should we simply cast aside the courageous companioning of the dying by medieval monks and nuns? To do so is to abandon the spiritual roots of hospice and to stand in danger of losing this great spiritual work. We owe so much to these practitioners of the ancient spiritual art of hospitality who lived so long ago. They teach us sacred care for the dying. They teach us what hospitality truly is. They teach us how to companion those at the end of life as one indivisible whole, in body, heart, and soul. They teach us what holistic care is all about in our health care teams. Truly, they teach us the spiritual nature of the work we now call hospice.

Conclusion. A Model of Companioning the Dying for our Times.

Our examination of the practice of medical palliative care in the Middle Ages reveals a ***holistic model of companioning the dying*** that is well suited to serve as the foundation for the proposed Medicare Family Companioning Benefit. In this ancient model, all companioning was spiritual, rooted in the offering of compassion for those in need. Such a spiritual foundation of hospice care reaches far beyond our current medicalized delivery of hospice services, for this ancient model opens the door for modern day faith communities to naturally be a vital part of companioning the dying. Also, included in this care for those on the journey to the end of life was the role of both the "professionals" (clerical and university physicians) and lay practitioners (trades people). Modern day companioning of the dying needs to be founded on such a comprehensive model. It should include both professionals, such as primary care physicians and the hospice health care team, as well family members who receive training and supervision in end of life care, much as the trades people of ancient times.

Above all, this model of companioning the dying derived from medieval culture is truly holistic. It is profoundly a companioning in body, heart, and soul. With this holistic model, modern medical palliative care can be incorporated as one essential dimension of a larger companioning on the journey to the end of life. Medicalization need not usurp the place of the other dimensions of companioning. The emotional and spiritual wisdom of the patient, family, and religious faith community are all given a valid and essential role to play. This eons old holistic model of care, and those who walked this path, can be our guide for how to companion at home today those on the journey to the end of life.

The hospice historian Sandol Stoddard speaks of the medieval view of dying and how much our modern times needs this ancient wisdom. He writes:

In medieval times, dying persons were seen as prophetic souls, voyagers and pilgrims to the community in a number of ways, not least in the opportunity they provided those around them for service and spiritual growth...We must begin to honor the labor of those pilgrims who journey on before us; and in being present for them during the part of their living which is called dying, we must learn better to honor life itself. This is what the hospice movement is all about.[79]

Chapter 9

Hospice Companioning in Modern Times

The historian James A. Corrick views the civilization of the Middle Ages as the direct ancestor of our modern Western culture.[1] It was an epoch period when forms and customs were in the making. For hospice, medieval times can be viewed as the bubbling spring of the hospice companioning of the dying. From out of this spring of hospitality flowed care that became a powerful river of compassion, as monks and nuns journeyed to the end of life with the dying. The living waters of hospitality flowed through monastic medicine, and were visible in the hospices, hospitals, leper houses, and monastic infirmaries of the era. Two great spiritual figures, St. Augustine and St. Benedict, inspired and informed this outpouring of hospitality. Such is the spiritual legacy of the modern hospice movement.

The French historian M. Paul Violett says:

> *"We issue from the Middle Ages…The roots of our modern society lie deep in them…What we are, we are in large measure because of the Middle Ages. The Middle Ages live in us; they are alive all around us."*[2]

As we companion the dying in hospice work today, the Middle Ages do live in us. The spiritual art of hospitality flows from an ancient spring and our work with the dying, while incorporating modern technology, draws on this timeless wisdom.

However, commencing with the 1500's, profound social changes began to occur that were to re-shape the Western world and change the hospice companioning of the dying. The Protestant Reformation challenged the Roman Catholic Church and the entire monastic way of life. In England, Henry VIII acted to break the power and control of the Church of Rome. This had a direct and highly destructive impact on monastic medicine, as the religious hospitals, hospices, leper houses and monastic infirmaries were dependent on the financial and spiritual support of the Roman Catholic Church. Most of all, Western secular medicine emerged in the 1600's as a profession apart from monastic medicine. Death became increasingly seen in the West as a physical event, with death and dying more and more within the realm of the medical profession.

An example of this profound shift in companioning the dying is seen in the architecture of hospitals. In the Middle Ages, religious chapels were normally attached to the main wards of hospitals. This graphically symbolized the hospital as a place for care of the soul and care of the body. From the Reformation on, the chapel began to disappear from this central place in the hospital. Today, most modern hospitals have the chapel tucked away on a hidden corridor, "out of sight and out of mind." Death has become an event that involves the body, and not the soul, in the modern Western view of medicine.

Cultural changes thus altered, and disrupted, the flow of hospice work as a river of care and compassion for the dying. Hence forth, this great hospice river of companioning the dying was to flow underground for the next four centuries. While care for the dying continued through hospices and hospitals run by religious monks and nuns, hospice work went largely unseen in Western society. It was not until the mid-1900's that the hospice river of care for the dying once more flowed above ground. Two charismatic figures, Elizabeth Kubler-ross in the United States and Cicely Saunders in England, were the leaders in the re-surfacing of the hospice river of spiritual hospitality.

Once again, there were mighty social forces at work in Western culture that brought about this new direction for hospice work. Especially important was the need to deal with Western medicine's deeply impersonal approach to death and dying that had developed to a crisis point by the mid 1950's. We also see a culture enamored with the advances of science and technology, and yet profoundly impoverished with regards to spiritual wisdom. There was a fundamental denial of death in Western society and a profound struggle with how to cope with the dying. Cancer emerged as a major cause of death. Western medicine had advanced many medical approaches to treat the disease, yet failed to offer adequate emotional and spiritual care for the terminally ill that could not be cured. In all these ways, there was an opening in Western society for hospice work where it could once more flow above ground as a river of care and comfort for the dying. But this is getting us ahead of our story. We will first turn to what I call "the Quiet Years" of hospice work. These are the little known years in the hospice movement from the 1500's to the mid 1900's.

The Quiet Years, 1550's- Late 1800's.

In the 1500 and 1600's, the forming of new hospices did occur but it was rare. Many of the older hospices were renamed as hospitals and much of the expression of monastic medicine was lost to the West. There was the closing of hospices and monastic hospitals.

The Roman Catholic Church continued to offer care and comfort for the dying through the spiritual art of hospitality. St. Vincent de Paul opened hospices in Paris.[3] These were places of care for the poor, sick, and the dying, much as in the middle ages. Hospice companioning of the dying was part of a compassionate outreach to those in need, especially the poor. The Sisters of Charity also embodied and carried forth these expressions of monastic medicine. "The common denominator of all these initiatives, activities and undertakings is the desire to help the lost and the have-nots by listening, friendship, spiritual, moral and material support; to give them back their dignity, to ensure their personal development, to give them back hope and, if possible, the joy of life."[4]

St. Vincent de Paul worked tirelessly to help those in need: the impoverished, the sick, the enslaved, the abandoned, and the ignored. He died in 1660 at St. Lazarus's house, Paris. His motto in life was: "God sees you." "Let us love God; but at the price of our hands and sweat of our face."[5]

Baron Von Stein of Prussia was inspired by the hospitality of Saint Vincent and worked with a Protestant pastor in his hometown to found Kaiserworth Hospice.[6] This hospice was unique in being run by an order of Protestant sisters. Both orders sent hospice workers to the Crimea during the 1850's, and work was done with Florence Nightingale.

Another important figure in this period of hospice work was Jeanne Garnier. As a young widow and bereaved mother, together with others in similar circumstances, she formed L'Association des Dames du Calvaire in Lyon, France, in 1842. The association opened a home for the dying the following year. The hospice was characterized by "a respectful familiarity, an attitude of prayer and calm in the face of death"[7] While Jeanne Garnier died in 1853, her influence led to the foundation of six other establishments for the care of the dying between 1874 in Paris, and 1889 in New York. We find today modern palliative care services that developed from the pioneering work of L'Association des Dames du Calvaire.

The Early Period of the Modern Hospice Era, Late 1800's-Mid 1950's

During the nineteenth century there was a rebirth in various forms of hospice care for the terminally ill in the West. The poverty and suffering of the potato famine in Ireland, and the poverty of other countries, clearly showed the need for care for those at the end of life. The clergy also became aware that secular hospitals were offering minimal care for the terminally ill, and there were few options.

Our Lady's Hospice, which began in Ireland in 1879, was the first modern hospice by a religious organization that offered palliative care specifically for the dying.[8] This was inspired by Sister Mary Aikenhead, a member of the Irish Sisters of Charity. Sister Mary had worked with Florence Nightingale and she also knew of the work of Saint Vincent DePaul. The term "hospice" was used by Sister Mary for her new facility. It was to denote death as life's final pilgrimage, "associated with pilgrims of yore."[9] The spirit of this hospice is expressed as meeting the need for "...a refuge for the sick poor of the city, an institution that took in the infectious, the destitute and the dying..."[10]

The Motto of the Congregation of the Religious Sisters of Charity

Caritas Christas Urget Nos- The Love of Christ Empowers Us.[11]

"Seeing and feeling how very hard it was to send away the poor, dismissed by the doctors as beyond hope of recovery, some having very poor homes and others no friends willing to receive them, they bethought themselves of having a hospice or home where these poor sufferers might be received."[12]

There were only two hospitals in Dublin, Ireland, that took fever patients. These were the Hardwick, which opened in 1803, and later St. Laurence's and Cork Street, opened in 1804. In the spirit of the Augustinian monks and nuns of the middle ages, Our Lady's Mount was opened as a place that "took in the poor, the sick and the dying."[13]

In England, there was the establishment of new hospices near the turn of the century. Many of these hospices are still active today and formed the foundation for the modern British hospice movement. Saint Luke's House of the Dying Poor in Bayswater, London, which was managed by the Methodist committee, was opened in 1893. It was here that Cicely Saunders volunteered in 1948.

Elizabeth Fry, a member of the English Sisters of Charity, developed hospices through her religious group in London. It was her hospice, St. Joseph's in London, that opened at the turn of the century, and provided the first medical position for Saunders in 1958.

It was during this same period of the late 1800's that American hospices began to emerge. Like those in Europe, they developed because modern hospitals were unable or unwilling to care for the terminally ill.

Father Gallwey

Father Gallwey, from Co. Kerry, Ireland, was the Rector of Farm Street Jesuit Mission. His greatest concern was the dire condition of the poor who suffered and died in the disease-ridden East End of London. He wanted to have a place for them where they could die in peace. He was aware of the hospitals, hospices and schools founded in Ireland by the Sisters of Charity, so over thirty years, he sent several requests for Sisters to work along side the poor in the east end.[14]

Rose Hawthorne Lathrop, Nathaniel Hawthorne's daughter, was a strong advocate of hospice care for cancer patients in the late 1890's. After the death of her husband, she took religious vows. Her title was Mother Alphonsa, and the organization she headed was the Dominican Sisters of Hawthorne.[15]

The Dominican Sisters of Hawthorne express their purpose in terms of hospitality: "We dedicate our lives to fulfilling our mission: "We must make our guests glad they crossed the threshold that is to be their last boundary. We must make them as comfortable and happy

---

The Dominican Sisters of Hawthorne

"Ours is a very special ministry. We share our patients' last months and days. To know they see your face one day and God's the next is an awesome occurrence."

"The Dominican mission is to preach God's love which we accomplish through our apostolate of nursing incurable cancer patient who cannot afford care. Our apostolate preaches the intrinsic value and dignity of each human being in their last stage of life. We care for the crucified and suffering Christ in each of our patients.

All of our Homes are supported by unsolicited donations from the public. We take no Medicare, Medicaid, private insurance or private funds from the patients or their families. Our dear foundress believed if she was doing God's work, He would provide...and He has!

...Our homes are God's homes and we are happy to welcome His poor so that we can shower His love upon them until He calls them to their eternal home."[16]

---

as if their own people had kept them and put them into the very best bedroom. We must love them." Each patient is given the physical, spiritual, and emotional support needed to accept the limitations imposed by illness.[17]

Another American hospice that combines hospice-like care with traditional medical treatment is Calvary Hospital, which was established in New York in 1899.

Calvary Hospital, New York City

Calvary Hospital is the only fully accredited acute care specialty hospital exclusively   providing palliative care for adult advanced cancer patients in the United States. Calvary Hospital is based in the Bronx, New York with a campus in Brooklyn. We provide palliative care-- the active treatment of the symptoms, not the cure of the disease, to make our patients as comfortable as possible.

Our programs include inpatient care, pain management, outpatient care, hospice, home care with bereavement and support programs for families and friends.

Calvary Hospital is committed to kindness, non-abandonment, and the importance of "caring" people who care for our patients.

The Modern Hospice Era, Mid 1950's-Today

In our times, medical care of the dying has fallen more and more within the realm of hospitals and secular Western medicine, and the holistic nature of monastic medicine has become less and less known. It has been stated that by the mid-twentieth century eighty percent of the people in the USA died in a hospital or nursing home.[19] Death became first and foremost a "medicalized" event in the West.

There were also profound social forces that led to the development of the modern hospice movement in the 1960's and 1970's. There was a widespread belief that Western culture had become a death-denying society. The mood of the 1950's toward the end of life can be summed up as "Death faces all of us, but few of us face death."[20]

Increasingly, the impersonal nature of secular medicine seemed to provide inadequate care for the terminally ill. It was during the 1950's and the 1960's that a "good death" or a "death with dignity" became a popular concept in society. Most of all, the 1960's were a time of social change and many causes were affirmed in the social chaos of the culture. It was a time in history when it became popular to stand "against the establishment," and secular medicine was a bulwark of the Western establishment.

In the 1950's one of the most important publications concerning the meaning of death and death with dignity was *The Meaning of Death,* by Herman Feifel.[21] The modern hospice era has been traced to the work by Feifel, who established the study of thanatology. (Thanatology is the academic study of death among human beings. It investigates the circumstances surrounding a person's death, the grief experienced by the deceased's loved ones, and larger social attitudes towards death such as ritual and memorialization).[22] The author Kenneth J. Doka speaks of the influence of Herman Feifel's work on the development of hospice. He stated that the writings of Fiefel fundamentally influenced how we think about death, treat the dying and bereaved, and view our lives.[23]

In the post World War II era, we also find music therapy and music thanatology developing as important modern forms of palliative care with the sick and dying. Music therapy was widely used in Veterans Administration Hospitals after World War I and II as an intervention to address traumatic war injuries. The first music therapy degree program was founded in 1944 at the University of Michigan. The National Association of Music Therapy was formed in 1950. Standards, clinical training and licensing requirements for the profession of music therapy were soon established.[24]

Music Therapy

"Music therapy can make the difference between withdrawal and awareness, between isolation and interaction, between chronic pain and comfort-between demoralization and dignity." Barbara Crowe (Past President of American Music Therapy Association).

"I regard music therapy as a tool of great power in many neurological disorders-Parkinson's and Alzheimer's-because of its unique capacity to organize or reorganize cerebral function when it has been damaged." Oliver Sacks, MD.[25]

Music Thanatology, in its modern form, began in 1973 with the ground-breaking work of Theresa Schroeder-Sheker.[26] However, as we have seen, this use of music as sacred palliative care with the dying traces back almost 800 years to the monastery in Cluny, France. The beginning work was the establishment of Ars Antiqua, a center for medieval musicology. It was in the 1970's that the School of Music Thanatology was formed in Denver, Colorado. The Chalice of Repose Project and the school were located in Missoula, Montana for many years, where there was a fruitful alliance with St. Patrick Hospital, (founded by the Sisters of Providence). It is one of four long-term geriatric care facilities of The Goodman Group/Sage Corporation, a local hospice, and peripherally, the Community Hospital.

It was in this post war era that the prophetic vision of Saunders and Kubler-Ross in companioning the dying, based on hospice work that stretches back to the fifth century or so in the early Middle Ages, became focused as a unique and special social movement in the West. Hospice emerges from the 1970's in the West as a spiritual work that stands apart from other expressions of spiritual hospitality, such as care for the poor and the homeless.

It is the spiritual art of hospitality that links the early companioning of the dying with the modern work of hospice. This is the thread that connects the spiritual work of monks and nuns as they practiced monastic medicine with the dying in the Middle Ages and the work of hospice today with modern medical technology. For over 1,500 years, hospice has existed as the practice of the spiritual art of hospitality in companioning the dying. It is, however, only in modern times that this spiritual practice of hospitality with those at the end of life has stood as an independent social movement. The great contribution of Saunders and Kubler-Ross was to establish hospice as a separate movement in the West, grounded in the holistic companioning of the dying and the practice of modern palliative medicine.

A contribution of Saunders and Kubler-Ross was to publicize the need for companioning the dying in general, and the work of hospice in particular. They brought to the general public an awareness of the need for our society to find ways to face our fear of death and companion the terminally ill with compassion. The "death with dignity" movement was an important part of their bringing a social consciousness to Western society.

We will now turn to the specific contributions of Saunders and Kubler-Ross in shaping the spiritual art of hospitality as a spiritual work with the dying in our society. What did they contribute to the spiritual art of hospitality to help form hospice as the movement that it is today?

Dame Cicely Saunders (1918–2005)

The life and work of Cicely Saunders (1918-2005) are well known. She opened the first modern hospice as a residential treatment center in London in 1967. The St. Christopher's Hospice she founded welcomes around 4,000 visitors annually and more than 50,000 health care professionals from all over the world visit and train there.[27] She was a visionary who transformed the spiritual consciousness of Western society in how we view death and dying in modern times. As has been written about Cicely Saunders as founder of the modern hospice (or palliative care) movement. "…she reshaped end-of-life care. In a deeper sense, Saunders transformed how we care for those with terminal illness as well as the bleak way we look at dying."[28] In a 2002 interview for *The Daily Telegraph of London*, she said, "I didn't set out to change the world; I set out to do something about pain." Saunders' work was a "personal calling, underpinned by a powerful religious commitment," wrote David Clark, an English medical school professor of palliative care and Saunders' biographer. [30]

A major contribution of her work to the spiritual art of hospitality was her concern for the dignity of the dying person combined with her spiritual presence. In a tribute to her, a colleague stated she conveyed a message of caring for those at the end of life.[31] As Saunders said, "You matter because you are you, and you matter to the end of your life. We will do all we can not only to help you die peacefully, but also to live until you die."[32]

This basic concern with the dignity and worth of each person is well expressed in a letter written to Dr. Saunders by the relative of a grateful patient at St. Christopher's Hospice in 1972.

As we have mentioned, a contribution Dr. Saunders made to the spiritual art of hospitality was this concern for developing the frontiers of medical palliative care with the dying. Her work at St. Christopher's Hospice in London established "total pain" as a basic palliative concept of all hospice work in the West. She taught that hospice should include the physical, emotional, and spiritual dimensions of pain and the entire experience of death and dying.[34] St. Christopher's introduced the pioneering approach of administering opiods "by the clock" on a scheduled basis to control pain before its onset. One of her legacies, it has been written, is the change in pain management care of the dying. Saunders' questioned practitioners' fear that their dying patients would become addicted to medications. Rather than respond to pain with intermittent sedation, Saunders' novel method of pain control provided a steady state in which a dying patient could remain conscious and maintain a good quality of life.

It has been said of her concern for providing palliative care through her understanding of total pain that this was," clearly anchored in a scientific approach to the use of analgesics, other symptom relief drugs, and non-drug measures."[35] In an article in the British Medical Journal ten years ago, entitled "A Personal Therapeutic Journey", Cicely mentioned a handout she prepared to accompany her lectures: "Drugs most commonly used at St Joseph's and St Christopher's Hospice."[36] It was four pages and covered two sides of folded foolscap. It was later updated and expanded by Mary Baines, and remained a key handout for many years. Now, the handout has been superseded by the one thousand, two hundred forty four pages of the *Oxford Textbook*

Correspondence to Dr. Saunders

Dear Dr. Saunders:

I would like to write to you and attempt to express something of the gratitude and admiration that I feel for St. Christopher's. In saying this I realize that St Christopher's is not just a building, but a way of living – an attitude towards people, their life and their death – that is so remarkable.

During those weeks which I spent with my father, and with you, it did seem very remarkable that the vision of one person, who had responded to a need, could be caught and sustained by so many others; so that the vision became a reality and the reality perpetuates itself creatively...

The men and women at the reception desk all greet you as if you belong and are welcome, the cleaners smile and look as if they enjoy playing their part in the scheme... The nursing staff have all the qualities that nurses are supposed to have and something extra as well. I don't quite know what it is – perhaps it's a dimension of personality which is free to flow out when a nurse is trusted to motivate from within and is not oppressed by bossy hierarchies.

So how did this affect my father who was brought into the Hospice too ill and too weak to be much aware of his surroundings? He benefited because St Christopher's is a happy place in spite of its sadness (perhaps joy is a more appropriate word because you can't experience joy without sadness). So those daily visits was marked by a feeling of serenity and calm as well as with humor and laughter, for which one is so grateful...

And I think I came to know my father better during those visits, as a man and not just my father! I have written more than I intended, but please accept it all as an attempt to say "thank you" for so much that has been good."[33]

---

of Palliative Medicine, and numerous other books, such as befits a full-blown medical specialty. But whether just four pages or over one thousand, the need for a thorough holistic evaluation of the patient remains essential. Cicely disparaged 'tender loving care'; she championed instead 'efficient loving care' in which attention to detail is the constant watchword.[37]

Dr. Saunders relates how she came to this concern for relieving the pain and suffering of the dying as her life's work. "My story in this field goes right back to 1948 when I was a social worker... meeting a young Polish Jew who had an inoperable cancer," Dr. Saunders says. "I became very fond of him." David Tasma had escaped the Warsaw ghetto and was dying in a London hospital. Tasma's pain, loneliness and anguish had a profound affect on Saunders. She visited Tasma frequently in the last two months of his life. As Saunders and Tasma spoke of his looming death, Saunders had a revelation: "I realized that we needed not only better pain control but better overall care. People needed the space to be themselves. I coined the term 'total pain,' from my understanding that dying people have physical, spiritual, psychological, and social pain that must be treated. I have been working on that ever since."

Pioneering research on the use of morphine as an effective drug for pain control was carried out at St. Christopher's, along with other detailed studies of new approaches to symptom control. In the 1970 book *Matters of Life and Death*, Cicely Saunders described chronic pain as "not just an event, or a series of events but rather a situation in which the patient is, as it were, held captive" In terminally ill patients, where the major challenge is to use active strategies of prevention to avoid the onset of such pain, she advocated in particular the regular giving of strong analgesia in anticipation of, rather than in response to, the onset of pain. Her oft-repeated maxim was "constant pain needs constant control."

At the beginning of the 1980s, she contributed a chapter to Mark Swerdlow's collection *The Therapy of Pain* (Saunders, 1981). Here she cited examples from studies conducted between 1954 and 1978, presenting evidence of patients suffering unrelieved terminal pain. By contrast, data on 3,362 patients cared for by St. Christopher's Hospice between 1972–1977 showed that only 1% of the patients reported continuing pain problems, although more than three quarters had been admitted to the hospice with pain. Saunders developed, in large measure, the modern hospice approach of medically controlling pain at the end of life.

Another contribution she made to the spiritual art of hospitality was the in the area of holistic care with the dying. Echoing monastic medicine, Dr. Saunders developed the understanding that a team approach to patient care could implement this holistic concept. This resulted in an inter-disciplinary approach, focusing on the physical, social, spiritual and psychological needs of the patient and the family. A nurse, social worker and doctor became part of a multi-faceted, holistic approach to care giving. This formed the foundation for the development of a new medical specialty, palliative care, which is an integral component of contemporary hospice care.

Dr. Saunders followed in the steps of the age-old Benedictine approach to companioning the dying in establishing a hospice as a place of care. St. Christopher's opened in 1967, a place that served, in her words as quoted by de Boulay, as "a hospital and a home." This was a "come structure" as a place of care for those at the end of life. At St. Christopher's Hospice, there was a home where the patient and their family became a focus of care.

A final contribution of Dr. Saunders that we will consider was the importance of spiritual presence in her life and work with hospice. Her autobiography is entitled, ***Watch with Me***. The work consists of contains five reflective articles written and delivered over a span of forty years. The last talk, "Consider Him", is dated 2003. Here she quotes from a book by one of her favorite theologians: "The crucified Jesus is the only accurate picture of God that the world has ever seen, and the hands that hold us in existence are pierced with unimaginable nails."

Tribute to Dr. Saunders

Cicely didn't just talk the talk,

She walked the walk.

She stayed the course, and in doing so she changed the world,

And is changing it still.

Although physically she has left us, her vision lives on.

To honor Cicely, we too must not just talk the talk,

But, like her, we must walk the walk,

And stay the course, and continue the task of changing the world.

Fear of death is instinctive,

So the task is unending.

For each new generation, the same battles to fight and to win.[45]

There is a popular misconception in hospice literature today that is also found on the web site of many hospices. The statement is made that for all practical purposes that Cicely Saunders founded the hospice movement. All that went before her under the name of "hospice" was simply archaic and of no real value. Saunders herself refutes this claim. She once said, "I did not found hospice. Hospice found me."[46] I believe Saunders "was found" by the ancient spiritual wisdom of the Hospice Way. She "was found" by the spiritual art of companioning the dying that stretches back to the so called Dark Ages in the West.

She gave this spiritual art of hospitality with the terminally ill a new face. She infused and renewed the art with a modern understanding of medical palliative care and a holistic team approach in caring for those at the end of life. Her vision and passion for alleviating the suffering of the dying was fundamental to establishing hospice as a modern social movement with its own profoundly spiritual legacy. In spite of all her great contributions Saunders was absolutely correct in saying, "I did not found the hospice movement." The spiritual roots of hospice work are ancient and run deep in Western culture. The spiritual art of hospitality in companioning the dying has been with us for well over a millennium and a half. In our times this great spiritual work found Cicely Saunders and this, in large measure, led to the birth of the modern era of hospice.

Elizabeth Kubler-Ross (1926-2004)

It has been written that perhaps the most enduring tribute that can be paid to Elizabeth Kubler-Ross is that "she brought the subject of death and dying out of the dark closet of fear in which it had been ensconced by society for so many years." Her great contribution was in changing the consciousness of Western society in accepting death with dignity.

As we have seen in our discovering of the ancient Hospice Way, observing the dignity of the patient is a fundamental spiritual practice. Kubler-Ross was a tireless advocate for patient dignity in the face of death.

"We live in a very particular death-denying society," Dr. Kubler-Ross told a U.S. Senate committee in 1972. "We isolate both the dying and the old, and it serves a purpose. They are reminders of our own mortality. We should not institutionalize people. We can give families more help with home care and visiting nurses, giving the families and patients the spiritual, emotional and financial help in order to facilitate the final care at home."[48] Kubler-Ross became a leading advocate of the Death with Dignity movement.

Another major contribution of Kubler-Ross to the modern form of hospice is seen in her statement to the Congress. She emphasized the importance of care in the home for the terminally ill, and the vital nature of a holistic health care team.

Kubler-Ross was also an advocate for sacred palliative care. In 1969, Elizabeth Kubler-Ross wrote *On Death and Dying*.[49] From her research and interviews with dying patients that began in 1965, she saw a pattern emerging in the dying process. The Swiss-born psychiatrist returned to the ancient spiritual understanding that death is an integral part of life, and that the terminally ill are best served in their final days with dignity and respect. She theorized that the terminally ill go through five stages of grief as they near death. She was able to express this pattern in the form of five stages that express the nature of grief and dying. These stages have become well known, and are now an accepted part of hospice work. While she believed that not everyone goes through each stage and the order may be different for each person, the stages are still seen as universal. These now familiar stages are (1) denial and isolation, (2) anger (3) bargaining (4) depression and (5) acceptance.

So how does the spiritual art of hospitality, as an expression of the Hospice Way of companioning the dying, relate to these stages of the dying process developed by Kubler-Ross? The primary difficulty with the Kubler-Ross stages theory is that it does not fully appreciate the spiritual practice of patient driven care. Her stage theory tends to prescribe rather than describe, and reflects her medical orientation. Her theory has become well known in our culture and patients may see spiritual and emotional growth, and also their well being, dependent on making it through the stages she set out.

The Kubler-Ross model seems to imply it is "better" or "healthier" to move beyond denial and find your way to acceptance. Patients may feel that they need to work through the stages, or they may be pressured by family members to move beyond one certain stage, such as anger. The model of Kubler-Ross brings the message that "the proper way to die" is to accept your own death. The process of dying has a *prescribed* way that it should occur, according to this theory, and is not simply *described* to us as we companion the dying.

By contrast, in practicing the ancient spiritual art of hospitality of the Hospice Way, the process of dying is left open as a wondrous mystery that simply cannot be prescribed ahead of time. The Kubler-Ross term "stages" implies a set order of set conditions. When companioning the dying through the spiritual art of hospitality, the focus is on palliative care that *responds* to the needs of the patient, rather than *prescribes* the stages a patient should go through their final days. The patient may have many emotional experiences that do not even fit into the Kubler-Ross stages. For example, I am not sure what stage would relate to one patient's conversation with the angels that was shared with me as a hospice chaplain.

It would be all too easy to misuse the Kubler-Ross stages to make value judgments about a patient without being fully aware of these judgments. I recall one patient I knew was a deeply spiritual lady who lived her whole life out of a profound Christian faith. She enjoyed talking about her faith, and we shared many hours discussing scripture. Toward her final days, there were times that she was angry and apparently delusional. She just could not figure out why some mean people had moved her bed, and she woke up to find herself away from her house. The patient was angry and "ticked off" (to say the least) about being moved; even though the staff of the facility where she was explained that she had not been moved. The hospice nurse working with this patient described her as "angry and slipping," as if this were a serious decline in her condition. In terms of Kubler-Ross stages, it may have be a set back to go from a serene spiritual acceptance of death (stage five) to being angry and hard to manage (stage one) in a residential facility. I prefer, however, the view of the spiritual art of hospitality of the Hospice Way that calls me to companion the dying according to *their* needs and according to how *their* spiritual journey unfolds in the last days. While the Kubler-Ross stages are helpful to be aware of, there is the danger of forcing the dying person into a mold into which that they do not fit. This patient seemed to find it very helpful to stay focused on her life of deep faith, and celebrate her spiritual journey as a whole through the years. Such a focus is very difficult if we focus too firmly on a particular stage or experience that the patient may be experiencing at the moment.

The spiritual art of hospitality calls for a more gracious and patient focused way to companion the dying. As a hospice chaplain, I try to let the patient describe their final journey to me, rather than assuming I know ahead of time how they are experiencing the end of life. Kubler-Ross's work is very helpful if we simply see it as simply a description of what some patients have felt and know as life draws to a close, rather than as definite stages of the end of life for all of us.

In a tribute to the work of Kubler-Ross, it has been written: "It is the responsibility of each of us to carry Elizabeth's light into the shadows of fear and ignorance so that everyone in every corner of the world will have the opportunity to die on their own terms, peacefully, without pain, surrounded by family and friends. The extraordinary Elizabeth Kubler-Ross did ultimately achieve a death with dignity—the kind of passage that even the most ordinary of human beings deserves."[50]

This brings us to the modern era of the hospice movement in the United States, which we will now consider.

The Modern Hospice Era in the United States, Mid 1970's-Today

In 1974, the first American hospice to provide patient services was founded by the Yale Study Group and located in Branford, Connecticut.[51] It went by the name of Hospice, Inc., and was funded for three years by The National Cancer Institute (NCI) to develop a national demonstration center for home care for the terminally ill and their families. It is known today as The Connecticut Hospice.

In 1980, Connecticut Hospice opened the nation's first specially-designed free-standing hospice inpatient care center in Branford, Connecticut. In 1988, Connecticut Hospice founded the Hospice Cottage as a residence and treatment center for homeless patients. Today, the hospice serves over 2,400 patients and families from across the state of Connecticut and beyond through home care, Inpatient, and cottage programs.[51]

> ### A Hospice Setting in Nature
>
> The Connecticut Hospice was the first hospice in the United States. It is built adjacent to a small island that the hospice also owns. At low tide, the island is accessible on foot each day.[52]

This hospice was based on Cicely Saunder's model of care, and was to become the only U.S. hospice with no direct ties to the acute health care system in the United States. We see the spiritual practices of the spiritual art of hospitality reflected very clearly in the United Way web site that details the work of this hospice. There is a concern for the dignity of the patient, sacred palliative care, concern for the family, care provided in the home, care determined by the patient, holistic care, and spiritual presence.

The Connecticut Hospice has similarities to the earliest form of hospice in the Middle Ages, where hospice care provided a place for the homeless. Also, care is open ended, as care is offered "for as long as life lasts." We also see that companioning of the dying is based on patient needs and not on the patient's or family's ability to pay for services.

> ### The Connecticut Hospice
>
> The Connecticut Hospice shall provide quality, compassionate and competent hospice care in Connecticut to patients suffering from irreversible illness, and to members of their families. Care shall be interdisciplinary in nature, allow for family decision-making and participation in care, and shall seek to enhance quality of life for as long as life lasts. With the support of the philanthropic community, care shall be offered based on need rather than ability to pay. Bereavement care shall also be offered for one year to all families. Home and Inpatient care shall serve as a clinical model for our national unique role as the founder of hospice care in America.[53]

The Medicalized Form of the Modern Hospice Movement.

In the United States, a defining moment for the modern hospice movement occurred in 1982. In September, the Tax Equity and Fiscal Responsibility Act (TEFRA) expanded Medicare benefits to create a new hospice benefit. An evaluation of hospice care was completed in September, 1986, and this benefit became permanent. Not only did this Medicare benefit offer more services to hospice patients, but it also moved hospice in the direction of medical palliative care dominating all other aspects of patient care in hospice. However, the government's financial support of the hospice movement has come at a great price. *The spiritual work of hospice today is in danger of being lost, as hospice workers across the United States increasingly devote immense time and energy to compliance with the standards and compliances set by Medicare benefits and abandon the ancient Hospice Way.*

As we saw with the stages model of Kubler-Ross, the spiritual art of hospitality of the Hospice Way brings a broader and more comprehensive understanding to hospice work. The ancient wisdom of hospitality allows us to understand sacred palliative care as *one* spiritual practice among the seven practices of this spiritual art. The spiritual art of hospitality, as the driving force of hospice care, can and should provide for compliance with all the standards required for Medicare benefits in hospice. What needs to occur, however, is modern medical care embracing ancient spiritual wisdom. Such an embrace provides for truly holistic care of the hospice patient and family in body, heart, and soul.

In the 1982 hospice Medicare benefit, the federal government supported the hospice approach to health care but limited reimbursement to specific services. Many of the spiritual practices of the spiritual art of hospitality were funded, but not all. The practice of sacred palliative care, with pain management and symptom control, is covered by Medicare. Also provided for in Medicare are the practice of the family as the unit of care, the home as a place of care with home care services, holistic patient care through a health care team and patient participation in the health care treatment.

It is interesting that other aspects of the spiritual art of hospitality were not covered. Spiritual and bereavement support are not part of the Medicare benefit. The Medicare regulations affirmed the importance of bereavement services as a necessary dimension of hospice care but did not reimburse them. In terms of pastoral care and spiritual support, not only did Medicare regulations deny funding, but they also specified that nurses, volunteers, or other team members could provide spiritual support for patients and families.

It has been suggested that the form hospice programs in the United

States have taken is primarily the result of funding priorities rather than the ancient spiritual ideals of the hospice movement. The spiritual art of hospitality in companioning of the dying that is the Hospice Way calls for a return to the ideals of hospice as a spiritual work in being with the dying at the end of life.

In the late 1970's popular interest in hospice care led to the formation of the National Hospice Organization to represent the hospice movement. It was decided that establishing standards for hospice care would allow providers to better promote the hospice concept and work with the Joint Commission on Accreditation of Hospitals and other health care organizations. This resulted in the first official standards for hospice care in the United States. These standards for hospice programs published in 1979 by the National Hospice Organization are as follows[54]:

Table Nine

Standards of a Hospice Program of Care

1. The hospice program complies with applicable local, state, and federal law and regulations governing the organization and delivery of health care to patients and families.

2. The hospice program provides a continuum of inpatient and home care.

3. The home care services are available 24 hours a days, seven days a week.

4. The patient/family is the unit of care.

5. The hospice program has admission criteria and procedures that reflect:

    a. the patient/family's desires and need for service.

    b. physician participation.

    c. diagnosis and prognosis.

Table Nine Continued

6. The hospice program seeks to identify, teach, coordinate, and supervise persons to give care to patients who do not have a family member available.

7. The hospice program acknowledges that each patient/family has its own beliefs and/or value system and is respectful of them.

8. Hospice care consists of a blending of professional and nonprofessional services, provided by an interdisciplinary team, including a medical director.

9. Staff support is an integral part of the hospice program.

10. Inservice training and continuing education are offered on a regular basis.

11. The goal of hospice care is to provide symptom control through appropriate palliative therapies.

12. Symptom control includes assessing and responding to the physical, emotional, social, and spiritual needs of the patient and family.

13. The hospice program provides bereavement services to survivors for a period of at least one year.

14. There will be a quality assurance program that includes:

    a. evaluation of services.

    b. regular chart audits.

    c. organizational review.

We can relate these standards established by the National Hospice Organization to the spiritual art of hospitality of the Hospice Way in companioning the dying. The following table shows how these modern standards can be seen in terms of the ancient spiritual wisdom of companioning the dying in the hospice tradition stretching back to the Middle Ages.

Table Ten

Relationship of The Seven Spiritual Practices that Form the Ancient Spiritual Art of Hospitality In Hospice Companioning of the Dying and with the National Hospice Organization Standards of a Hospice Program of Care

1. Observe the Dignity of the Patient above all else.

> NHO Standard 7. "The hospice program acknowledges that each patient/family has its own beliefs and/or value system and is respectful of them."

Total of one standard

2. Provide Sacred Palliative Care.

> NHO Standard 1. "The hospice program complies with applicable local, state, and federal law and regulation governing the organization and delivery of health care to patients and their families."

> NHO Standard 5. The hospice program has admission criteria and procedures that reflect:

>> b. physician participation.

>> c. diagnosis and prognosis.

> NHO Standard 11. "The goal of hospice care is to provide symptom control through appropriate palliative therapies"

> NHO Standard 14. "There will be a quality assurance program that includes:

>> a. evaluation of services.

>> b. regular chart audits.

>> c. organizational review.

> NHO Standard 15. "The hospice program maintains accurate and current integrated records on all patient/families."

> NHO Standard 16. "The hospice program complies with all applicable state and federal regulations."

Total of six standards.

Table Ten Continued

3. Offer Compassionate Care for the Family of the dying.

> NHO Standard 4. The patient/family is the unit of care.
>
> NHO Standard 13. The hospice program provides bereavement services to survivors for a period of at least one year."

Total of two standards.

4. Provide Care in the Home of the Patient or a Home-Like Residential Facility.

> NHO Standard 2. The hospice program provides a continuum of inpatient and home care services through an integrated administrative structure.
>
> NHO Standard 3. The home care services are available 24 hours a day, seven days a week.
>
> NHO Standard 17. "The hospice inpatient unit provides space for:
>
> > a. patient/family privacy.
> >
> > b. visitation and viewing.
> >
> > c. food preparation by the family.

Total of three standards.

5. Let all Care Be Determined By the Needs of the Patient, as much as possible.

> NHO Standard 5. The hospice program has admission criteria and procedures that reflect:
>
> > a. the patient/family's desire and need for service.

Total of one standard.

6. Provide Holistic Care Through a Health Care Team.

> NHO Standard 6. The hospice program seeks to identify, teach, coordinate, and supervise persons to give care to patients who do not have a family member available."
>
> NHO Standard 8. "Hospice care consists of a blending of professional and nonprofessional services, provided by an inter-disciplinary team, including a medical director."

Table Ten Continued

NHO Standard 9. "Staff support is an integral part of the hospice program."

NHO Standard 12. "Symptom control includes assessing and responding to the physical, emotional,, social, and spiritual needs of the patient/family."

Total of four standards.

7. Foster Sacred Presence Through Nature and all Creation.

NHO Standard 12. "Symptom control includes assessing and responding to the physical, emotional, social, and spiritual needs of the patient/family."

Total of one standard.

Be Spiritually Present as a Companion to the Dying On the Journey to the End of Life.

NHO Standard 12. "Symptom control includes assessing and responding to the physical, emotional, social, and spiritual needs of the patient/family."

Total of one standard.

The above table is very revealing in terms of how hospice work is understood today as compared to the ancient tradition found in the Hospice Way. Today, palliative care is emphasized, with six NHO standards established for this practice. There is only one NHO standard that refers in part to fostering a spiritual presence with nature; and also only one NHO standard that relates to a spiritual presence with the dying. The table reveals clearly the far reaching medicalization of hospice work by the National Hospice Organization in the late 1970's.

This medicalization is stated sharply in NHO Standard 11, which states *"The goal of hospice care is to provide symptom control through appropriate palliative therapies."* This presents hospice work as not a companioning of the patient in the dying process but rather a control of symptoms as the body declines. As a hospice chaplain and ordained Protestant minister, I do not see how it is possible, for example, to view the sacraments of the church as a response to a symptom in the life of a patient. The spiritual dimension of life, such as prayer and sacred scripture seem to have no relation to symptoms.

In the view of NHO Standard 11, the emotional, social and spiritual needs of the patient become important only as they relate to symptoms. The underlying view of the patient here is that patients are seen as a complex machine that needs appropriate fixing as symptoms of decline appear. NHO Standard No. 12 states this clearly, *"Symptom control includes assessing and responding to the physical, emotional, social, and spiritual needs of the patient/family."* The understanding of hospice work reflected here is one dimensional; the work of hospice is simply symptom control. By definition, *what is not present as a symptom has no place in the modern hospice way of care.*

The spiritual art of hospitality of the ancient Hospice Way offers the alternative of a truly holistic understanding of the dying process as part of the natural mystery of life. It holds that hospice is a spiritual work which includes the companioning of the patient and the family in their body, heart, and soul. In companioning, hospice work does not have to force, in a reductionistic way, all of its comfort and care through the narrow door of symptom control. The spiritual art of hospitality is truly a holistic companioning of the dying that holds sacred not only the control of symptoms, but also the heart and the soul of the patient and their family.

Viewed in terms of the spiritual art of hospitality of the Hospice Way, NHO Standard 11 needs to be rewritten to express more fully a truly holistic understanding of hospice work that is in keeping with the rich spiritual heritage of hospice. Such a suggested revised NHO Standard 11 could be: *"The goal of hospice work today is to provide palliative comfort and care through the spiritual art of hospitality, as patients and families are companioned on the journey to the end of life as one indivisible whole in body, heart and soul."* Such a revision of this standard calls for a fundamental shift from a narrow medical view of modern hospice care to a holistic companioning of the patient and family. It creates a valid place for the hospice health care team, for team members may companion the patient and family in the infinitely varied dimensions of life. This revision provides for both the ancient spiritual wisdom of the Hospice Way and modern medical palliative care to be incorporated in the work of hospice. It is an approach which embraces all that our hospice brothers and sisters have understood as hospice work for over 1,500 years. It opens the door to our spiritual heritage of hospitality while at the same time allowing for symptom control through appropriate palliative therapies. Such a revised standard connects us to the past and speaks to the present.

So where has our journey through the modern era of hospice care taken us? We can summarize the contributions to the ancient Hospice Way in the following table.

Table Eleven

The Modern Form of the Ancient Hospice Way
Modern Developments of the Ancient Spiritual Art of
Hospitality In Hospice Companioning of the Dying

1. Observe the Dignity of the Patient above all else.

- Herman Feifel's *The Meaning of Death*, published in 1959.

- Elizabeth Kubler-Ross and the Death with Dignity Movement.

- U.S. Senate hearing on "Death With Dignity" in 1972.

2. Provide Sacred Palliative Care, Focusing on Pain Management and Symptom Control.

- Elizabeth Kubler-Ross and the Stages of Grief Theory.

- Cicely Saunders and the concept of "Total Pain" and giving pain medication "by the clock."

- St. Luke's Hospice in New York City, the second hospice in the U.S., opened in the 1970's. It emphasized pain management and symptom control.

- Symptom Control established as a standard of hospice care by the National Hospice Organization in 1979.aion in 1979.

- Pain management and symptom control funded under the Medicare hospice benefit in 1982.

- Music Therapy begins as modern profession in the post World War II era.

- Music Thanatology as a profession begins in the early 1970's.

---

3. Offer Compassionate Care for the Family of the dying.

- Modeled by Cicely Saunders at St. Christopher's Hospice.

- The family as a unit of care established as a standard of hospice care by the National Hospice Organization in 1979.

- Family as a unit of care funded under the 1982 Medicare Hospice Benefit.

4. Provide Care in the Home of the Patient or A Home-Like Residential Facility.

- Modeled by Cicely Saundres at St. Christopher's Hospice..

- Hospice Inc., in Branford, Connecticut, is the first modern American Hospice. It began home care services in 1973, and inpatient services later.

- Hospice of Marin in California, the third hospice in the U.S., opens in the late 1970's as a home health agency.

- Home care established as a standard of hospice care by the National Hospice Organization in 1979.

5. Let all Care Be Determined By the Needs of the Patient, as much as possible.

- Elizabeth Kubler-Ross and the Death with Dignity Movement.

- Modeled by Cicely Saunder's at St. Christopher's Hospice.

- Established as a standard of hospice care by the National Hospice Organization in 1979.

- Funded as a Medicare hospice benefit in 1982.

6. Provide Holistic Care Through a Health Care Team.

- Connecticut Hospice opens in 1980 as the first hospice in the US. and emphasis the role of a health care team.

- Modeled by Cicely Saunders at St. Christopher's Hospice in London, 1967.

- Modeled in the U.S. by Kubler-Ross at the teaching center, Shanti Nilaya, in California in 1977.

- Established as a standard of hospice care by the National Hospice Organization in 1979.
- Funded as a Medicare hospice benefit in 1982.

7. Foster Sacred Presence Through Nature And All Creation.

- Modern use of morphine as an effective means of pain control.
- Hospice Gardens established worldwide and new hospices built in natural settings.

Be Spiritually Present as a Companion on the Journey to the End of Life through each Spiritual Practice.

- Personal philosophy of Cicely Saunders.

Conclusion

The modern hospice movement can be seen as a "rediscovery" in our time of certain dimensions of the ancient Hospice Way of companioning the dying. Most notably, contemporary hospice work rests on the foundation of companioning on the journey to the end of life with dignity and respect for the patient and family (Kubler-Ross) and medical palliative care through a team approach (Cicely Saunders). The concern with the management of patient symptoms through palliative therapies is a central motif of hospice today, and indeed dominates modern hospice work. The very language of hospice today reveals this deep medicalizing. We speak of patients and not companions. The hospice worker reflects on problems and interventions, and not the not the needs of the body, heart, and soul.

The modern hospice movement has yet to discover and appreciate that hospice is, in its very essence, a unique and life-transforming *spiritual tradition*, rooted in ancient times and possessing a deep well of wisdom. The Hospice Way of old is a profoundly holistic companioning of patients and their families, and this companioning in body, heart, and soul has been the lifeblood of hospice work down through the ages. Monastic medicine of the Middle Ages presents the shinning ideal of holistic care. We stand in danger today of losing this holistic companioning as we go down the road of radically medicalizing all our companioning of the dying.

We will now bring the medical approach of modern hospice companioning into sharp relief with the ancient wisdom of companioning the dying. In presenting *A Spiritual Manifesto*, there is a call for the embrace of modern medical palliative care and this eons old way of companioning the dying. It is through this embrace that we can find the depth and power of a Beautiful Death becoming a living reality in our life and that of our loved ones.

Chapter 10

A Spiritual Manifesto:
A Call for an Embrace of Medical
Palliative Care and Ancient Spiritual
Heritage in Modern Hospice Work

In our modern times, the Western hospice movement has become, as we have seen, thoroughly medicalized. The holistic companioning of the dying, in body, heart, and soul, which is the lifeblood of the ancient Hospice Way, stands in danger of disappearing from the scene. Above all, hospice as an eons old *spiritual tradition* which contains a great depth of wisdom has yet to be recognized and appreciated by the hospice movement today.

The medicalization of hospice in the West can be clearly seen in the standards of the National Hospice Organization set in the late 1970's that forced all hospice care through the narrow door of symptom control. Rather than focus on *companioning* in hospice work, we are primarily concerned with the *management of symptoms*. In spite of the efforts of reformers such as Elizabeth Kubler-Ross, the care for the dying in Western society is dominated by the medical profession with its emphasis on problems and symptom management. This is understandable in terms of the funding of hospice care through Medicare and Medicaid.

The decisions being made by hospice staff regarding the suitability of patients to either enter a hospice program or remain in hospice are principally medical decisions. Whether or not a patient is appropriate for hospice care is not a question open to debate about social, emotional, or spiritual patient, or family needs. Guidelines have been established for federal funding of patient care in hospice, and these guidelines must be followed if hospices are to operate on a sound financial footing.

Zelda Foster has reviewed the book, ***The Hospice Movement, Easing Death's Pain***, In her review, Ms. Foster states that the author "presents a compelling case for how the insertion of a cost-effective, government-controlled model of hospice care conspires to diminish and distort the driving force of hospice as a health care reform for dying patients and their families....This scholarly work calls on us to revisit the ideals and principles that gave life to hospice."[1]

Are we in danger of losing the true heart and soul of the ancient Hospice Way in adapting the modern hospice movement to federal government sources of funding? I believe we are. The time has come in the West for the hospice movement to re-examine its spiritual roots and engage in a soul searching review of how patient care is offered in hospices. This touches every single aspect of hospice; from the philosophy and orientation of hospice administrators and CEO's, to the training and hiring of staff, to the very nature of care that is offered every day in hospices.

The spiritual art of hospitality of the Hospice Way calls for a return to an ancient historical model as we companion the dying in hospice. Such a return can be done without rejecting either the technology of modern medical palliative care or the standards for licensing, funding and patient care established by state and federal authorities. This spiritual homecoming has five profound and indeed radical implications for the hospice movement today in the West, particularly in the United States. These calls for spiritual renewal are presented as a spiritual manifesto; a call for true change in the course of the modern hospice movement.

- ***First, we need to recognize a fundamental spiritual dimension in the Hospice Way of companioning the dying.***

From the very first historical records of hospice work in the West, being with the dying at the end of life has been understood in our heritage as a spiritual work. While the hospice movement is not affiliated with any religion or religious group, it is spiritual in nature.

It is a profoundly spiritual work to companion the dying and their loved ones in body, heart and soul as one indivisible and sacred whole. It is spiritual in that it ***connects*** the dying with the vital dimensions of human existence. Palliative care is sacred care for the body in hospice work as it connects the dying to relief of pain and provides comfort

212

in the midst of distress. Hospice care for the heart is sacred care as it connects the dying with those they love and who love them. Hospice care for the soul is sacred care as it connects those at the end of life with what gives their life a true sense of meaning, purpose and value. This may or may not involve what we know as traditional religion.

Hospice work of companioning the dying should be seen today as it has been through the ages: a sacred spiritual work.

• *Second, hospice companioning of the dying today is grounded in modern medical palliative care. However, medical palliative care in hospice should be contained within the ancient wisdom of the Hospice Way, rather than having the Hospice Way contained within medical palliative care.*

What is it that drives hospice care today? In the West we would have to answer that it is medical palliative care. In the ancient model of the Hospice Way, each discipline has its own unique and distinctive place in providing for the care of the patient. The spiritual manifesto calls for a return to a broader umbrella of care; that of the spiritual art of hospitality in companioning the dying.[2] Medical palliative care is **one practice** in this ancient spiritual art but should no longer be **the** determinative practice in patient care. All seven practices of the spiritual art of hospitality have their place and must be respected as hospice companions the dying at the end of life.

In very practical terms, medical palliative care in hospice should be defined and qualified by the other six spiritual practices of the art of hospitality. For example, all hospice medical staff, regardless of education and training, should strictly observe the first spiritual practice of holding the dignity of the patient in the highest regard. It is never appropriate to belittle or make fun of patients or disregard their dignity in any matter. The spiritual art of hospitality provides a framework in which medical palliative care is practiced in hospice.

• *Third, this spiritual manifesto calls for a return to the spiritual heritage found in the ancient wisdom of the Hospice Way.*

Hospice simply cannot be true to its historical roots through the ages without a deep appreciation and regard for the spiritual heritage from which it developed. Such an appreciation is lacking today. The Western model of palliative care does not have the ability to provide this spiritual foundation for the hospice movement. Spiritually, the modern hospice movement is headed toward a dead end in the West. The need is to retrace our steps and follow again the path of our forefathers who understood the nature of sacred palliative care. Hospice care in companioning the dying is intrinsically spiritual in nature and this spiritual nature can only ignored at the cost of a spiritually dead hospice movement. We need to reclaim our heritage of the spiritual art of hospitality offered as holistic sacred care for those at the end of life.

- *Fourth, the ancient wisdom of the Hospice Way calls all hospice caregivers to understand that they are first and foremost practitioners of the ancient spiritual art of hospitality. They companion the dying as practitioners of this art. Their identity in hospice is secondly that of a skilled Western specialist, such a doctor, nurse, social worker, music therapist, volunteer or chaplain.*

This has far reaching implications for the training, recruitment, and continuing education of all involved in the Western hospice movement. It radically re-defines hospice care today.

Those who are hired to do hospice work, for example, should be seen as qualified to offer hospice care not just by meeting professional standards in their chosen field. More importantly, do they know and practice the spiritual art of hospitality of the Hospice Way as they companion the dying? Specifically, are the practices that make up the spiritual art of hospitality demonstrated in the life of a hospice caregiver? This means asking hospice caregivers questions such as those found in table twelve below:

Table Twelve

Qualifications for A Hospice Companion following the Ancient Hospice Way

• **First Spiritual Practice**

Does this caregiver show respect for the dignity of patients? Are patients treated with real care and concern as they are companioned in hospice work?

• **Second Spiritual Practice**

Does the caregiver practice sacred palliative care? Is there awareness of pain and discomfort, and a willingness to respond compassionately to patient and family needs?

Table Twelve Continued

• Third Spiritual Practice

Is there a place in the heart of the caregiver for the family of the dying? Is there compassionate care extended to the family?

• Fourth Spiritual Practice

Does the caregiver value the home of patients? Do they honor and respect this place, even when it may contrast strikingly with their own life style?

• Fifth Spiritual Practice

Is the caregiver open to listening to the needs of the patient and responding to these needs in a caring way? Is there a willingness to let care be patient directed, as much as is practical? Or is care forced on the patient by a caregiver who assumes they know what is best in all situations?

• Sixth Spiritual Practice

Is the caregiver committed to being a part of holistic care with the patient?

Is there an attitude that others have important lessons to teach me as a caregiver, and I am available to share with others on the hospice team?

• Seventh Spiritual Practice

Does the caregiver have an appreciation for nature and all of creation? Will they foster a sacred presence through nature as they companion the dying?

• Spiritual Presence in Companioning the Dying

Most importantly, how spiritually present is the hospice caregiver? Do they "show up" in the patient's and family's life as someone that has an open heart and soul? Do they have spiritual presence or are they just "going through the motions" of being a professional caregiver? What do patients and their families say about this caregiver's companioning?

These question raise the age old qualifications for hospice work in companioning the dying. These questions should be asked of every hospice caregiver in every hospice in the West as the minimal entrance standard for hospice work. This spiritual manifesto calls on the hospice movement to implement these qualifications for all hospice workers.

• *Fifth, the practice of the spiritual art of hospitality of the ancient Hospice Way in companioning the dying should drive all hospice patient care.*

This is where "the rubber meets the road." As a practical matter, all hospice admissions should be based on the practices of the spiritual art of hospitality in considering a patient as appropriate for hospice care. This would carry over as to how patient charts are organized and how interdisciplinary team meetings are conducted in hospices in the West. At a hospice team meeting, for example, there would be a review of the patient plan of care in terms of the spiritual art of hospitality, and not in terms of the individual disciplines of the hospice team members. Each of the practices of the spiritual art of hospitality would be raised in terms of the care of each patient in hospice.

The team meeting would focus on questions such as those shown in table thirteen below:

Table Thirteen

Team Meeting following the Ancient Hospice Way

• **First Spiritual Practice**

What issues of dignity are there for this patient? These could be physical,, emotional, or spiritual issues.

• **Second Spiritual Practice**

What are the issues of sacred palliative care? Doctors, nurses, and nurses aides may guide the team in this practice.

• **Third Spiritual Practice**

What are the family issues that hospice needs to be concerned about? Social workers and bereavement team members may provide leadership for the team in this practice.

• **Fourth Spiritual Practice**

Are there home issues that need to be addressed? Social workers may have keen insight in this practice.

• **Fifth Spiritual Practice**

What do we see as the needs of the patient, physically, emotionally, and spiritually? How are these needs being met by hospice care? Music therapists and practitioners of other healing arts may have special insights in companioning of the patient. All team members may participate from their unique discipline.

• **Sixth Spiritual Practice**

Who are the members of the hospice holistic health care team, and what care is being provided for the patient and family by the team?

• **Seventh Spiritual Practice**

Would the patient benefit from companioning by animals? Is the patient given the opportunity to sit by a window and see out, and be outside as much as they desire?

• **Spiritual Presence in Companioning the Dying.**

What of our spiritual companioning of the patient and the family in hospice? Is it effective and meeting their needs? The focus should be on the team as a whole seeing itself as practicing the spiritual art of hospitality in companioning the dying.

This spiritual manifesto calls for the spiritual art of hospitality to drive team meetings and indeed all hospice care. This age old way of caring should serve as the blueprint for hospice companioning of the dying.

The time has come in the West for the ancient spiritual wisdom of hospice work to be wedded to modern medical palliative care. It is not a question of either/or, but rather both/and. It is a question of shaping our medical technology with the spiritual wisdom of our hospice brothers and sisters who have gone before us in this hallowed tradition of companioning the dying. The spiritual art of hospitality shows us how this can be done practically in our world. The spiritual art of hospitality may serve as a blueprint for understanding the past, present and future of hospice work. The hospice movement of companioning the dying is profoundly spiritual in nature. The time has come to recognize our spiritual heritage as we also recognize the latest advances in medical palliative care.

A holistic spiritual companioning of patients and their families is our ancient tradition in hospice work. The secular medical model in the West simply does not have the ability to hold the full wonder, mystery and awe of the incredible natural experience of death and dying. It is a container too small for such a sacred event. Ancient spiritual wisdom by itself, while holistic in nature, does not have the ability to provide physical comfort and care at the end of life without modern medical palliative care.

This spiritual manifesto calls for the modern hospice movement to companion the dying not just in their body, which is critically important, but also in their heart and soul as one indivisible whole. This sacred care of the dying and their loved ones in body, heart, and soul is our hospice legacy, one that has endured in Western culture for over 1,500 years.

Companioning the dying in hospice work today comes to us as an embrace. It is the embrace of the most contemporary medical palliative care and ancient spiritual wisdom expressed in the spiritual art of hospitality. From this embrace comes a beautiful dance of true comfort and care as we journey with the dying to the end of life.

This creative embrace opens the way for a Beautiful Death to be the natural end of the journey of life on earth. Medical palliative care becomes sacred palliative care through the embrace. The true spiritual nature of hospice companioning is revealed in the embrace. The embrace opens up the holistic nature of companioning; the journey to the end of life is not simply a journey of companioning the physical body, but also the heart and soul of the patient and their family. The local faith community becomes included in the companioning through the embrace, and the family takes it place as true team members, true companions on the journey. The embrace allows the modern hospice movement to have a new vision of even death itself: death is not just a physical event, but the conclusion of a journey that encompasses the body, the emotions, and the spirit of both those companioned as well as the caregivers.

Those at the end of life deserve the best care that is available in our world today. This spiritual manifesto calls for that care to be provided; care that offers the centuries old spiritual wisdom of the Hospice Way and also modern medical technology in palliative care. From this embrace of ancient and modern emerges in our world the beautiful spiritual work of companioning those at the end of life called hospice. It is as we walk this eons old and yet ever new path that the way to a Beautiful Death becomes a living presence.

Appendix A

Historical Time Line of Hospice Companioning In the West

First hospices organized by Roman Catholics (Augustinians) in Europe	Roman Catholic hospices/hospitals/ leper houses Monastic Medicine	Hospices/hospitals/ leper houses Knights Hospitaller Monastic Medicine
Ancient (300 A.D.)	**Early Medieval (500-1000 AD)**	**Crusades (1095-1291)**

Closing of Catholic Monasteries- Ending of monastic medicine Separation of hospices and hospitals	Death increasingly medicalized in the West	St. Vincent De Paul opens hospices in Paris
Reformation (1500's)	**Renaissance (1400-1600's)**	**Quiet Period 1700- 1800's**

Our Lady Hospice opens in Dublin, Ireland First modern religious hospice to offer medical palliative care	Religious Orders in London open Hospices: St. Joseph's Hospice, St. Luke's Hospice, Hospice of God
Early Modern (late 1800's)	**Early Modern (early 1900's)**

Pioneering Work Kubler-Ross and others - Death & Dying	Dr. Cicely Saunders founds St. Christopher's Hospice in London Model of the modern hospice	Free-Standing Hospice opens in England separate from hospitals
Modern 1960's	**Modern 1967**	**Modern 1968-1975**

First modern hospice program in U.S. Hospice Inc. in Branford, Connecticut	Hospices formed across North America	National Hospice Organizational formed
Modern 1974	**Modern 1970's- 1980's**	**Modern 1977**

National Hospice Accreditation JCAHO (Joint Commission on Accreditation Of Healthcare Organizations)	Permanent Medicare Hospice Benefit in U.S.	2,884 Hospices Identified by Medicare in U.S. Hospices in Canada, Western Europe, and much of Asia
Modern 1984	**Modern 1986**	**Contemporary 2006**

Appendix B

Reflections on St. Augustine and Companioning the Dying

The Spirit of St. Augustine

In the Middle Ages, Augustine of Hippo was a towering figure not just for the church but for the entire culture. Robert Crouse, quoted in **Our Restless Heart**, The Augustinian Tradition, noted that, "in the intellectual and spiritual life of Europe in the Middle Ages, the influence of St. Augustine was all-pervasive."[1] St. Augustine was "the magister par excellence of Christian theology and spirituality in Latin Christendom in the Middle Ages."[2]

It is difficult to grasp the complexity of Augustine's voluminous teachings. In his lifetime, Augustine was one of the most prolific Latin authors. The list of his writings consists of more than a hundred separate titles. There are thousands of books dealing with the thought, life and times of this pillar of the Middle Ages.

It may be helpful to lift up some major themes of Augustine's thought that helped shape the founding of hospices, hospitals and leper houses all throughout Europe in the medieval period. These themes had a profound influence on the practice of hospitality as a spiritual art in the early centuries.

Life is a Journey in a Hospice

Thomas F. Martin, OSA, suggests the theme of the journey (peregrination) as a basic metaphor or image for the spirituality of Augustine. In this metaphor is a "key to understanding and living Augustinian spirituality."[3] The journey is more than the trip itself. It also involves all that goes to make the journey unfold. It is the planning and preparations for the trip, the places to stay for the night while out on the trip, the needs and concerns of the weary traveler and the choice of companions as fellow travelers. Most important of all is knowledge about where the journey is to lead. As Augustine states, "Everyone knows what the journey demands."[4] There are rich Biblical themes of the journey, such as the call of Abram to go to the land of Ur as the basis of God's covenant with His chosen people. It is as the children of Israel leave the land of Egypt and go through the journey which will lead to the Promised Land, that they are given the Ten Commandments and become the nation of Israel. Jesus speaks of the theme of the journey when He proclaims Himself as "the Way."

In the medieval world, a journey was a difficult and arduous undertaking. A spiritual pilgrimage would mean leaving behind the safety and security of the walled city and going through dangerous and unpredictable territory until the destination was finally reached. It was into the unknown that the pilgrims stepped as they began a journey; there was the risk of accidents and sickness, storms and illness, not to mention thieves and vandals that could be lurking along the way.

In his work **The Confessions**, Augustine tells the story of how his mother Monica's sea voyage from Africa to Italy to join her son in Milan almost met with shipwreck.[6] For Augustine, there were those who planned to ambush him who opposed his teachings, but Augustine's party made a wrong turn and escaped the danger to their lives.

Much of what we understand today as spirituality in general and the spirituality of hospitality in particular, can be found in the needs and concern of the pilgrims as they undertook the dangers and risks of the unknown as seen in Augustine's motif of the journey. As St. Augustine has written:

Alas, that I am a stranger in a distant land. I have gone far from you, my pilgrimage has become long in duration. I have not yet come to that homeland where I will not be overcome by some misfortune; I have not yet arrived in that community of Angels where I need fear no scandal. Why am I not there? Alas, that I am a stranger in a distant land.[6]

The central place of hospitality is clear when we see that Augustine understood all our days on this earth as one great journey to our true home which lies beyond the grave. Each of our days is terminal, as indeed every moment our life is terminal in this hospice. We live each day now in a great hospice called earth, each one of us having our own room. We are to be gracious hosts to all we meet, for we are guests in this hospice.

Bringing Christ to the World

For Augustine, as we have seen, each of us is dwelling in a little room in this hospice on earth. It is important that we not pass our days alone in our room, but that we bring a spiritual presence into this place. We are to make known the presence of Christ in our rooms. He calls us to be "Christ-bearers" in our hospice rooms. Augustine writes to the Christian faithful:

The mother Mary bore Jesus in her womb; let us bear him in our hearts. The virgin became pregnant with his presence through our Faith in him."[7]

For Augustine, Christians are to make the divine Jesus live in us as a spiritual presence as powerfully as he once lived in Mary. When Mary encountered the angel who announced that she was to receive into her womb the incarnate God, her response was a profound "Yes". As recorded in the Gospel of Luke the angel Gabriel announces the birth of the savior through Mary. When it was explained to her how this was to take place, Mary responded:

"I am the Lord's servant," Mary answered. "May it be to me as you have said." Then the angel left her." *Luke* 1:38.

The monks and nuns who followed in the teaching of Augustine understood it as their task to bring Christ to the world in their life, especially as they cared for the poor, the sick and the dying.

Death as the Door out of the Hospice on Earth

Augustine understood that there is a natural place for death as part of the human condition. He wrote:

To the degree that anything is no longer what it was, and is now what it once was not, it is in the process of dying and beginning anew.[8]

It is natural to enjoy our little room in this hospice on earth. We fear change and want life to continue and to love what brings us pleasure and joy.

However, there is a time to "check out" of this hospice and leave our little room on earth. In the thought of Augustine, death is seen as leaving the hospice room that we have and going through a door that leads to eternal life. It is a natural part of dwelling in the earthly hospice that there will come a time to walk through the passageway that leads onward. As Augustine writes:

From the first moment that life begins every movement made hastens the approach of death. Every moment that is lived subtracts from the length of life and day after day less and less remains. Life now is nothing but a race toward death, a race in which no one can stand still or slow down even for a moment. All must run with equal speed and never-changing stride. For those who live a short time and those who live a long time, each day passes with unchanging pace. Both run with equal speed, one to a nearer, the other to a farther end. For both equally the lengthening minutes of passing life are left behind. Just as a long journey does not mean that travelers slow their steps, so on the way to death those who take more time, proceed no more slowly than those who seem to reach the goal more quickly. Indeed, all of us are in the process of dying from the moment of our birth.[9]

For Augustine, each moment our life is a "dying" to the past so that we might "live" in the new moment that is present for us. There is a transitory nature to our lives just as this hospice in which we live is passing away. Augustine calls us to "lean into the future," so that we can accept and celebrate that which is yet to be. We do not forfeit the ages that are past, for we have the ability to build on top of them. Life calls us to a grand new beginning as we leave this hospice on earth. This new beginning is so wondrous that it makes our life on earth seem not even to exist. As Augustine writes:

*Does that day in which you **are** now not exist? Well, I have to say that if I look hard, it does not exist. If I compare the passing things of this life with those eternal things that abide forever, I can clearly see what has true being and what has more the **appearance of being.** Am I to say that these present days of mine have **true being**? Shall I be so rash as to use the great word "BEING" of this flux of things that slide toward extinction? For myself, in my weakness, I am so nearly **non-existent** that I cannot even understand the God who said: "I AM WHO AM"!*[10]

For Augustine, death as the door out of the hospice on earth leads for faithful believers to a brilliance in a land of eternal light where there is no past or future and no "coming and going". What is known is an eternal "now" in the presence of the infinite God who is the true "I AM".

Conclusion

As we have seen, Augustine understood that we live each moment of our existence, and every day of our life, as a fleeting experience in this great inn for travelers, this hospice on earth. We are all terminal, for a "check out" from the hospice awaits everyone who is born. In this hospice, we are to extend hospitality as a gift. The greatest hospitality is to bring the presence of Christ into our little room in this inn. We are to extend this spiritual presence in being with those as they leave the earthly hospice. It is this spiritual presence that allows travelers to leave the hospice peacefully as they journey on to life eternal.

A scholar of Augustine's thought, Donald X. Burt, expresses so beautifully in his book, ***Reflections on a Dying Life***, the deep message of Augustine for each of us. He states: "The encouraging message from Augustine's death is that if we have tried to live with love for others and love for God, at the end of life we will have the divine support to die without fear. And, if we are ***really***... [blessed], we will be surrounded by some who loved us and stood by us as we lived out our days in this Hospice, this Inn for Travelers."[11]

Even though it has not been fully recognized, the spiritual legacy of Augustine is cemented into the very structure of hospice work today. It forms in large part the ancient spiritual wisdom that is the foundation of our sacred companioning of the dying.

Appendix C

Reflections on St. Benedict and Companioning the Dying.

St. Benedict was another landmark figure of the Middle Ages. His spirit and teachings have touched countless lives and influenced the course of Western history through the establishment of monasteries that bear his name as Benedictine. In the Middle Ages these monastic institutions emerged as places that offered great hospitality for weary pilgrims.

Social Nature of the Monastic Life

The religious life, as understood by St. Benedict, is essentially social.[1] *The Rule of St. Benedict* is focused on establishing the nature of a community where men of faith live and work and pray and eat together. Much of the spiritual teaching of the Rule is concealed under legislation which seems to deal with social and domestic organization.

The Guest as Christ

The *Rule of St. Benedict* reveals various attitudes about guest.[2] On the one hand, guests "are to be welcomed as Christ." Yet on the other hand, Benedict establishes ritual and practical restrictions on the reception of guests. These include prayer to avoid the devil, a special kitchen, and a restriction about conversing with guests. Benedict's foresight, and indeed, wisdom approach to community is even evident in the "negative" prescriptions and the negative prescriptions of the *Rule* to establish some basis for maintaining the balanced life of the monastery.

Benedict saw the monastery as being **in** the world, but not **of** the world. The world for Benedict did not mean simply the physical world, because all of God's creation was sacred for Benedict. By the term world was meant everything that did not center on God. Benedict saw much in the beliefs and ways of society that were opposed to the Christian way of life. For Benedict, the monastery was to be a place in the physical world where God's creative love was experienced; and this love was to have a redeeming presence for all who knew it.

This understanding of God's creative love as gracious gift is at the heart of Benedictine hospitality. Benedict saw every person as a unique gift that God had created. The greatest gift to mankind was the person of Jesus, whom we know as the Christ of the world. Every human being, like Jesus, was a gift who resembled the greatest gift. Jesus was spiritually present as a gift in each person because Jesus had taught: "I was a stranger, and you welcomed me" (*Matthew* 25:35 and *Rule of St. Benedict* 53.1).

Monastic Hospitality

Hospitality is the glue which holds together the monastic community because every person in the monastery is a guest. This is true even of the monks themselves. Each of them has been invited by grace to come into this house of God, this dwelling place of God's presence. The rituals of the monastery reveal clearly that all are guests, and all are Christ to whom love and respect are to be shown. The monastery shows this basic hospitality in the washing of the feet of the brothers, in their respect in greeting one another, as well as in the care of the sick.

While hospitality is offered to guests in Benedictine monasteries, it is always in the context of the balanced life of the community. As one Benedictine has written: "Each monastery, with its own life, offers something unique to guests, so its style of receiving them must be such that the uniqueness of the monastery is able to be experienced by the guests." What we see in Benedictine hospitality is a receiving of the guest as Christ's presence into the balanced life of the monastic spiritual community.

In hospice work today, we inherit the Benedictine tradition of a community that welcomes the guest into their midst with spiritual presence. This is the ancient spiritual wisdom that undergirds the hospice residential center as it companions the dying in our modern world.

End Notes

Front Cover

Figure One Cover Image "walking in winter", by Paul Maguire. Used with permission from www.dreamstime.com.

Section Separator Image "Snow Footprint"@Icefields. Used with permission of Dreamstime.com.

Introduction. *The Challenge of Death and Dying Today*

[1] U.S. Census Bureau. Facts for Features. ***"Oldest Baby Boomers Turn 60"*** http://www.census.gov/Press-Release.

[2]Ibid.

[3] FASTSTATS-Nursing Home Care. Centers for Disease Control and Prevention. http://www.cdc.gov/nchs/faststats/nursingh.htm.

[4] Quoted in **"Tennessee End of Life Report, *Location of Death.*"** http://www.sewanee.edu/philosophy/TELR/Components/q2-home2B.html.

[5] Ibid.

 Consider also the statement in an article in ***The Street***.com:

 "Given their druthers, older people want to stay put and age in place," says Tom Otwell, spokesman with the AARP, a service organization for the elderly. He cites a recent AARP study in which 83% of those over age 45 said they would like to stay in their current residence for as long as possible.

Only 4.2% of households headed by those older than age 65 moved between 1998 and 1999, according to the most recent statistics available from the Administration on Aging. In comparison, 16.5% of those households headed by people younger than age 65 changed location during the same period.

[6] Ibid.

[7] Ibid.

[8] The statement by Mother Teresa from which I take a Beautiful Death is: "A beautiful death is for people who lived like animals to die like angels — loved and wanted." Quoted in   Kathryn Spink, *Mother Teresa: A Complete Authorized Biography* *(New York :HarperCollins , 1997).*

[9] *The MetLife Market Survey of Nursing Home & Assisted Living*, October 2007. http://www.metlife.com.

[10] *"Assisted Living and in Home Care increase as Nursing Home Beds Decline"*, EmaxHealth. August 11, 2005. http://www.emaxhealth.com.

[11] See the *LIFE* website: http://www.lifeupenn.org.

[12] Ibid.

[13] See the PACE website: http://www.npaonline.org.

[14] See the website, *"Innovative Care Models"*. http://innovativecaremodels. com. As the website states" Launched in April 2008, Innovative Care Models provides detailed profiles of 24 successful care delivery models. These profiles were developed as part of a research project by Health Workforce Solutions LLC and funded by the Robert Wood Johnson Foundation".

[15] Paul R. Brenner, *"Spirituality in Hospice". The Challenge of Success*. The Park Ridge Center for Health, Faith and Ethics.6/15/2007. http://www. parkridgecenter.org.

[16] Richard Smith, editor of the *British Medical Journal*, in commenting on Illich's radical polemic of 1975 states:

"Health, argues Illich, is the capacity to cope with the human reality of death, pain and sickness. Technology can help, but modern medicine has gone too far – launching into a god-like battle to eradicate death, pain and sickness. In doing so, it turns people into consumers or objects, destroying their capacity for health....

Illich sees three levels of iatrogenesis (doctor-induced disease). **Clinical iatrogenesis** is the injury done to patients by ineffective, toxic and unsafe treatments... Illich points out that 7% of patients suffer injuries while hospitalised... **Social iatrogenesis** results from the medicalisation of life. More and more of life's problems are seen as amenable to medical intervention. Pharmaceutical companies develop expensive treatments for non-diseases...

Worse than all this is **cultural iatrogenesis**, the destruction of traditional ways of dealing with and making sense of death, pain and sickness. "A society's image of death," argues Illich "reveals the level of independence of its people, their personal relatedness, self-reliance, and aliveness." For Illich, ours is a morbid society..." Richard Smith, *Limits to Medicine. Medical Nemesis: the Expropriation of Health*, *Journal of Epidemiology and Community Health* #57 – 2003

Quotes from Ivan Illich:

"On Health – a manifesto for 'hygienic autonomy':

Let us look at the conditions of our households and communities, not at the quality of "health care" delivery; health is not a deliverable commodity and care does not come out of a system.

I demand certain liberties for those who would celebrate living rather than preserve "life":

- the liberty to declare myself sick;
- the liberty to refuse any and all medical treatment at any time;
- the liberty to take any drug or treatment of my own choosing; the liberty to be treated by the person of my choice, that is, by anyone in the community who feels called to the practice of healing, whether that person be an acupuncturist, a homeopathic physician, a neurosurgeon, an astrologer, a witch doctor, or someone else;
- the liberty to die without diagnosis.

I do not believe that countries need a national 'health' policy, something <u>given</u> to their citizens. Rather, the latter need the courageous virtue to face certain truths:

- we will never eliminate pain;
- we will not cure all disorders;
- we will certainly die.

Therefore, as sensible creatures, we must face the fact that the pursuit of health may be a sickening disorder. There are no scientific, technological solutions. There is the daily task of accepting the fragility and contingency of the human situation. There are reasonable limits which must be placed on conventional 'health' care. We urgently need to define anew what duties belong to us as persons, what pertains to our communities, what we relinquish to the state.

Yes, we suffer pain; we become ill, we die. But we also hope, laugh, celebrate; we know the joy of caring for one another; often we are healed and we recover by many means. We do not have to pursue the path of the flattening out of human experience.

[17] David H. Gustafson, *"A Good Death". Journal of Medical Internet Research.* http://www.jmir.org/2007/1/e6.

[18] Ibid.

[19] Ibid.

Chapter One. *The Path*

[1] *Online English to Latin to English Dictionary.* http://www.freedict.com/onldict/at.html

[2] *"Spirituality. A White Paper of the Association for Spiritual, Ethical, and Religious Values in Counseling."* April 6, 1998. http://www.anglefire.com/nj/counseling/Whotepper1.htm.

We can consider the question of the nature of spirituality in more depth. There is an excellent article that contains a section titled, *"What is Spirituality?"* written by the staff of the Shalem Institute for Spiritual formation, and presented on the Shalem website. The article states:

What Is Spirituality?

"In many traditions, the word "spirit" refers to life-force, the basic energy of being. Symbolically, spirit is the breath of life. The Hebrew ruah, Greek pneuma, Latin spiritus, and Sanskrit prajna all mean both "breath" and "spirit." Traditionally, this life force is seen as manifest in our love--in the passions and inspirations that motivate us and connect us with the world and with one another.

In this view, spirituality has to do with the fundamental propelling forces of our lives, our most profound loves, passions and concerns. It is the wellspring of our sense of meaning and of our will to live, the source of our deepest desires, values and dreams. Spirituality, then, is not a thing apart from our daily lives, but rather the fundamental energy source that fuels all our emotions, relationships, work, and everything else we consider meaningful.

Contrary to popular belief, spirituality is not something special or extraordinary. It is instead absolutely ordinary and completely natural. Everyone has a spiritual life. We express it in many different ways: not only in places of worship but also in work, community and family, in all our creativity and commitments.

The spiritual life is like a deep ocean current, often unseen, but flowing through all our experience, moving us to seek fulfillment and connectedness, impelling us towards truth, goodness and beauty. As William Wordsworth said, it is something "deeply interfused" that "rolls through all things." Spirituality is the living heart of all the great world religions…"

Carole Crumley, Bill Detrick, Ann Kline, Gerald May, *"Contemplative Spirituality"*, March 2004. http://www.shalem.org/resources/publication/articles/contemplativespiritualty.html.

[3] *"Spirituality. A White Paper of the Association for Spiritual, Ethical, and Religious Values in Counseling."* April 6, 1998. http://www.anglefire.com/nj/counseling/Whotepper1.htm.

[4] "Approaching death and death itself, the dissolution of the physical form, is always a great opportunity for spiritual realization. This opportunity is tragically missed most of the time, since we live in a culture that is almost totally ignorant of death… Every portal is a portal of death, the false self…The end of the illusion-that's all death is. It is painful only as long as you cling to illusion". Eckhart Tolle, *The Power of Now* (New World Library, 1999), pp. 118-119.

[5] For information on the Zen hospice, see their website at: http://www.zenhospice.org. The Zen hospice was founded in 1987 as a program of the San Francisco Zen Center.

[6] Kathy Kalina, *Midwife for Souls. A Pastoral Guide for Hospice Care Workers and All Who Live With the Terminally Ill.* (New York: Pauline Books and Media, 1993).

[7] Ernest Beckner, in his book, *The Denial of Death*, presents a classic study of how much death is feared and denied in Western society. He writes"… this whole book is a network of arguments based on the universality of the fear of death, or "terror" as I prefer to call it, in order to convey how all-consuming it is when we look it full in the face." Enest Beckner, *The Denial of Death* (New York, New York: Free Press. Simon & Schuster, Inc., 1973). p. 15.

[8] Understanding exactly what constitutes the hospice tradition through the

ages is not easy to state. The essence of the hospice has been expressed by the Hospice Education Institute in a 1998 brochure. The hospice movement is united by...a *philosophy of caring* (my italics) which respects and values the dignity and worth of each person, and good hospice care is the practical expression of that personal and professional commitment. Hospices care for people approaching death, but hospices cherish and emphasize life, by helping patients (and those who love and care for them) live each day to the fullest". (http://www/hospiceworld.org).

The American Cancer Society also places the emphasis on hospice as a unique *philosophy of caring*, that has several distinctive features. They state: "Hospice is a philosophy of care". They go on to express the primary characteristics of this means of care. Following their writing, we can outline the major tenets of this philosophy as:

Tenets of a Hospice Philosophy

- Death is recognized as the final stage of life.
- The dignity and quality of the patient's life is affirmed.
- The goal is to make life pain-free for the terminally ill, and manage other symptoms.
- Hospice treats the person rather than the disease.
- Care is family centered, with the patient's last days surrounded by loved ones.
- Care is provided for the patient and family 24 hours a day and 7 days a week.
- Care may be provided in the patient's home or a hospice facility.

  (http://www.cancer.org.)

Understanding the hospice movement as a unique philosophy of care in companioning the dying has several important implications.

First, this hospice philosophy of care in companioning the dying is the connecting link to the past. Here we find what unites the various times and places that end of life care have been offered that can be called hospice. It is this philosophy which unites hospice as a historical movement dating back to the early centuries of Western society. The modern expression of hospice may be very unique, with the role of medical technology, and yet this expression is part of the hospice historical movement due to the philosophy of care that informs the use of this technology.

234

Second, this hospice philosophy of care in companioning the dying is the connecting link to the future. There is a great diversity in the specific means of care that can be employed in this movement called hospice. The hospice movement can be developed in ways that embrace both traditional Western medical means of care as well as Eastern forms of prayer and mediation, music therapy, and other healing modalities. The defining nature of the hospice movement is not a specific type of care or means of caring, such as Western medical care .It is not a specific place of care, such as residential unit. Rather, the hospice movement is a based on a philosophy that expresses the central value of caring for persons and families at the end of life, and providing for death with dignity, regardless of the specific means of .providing this care. There may indeed be many unique ways in the future that this philosophy of caring for those at the end of life may be expressed in our world.

The ways that this hospice philosophy of care has been implemented through the ages has been rich and varied. Hospice can be seen as a philosophy of care that embraces the Western medical model, as hospice offers palliative care. However, hospice is not limited to the confines of this model Also, while Medicare and Medicaid government financial support are the current basis of hospice economically today, the hospice philosophy of care is not limited to the requirements of this financial base of support.

Third, this study attempts to show there is a fundamental spiritual dimension to this hospice philosophy of care in companioning the dying. The spiritual art of hospitality is presented as the spiritual foundation of the hospice philosophy of caring for those at the end of life. This spiritual art is integral to expressing the hospice way of caring through the centuries and in our world today.

In summary, we can see that what provides hospice its unique and distinctive character as a historical movement is the age old philosophy of care in companioning the dying that under girds this movement.

[9] Greg Yoder and Alan D. Wolfelt, *Companioning the Dying: A Soulful Guide for Caregivers* (Independent Publishing Group, 2005).

[10] An excellent historical study of attitudes toward death and dying in western society through the ages is found in the book by Philippe Aries, *The Hour of Our Death* (New York: Alfred A. Knof, 1981).

[11] There have been hospices that stretch back to Oriental, Egyptian, Greek, and Roman origins, when temples or churches would be used to provide refuge for those in need. (Siebold, 1992). However, a review of the literature in the hospice movement shows, as Maggi Budd states in *"Evolution of the Modern Hospice Movement"*, that "…the notion of creating hospices specifically for the sick, the poor, and the homeless is attributed to the Christians". The hospice movement as a philosophy of care for the sick and dying is generally dated to the Middle Ages.

Maggi Budd, *"Evolution of the Modern Hospice Movement,"* University of North Texas. Available on the web at: http://unt.edu/bmed/EvolutionofHospice.htm. An excellent article of 31 pagers, complete with outline and full references.

The Hospice Education Institute (1998) begins their history of hospice in the Middle Ages when "hospices" were found on main crossroads on the route to religious shrines, such as Santiago de Compostela, Chartres, and Rome. http://www/hospiceworld.org.

[12] The University of Norte Dame, *Latin Dictionary and Grammar Aid,* defines *hospes* as follows:

-pitis m. and hospital –ae, f. (1) [a host, hostess]. (2) [a guest]. (3) [a guest-friend, friend]. (4) [a stranger]; used also like adj., [foreign].

The American Cancer Society states that: "Hospice, in the earliest days, was a concept rooted in the centuries-old idea of offering a place of shelter and rest, or"hospitality" to weary and sick travelers on a long journey"." What Is Hospice Care ?". http://www.cancer.org.

[13] Marjorie J. Thompson, *Soul Feast. An Introduction to the Christian Spiritual Life* (Louisville: Westminster John Knox Press, 1995, 2005).

[14] The primary source for this information is the article, *"St. Maximilian Kolbe. Priest hero of a death camp"*. Found on the web site of catholic-pages.com. http://www.catholic-pages.com/saints/st-maximilian.asp.

[15] Ibid. p. 4 of 7.

[16] Ibid. p. 5 of 7.

[17] *"St. Maximilian Kolbe. Priest hero of a death camp"*. Found on the web site of catholic-pages.com. http://www.catholic-pages.com/saints/st-maximilian.asp, p. 6 of 7.

[18] Fr. Jeremiah J. Smith. *Saint Maximilian Kolbe. Knight of the Immaculta* (Rockford, Illinois: Tan Books and Publishers1998), p.95. See also the article http://www.kolbnet.com. Article, *"St. Max Kolbe"*.

[19] Ibid, pp. 95-96. There are several accounts by witnesses at Auschwitz of this heroic act by Kolbe. All accounts report essentially the same thing, with minor difference. The accounts are stated by Andre Frossard in his book, *Forget Not Love, The Passion of Maximilian Kolbe*, translated by Cendrine Fontan (San Francisco: Ignatius Press, 1987), pp.194-196.

[20] *"St. Maximilian Kolbe. Priest hero of a death camp".* Found on the web site of catholic-pages.com. http://www.catholic-pages.com/saints/st-maximilian.asp, p. 6 of 7.

[21] *"St. Maximilian Kolbe. Priest hero of a death camp".* Found on the web site of catholic-pages.com. http://www.catholic-pages.com/saints/st-maximilian.asp, p. 6 of 7.

[22] Ibid, p. 6 of 7.

[23] Ibid, p. 6 of 7.

[24] Article, *"Lifesaver Hero: Maximilian Kolbe"*, by Richard Grimm. http://www.myhero.com.

[25] Father Daniel Homan and Lomi Collins Pratt. *Radical Hospitality. Benedict's Way of Love* (Brewster, Massachuchetts: Paraclete Press, 2002), p. 10.

[26] Ibid, p.11.

[27] We can point to the basic importance of hospitality in several world religions by presenting quotations from sacred writings of each religious tradition that speak of the central importance of hospitality for that tradition. It would be possible, of course, to write an entire lengthy book on the subject of hospitality as reflected through the religions of mankind. In the religions of the world, hospitality is closely linked to compassion, as it flows from a peaceful and grateful heart.

Hospitality Reflected in the Sacred Writings of Religions of the World

Christianity

"Offering welcome is basic to Christian identity and practice. For most of the church's history, faithful believers located their acts of hospitality in a vibrant tradition in which needy strangers, Jesus, and angels were welcomed and through which people were transformed." Christine D. Pohl, "Hospitality, a practice and a way of life".*Vision,* Spring 2002. http://www.mennovision. org/Vol 3 No 1/Pohl_Hospitality.pdf

"Lord, when did we see you hungry or thirsty or a stranger or needing clothes or sick or in prison, and did not help you?' He will reply, "I tell you the truth, whatever you did not do for one of the least of these, you did not do for me." **Matthew** 25: 44-45.

"Do not neglect to show hospitality to strangers, for thereby some have entertained angels unawares." **Hebrews** 13:1.

Judaism

The "ger," the sojourner who lived with a Hebrew family or clan, was assured by the Biblical law not only of protection against oppression (Ex. xxiii. 9) and deceit (Lev. xix. 33), but also of love from the natives (Deut. xvi. 14), who were to love him even as themselves (Lev. xix. 34). He was to be invited to participate in the family and tribal festivals (Deut. l.c.), the Passover excepted; and even in the latter he could take part if he submitted to circumcision. He received a share in the tithes distributed among the poor (ibid. xiv. 19); and "one law and one statute" applied equally to the native and to him (Ex. xii. 49). God Himself loves the stranger (Deut. x. 18) and keeps him under His special protection (Ps. cxlvi. 9). Abraham, the archetype of the Hebrew race, entertained three strangers at his house and showed them many kindnesses (Gen. xviii. 1-8). "Abraham looked up and saw three men standing nearby...Let a little water be brought, and then you may all wash your feet and rest under this tree..."http://www.JewishEncyclopedia.com

Hinduism

"Offering hospitality is fundamental to Hindu culture and providing food and shelter to a needy stranger was a traditional duty of the householder. The unexpected guest is called the atithi, literally meaning "without a set time." Scripture enjoins that the atithi be treated as God. It was especially important to extend hospitality towards brahmanas, sannyasis and other holy people. There are many stories regarding the benefits of offering a suitable reception and the sins that accrue from neglecting one's guests. Tradition teaches that, no matter how poor one is, one should always offer three items: sweet words, a sitting place, and refreshments (at least a glass of water). The flower garland

238

is offered to special guests and dignitaries, as a symbol of loving exchange. "http://www.hinduhttp://hinduism.iskcon.com.

Islam
"Muhammad was also a very hospitable person, even before he was raised to the status of a Prophet. Nobody ever went away from him empty handed. He used to feed the poor, the needy, the widows and orphans and was very popular among the people of Makkah. In Madinah, his hospitality knew no bounds and his house was open to all, rich and poor, friend and foe. All came to him and were treated very generously. People used to come in large numbers from all directions, and he entertained them all and served them personally.

His hospitality was not confined to Muslims alone, but was extended to all human beings, irrespective of status or creed. The poorest and the most destitute among the Companions were the Ashab As-Suffah, who were homeless and lived in the mosque as permanent guests of the Muslims. Most of the time they were the guests of Muhammad. Once he said, "Anyone who has enough food for two persons should take three of them, he who has enough for four should take five of them with him." Abu Bakr took three of them with him while Muhammad took ten of them with him." …As in all he did, Muhammad taught his Companions by his words as well as his deeds. http://www IsalemOnline.net.

Native African Religions
Among Africans, there is no need to book an appointment in advance for a visit to or a meal with a neighbour. In most societies, hospitality is considered a duty. Visitors are welcome, even when the motive for the visit is not clearly defined. This explains why it was easy for the first European Christian missionaries to gain a foothold in many African villages .." http://www.africansocieties.org.

Buddhism
There are three kinds of persons existing in the world: one is like a drought, one who rains locally, and one who pours down everywhere.

How is a person like a drought? He gives nothing to all alike, not giving food and drink, clothing and vehicle, flowers, scents and unguents, bed, lodging and light, neither to recluses and brahmins nor to wretched and needy beggars. In this way, a person is like a drought.

How is a person like a local rainfall? He is a giver to some, but to others he gives not.

In this way, a person is like a local rain-fall.

How does a person rain down everywhere? He gives to all, be they recluses and brahmins or wretched, needy beggars; he is a giver of food and drink, clothing, lodging and lights. In this way a person rains down *Dhammapada* 224.

239

Jainism

To be moved at the sight of the thirsty, the hungry, and the miserable and to offer relief to them out of pity -- is the spring of virtue. *Kundakunda, Pancastikaya* 137.

Taoism

Relieve people in distress as speedily as you must release a fish from a dry rill [lest he die]. Deliver people from danger as quickly as you must free a sparrow from a tight noose. Be compassionate to orphans and relieve widows. Respect the old and help the poor. *Tract of the Quiet Way.*

[28] *"Spirituality. A White Paper of the Association for Spiritual, Ethical, and Religious Values in Counseling."* April 6, 1998. http://www.anglefire.com/nj/counseling/Whotepper1.htm.

[29] Kathleen Dowling, Singh, *The Grace In Dying. A Message of Hope, Comfort and Spiritual Transformation* (New York, New York: Harper Collins Publishers, Inc., 2000).

[30] Ibid, 218.

[31] *Hospice Education Institute.* http://www/hospiceworld.org.

[32] *Time Magazine.* "The Time 100". "Elizabeth Edwards". http://www.time.com

[33] Ibid.

[34] Basic aspects of the hospice tradition of care have been well expressed by Maggi A. Budd, in the article, *"Evolution of the Modern Hospice Movement".* She states that there are unique goals that set hospice services apart from other forms of health care. She writes: "Modern hospice care is a holistic approach to health care (Archer & Boyle, 1999;Hayslip & Leon, 1991; Munley, 1983)...Hospices are differentiated from other forms of health care in that hospices's primary goals are to: promote patient autonomy with a focus on the family, have an interdisciplinary team offer services to both the dying person and the family, make both home-care services and inpatient care available, thereby maintaining continuity of care, aid patients in controlling their pain and maintaining quality of life, keeping hospice services available 24 hours per day, 7-days a week, and offer

support to the patient's family during the dying process and in the bereavement period. All hospice programs have core values of treating the whole person while at the same time respecting the right and autonomy of the dying person as well as including the family in the unit of caring (Jennngs, 1997; Leming & Dickinson, 1994; Saunders & Baines, 1989; Siebold, 1992".

[35] The World Health Organization defines palliative care as "…an approach that improves the life of patients and their families facing the problem associated with life-threatening illness, through the prevention and reflief of suffering by means of early identification and impecciable assessment and treatment of pain and other problems, physical, psychological and spiritual". http://www.who.int.

[36] Ibid. *"Palliative Care"*. http://www.who.int.

[37] Mai Amy Ha, MD. *"Physician Newsletter"*, November 2007. http://www.blueridgehospice.org.

[38] Ibid.

[39] Ibid.

[40] Russell E. Hillard. *"Music Therapy in Hospice and Palliative Care: A Review of the Empirical Data.* Advance Access Publication, 7 April, 2005. Published on the web: ecam.oxfordjournals.org/cgi/content/full/2/2/173.

[41] Ibid.

[42] Ibid.

[43] Christine D. Pohl, *"Hospitality, a practice and a way of life"*. Vision, Spring 202. Available on the Web at: http://www.mennonvision.org.

[44] Stephen Verderber & Ben J. Refuerzo, *Innovations in Hospice Architecture* (Taylor & Francis :Canada, Abingdon, Oxon, 2006), p. 33.

[45] Roger S. Ulrich, *"Health Benefits of Gardens in Hospitals"*, Paper for Conference, Plants for People. International Exhibition Floriade 2002. http://www.planterra.com/research/SymposiumUlrich.pdf.

See also Nancy Gerlach-Spriggs, Richard Kaufman, and Sam Bass. *Restorative Gardens. The Healing Landscape* (Yale U. Press: New Haven, Ct., 2005). The book concludes with a plea for the garden, rather than the shopping mall atria, to be incorporated into places of healing, health, and wholeness.

[46] Roger S. Ulrich, *"Health Benefits of Gardens in Hospitals"*, Paper for Conference, Plants for People. International Exhibition Floriade 2002. http://www.planterra.com/research/SymposiumUlrich.pdf.

[47] *"Medieval Gardens"*. Europa Medievale. website: http://www.italmedievale.org/2007/05/medieval-gardens.html.

[48] *"Morphine"*. http://en.wikpedia.org/wlk/mprphia.

[49] *"Morphine: An Introduction. Discovery and Synthesis of Morphine"*. Website: http://itech.dicinson.edu/chemistry.

[50] *Morpheus* (mythology). Website: http://en.wikpedia.org/wlk/Mprphia_(god).

[51] *"Opium, Morphine and Heroin"*. Website: http://www.ch.ic.ac.uk/rzepa/mim/drugs/html/morphine_text.htm.

[52] Ibid.

[53] Christine D. Pohl, *"Hospitality, a practice and a way of life"*. Vision, Spring, 2002. Available on the web at: http://www.mennovsion.org.

[54] *"Quotations"*. Shalem.org.

[55] Cathy Siebold, *"The Hospice Movement, Easing Death's Pains"*. (New York, New York: Twayne Publishers, 1992), p.187.

[56] James E. Miller and Susan C. Cutshall. *The Art of being a Healing Presence. A Guide for Those in Caring Relationships* (Fort Wayne, Indiana: Willowgreen Publishing, 2001), p.35.

[57] Ibid., 37.

[58] Movie, *"Shall we Dance?"* Miramax, starring Richard Gere and directed by Peter Chelsom. October 15, 2004.

[59] The seven spiritual practices that form the spiritual art of hospitality fully embody and express the hospice philosophy of care. As we have seen, it is this philosophy of care that is the foundation of the hospice movement down through the ages.

We can relate the spiritual art of hospitality to the hospice philosophy of care in the following manner:

Tenet of Hospice Philosophy	Way Embodied in a Spiritual Practice in the Art of Hospitality
•Death is recognized as the final need Stage of life.	Provide Sacred Palliative Care (Recognition of the for care, and not cure in the face of death as the finalStage of life.) Practice Being Spiritually Present as a Companion to the Dying.
•The dignity and quality of the patient's Life is affirmed.	Observe the Dignity of the Patient above all else. Practice Being Spiritually Present as a Companion to the Dying
•The goal is to make life pain-free for the terminally ill, and manage other Symptoms.	Provide Sacred Palliative Treatment. Practice Being Spiritually Present as a Companion to the Dying
•Hospice treats the person rather than the disease.	Practice Holistic Care-through a Health Care Team. Practice Being Spiritually Present as a Companion to the Dying

•Care is family centered, with last days surrounded by loved ones.	Offer Compassionate Care for the Family of the dying.
	Practice Being Spiritually Present as a Companion to the Dying
•Care is provided for the patient and family 24 hours a day and 7 days a week.	Let all Care be Determined by the Needs of the Patient,as Much as Possible (Need for constant care at the end life.)
	Practice Being Spiritually Present as a Companion to the Dying
•Care may be provided in the patient's Home or a hospice facility.	Provide Care in the Home of the Patient or a Home-like Facility.
	Practice Being Spiritually Present as a Companion to the Dying

[60] The World Health Organization states that palliative care includes the following types of care:

- Provides relief from pain and other distressing symptoms.
- Affirms life and regards dying as a normal process.
- Intends neither to hasten nor postpone death.
- Integrates the psychological and spiritual aspects of patient care.
- Offers a support system to help patients live as actively as possible until death.
- Offers a support system to help the family cope during the patient's illness and in their own bereavement.
- Uses a team approach to address the needs of patients and their families, including bereavement counseling, if indicated.
- Will enhance quality of life, and may also positively influence the course of illness.

The spiritual art of hospitality offers us a practical framework that expresses all these many aspects of palliative care. See the article, *"Palliative Care"*. http://www.who.int.

[61] Parker J. Palmer, *The Company of Strangers: Christians and the Renewal of America's Public Life* (New York: Crossroad, 1986), p. 69.

Chapter Two. *Being a Spiritual Companion on the Journey*

[1] The importance of St. Benedict and the Rule as a vital dimension of our modern companioning of the dying is explored in depth in Chapter Eight, The Historical Roots of Hospice Companioning", as well as in Appendix III, "Reflections on St. Benedict and Companioning the Dying".

[2] *Matthew* 25: 37-40.

[3] The concept of bringing an "Inner Yes" is from the teaching of Eckhart Tolle. The book, *The Power of Now* emphasizes this theme. In Chapter One, for example, Tolle tells us to simply "say yes to life, and see how life suddenly starts working, for you rather than against you" .Eckhart Tolle, The Power of Now: A Guide to Spiritual Enlightenment (New World Library. Novata, Ca, 11999), 28.

[4] Ibid.

[5] *Merriam-Webster OnLine Dictionary.* "sacred".   http://www.merriam-webster.com.

[6] Ibid.

[7] Thomas Merton. Quoted in *"Allowing God to Catch Us"*, by Paula Killough, May 4, 2003. http://seattle.wa.us.mennonite.net/sermons/2003/May403sermon.htm

[8] Ibid.

[9] http://www.brainyquote.com.

[10] Oprah.com Community site, 08/16/2008.

[11] Used by permission of the author.

Chapter Three. *Companioning the Dying as a Spiritual Art*

[1] Alfred Lord Tennyson, ***Crossing the Bar.*** http://www.victoriaweb.org/authors/Tennyson/crossing.

[2] Father Daniel Homan and Lomi Collins Pratt. ***Radical Hospitality. Benedict's Way of Love*** (Brewster, Massachuchetts: Paraclete Press, 2002), p. 10.

[3] Henri Nouwen. Quoted on *"Wisdom Quotes"*. http://www.wisdomquotes.com/000584.html.

Chapter Four. *Journey's End: A Beautiful Death*

[1] Edwin Shneidman, *"Criteria for a Good Death"*. Suicide and Life-Threatening Behavior 37(3), June, 2007. The American Association of Suicidology.

[2] There is a considerable body of literature today concerning a "good death". The distinction can be made that in a good death, one or more of the spiritual practices of the spiritual art of hospitality are present, but not all the seven practices are fully expressed. For example, the Institute of Medicine defines a good death as "one that is free from avoidable death and suffering for parents, families and caregivers in general accordance with the patients' and families' wishes." Here, in terms of the Hospice Way, a good death is understood in terms of sacred palliative care, care for the family, and patient driven care. The other practices of the spiritual art of hospitality are not mentioned. See the ***Journal of Medical Internet Resources*** 2007; 9(1):e6 See http://www.jmir.org.

A Beautiful Death stands as all encompassing: it understands death as a biological event involving the functions of the body, an emotional event involving the relationships of the patient and loved ones, and a spiritual event involving what gives meaning, purpose, and value to the patient and family.

Chapter Five. *A Vision For a New Face of Death and Dying in America*

[1] The addition of a small suite to an existing home meets the definition of a house. According to Webster's a house is: "any place of abode". A hospi-

tality house can be a place of abode where hospitality is offered. *The New American Webster Dictionary* (Signet: 1995, New York, New York, 1995), p.338.

[2] *"An Informed Consumers Guide to Accessible Housing"* . http://www. abledata.com/abledata_docs/icg-hous.htm.

[3] Website. Quality of Life Technology Center. http://www.qolt.org.

[4] Website. Quality of Life Technology Center. http://www.qolt.org.

[5] Ibid.

[6] Ibid.

[7] Ibid.

[8] Ibid.

[9] *"The MetLife Market Survey of Nursing Home & Assisted Living,"* October 2007. http://www.metlife.com

[10] Ibid.

[11] National Caregivers Library. *"Paying for Residential Care"*. The statement on the web site is: "About one-half of all residents pay for costs out of personal resources". http://www.caregiverslibrary.org

[12] See endnote #29 in Chapter One for a brief statement of the basic importance of hospitality in several major religious traditions o the world.

Chapter Six. *Stories From the Path*

[1] *Anthony De Mello. Writings* Selected with an Introduction by William Dych, S.J. (Orbis Books, Maryknoll, New York, 1999). Modern Spiritual Masters Series, p.72

[2] All quotes on the work of music therapy are taken from this source: *"Music Therapy May Help Ease Pain",* by Korva Coleman. Your Health. June 3, 2008. http://www.npr.org/templates/story/story.php?Id=5519661.

[3] Ibid.

[4] Ibid.

[5] Ibid.

[6] Ibid.

[7] This lengthy quotation is taken from the website of The Chalice of Repose Project, Inc. The Voice of Music-Thanatology. *"The First Vigil: The Birth of Music-Thanatology".* http://www.chaliceofrepose.org.

Chapter Seven. *The Dying Speak To Us as Companions*

[1] The idea of using the Wizard of Oz to express hospitality is taken from the book: Father Daniel Homan, O.S.B., and Lonni Collins Pratt, Radical Hospitality. *Benedict's Way of Love* (Paraclete Press, Brewster, Massachusetts, 2002), pp.206-207.

Chapter Eight. The Historical Roots of Hospice Companioning

[1] Guenter B. Risse, *Mending Bodies, Saving Souls*. A History of Hospitals (New York: Oxford University Press, 1999), p.82.

[2] Matthew 25: 37-40.

[3] Anthony C. Meisel and M.L. del Mastro, translators, *The Rule of St. Benedict* (New York: Imago Books, Doubleday, 1975), p.89.

[4] "Charity," Dorothy insisted, "was a word to choke over," and she recommended "the spiritual and corporal works of mercy and the following of Christ to be the best revolutionary technique and a means of changing the social order rather than perpetuating it."(p.9). *"The Catholic Worker After Dorothy Day,"* a book review by Brian Terrell, March 26, 2008.

[5] Heinrich Pompey, *"Biblical and Theological Foundations of Charitable Works"*. Acts of the World Congress on Charity. Rome, 12-15 May, 1999, p.12.

[6] Ibid., p.13.

[7] Ibid., p.14.

[8] Ibid., p. 15.

[9] Ibid., p. 15.

[10] The corporal and spiritual acts of mercy can be historically traced to the Middle Ages. The early references to the Seven Corporal Works of Mercy include their being a part of the 1281 Lambeth Constitutions which set out the syllabus to be taught to the laity in the Archdiocese of Canterbury. University of Leicester web site, *"Frequently Asked Questions: Seven Corporal Works of Mercy."* http://www.leac.arthistory.html   Thomas Aquinas (1225-1274), in his Summa Theologie, faithfully records and describes the spiritual works of mercy.

[11] D.W. Amundsen. *Medicine, Society, and Faith in the Ancient and Medieval Worlds.* Quoted in Benjamin C. Silverman, *"Monastic Medicine: A Unique Dualism Between Natural Science and Spiritual Healing".* HURJ, Spring 2002, Issue 1. Websource: http://www.jhu.edu/hurj, page 11.

[12] Ibid, p. 11.

[3] Ibid., p. 13.

[14] Ibid., p. 11.

[15] Ibid.

[16] *Mother Teresa: A Complete Authorized Biography* (New York: Harpers Collins, 1997)

[17] Image from: http://www.patbenincasa-art.com/paintings.htm.

[18] John Paul II (October 22, 2005). *Address of John Paul II to the Pilgrims Who Had Come to Rome for the Beatification of Mother Teresa*. http://www.vatican.va.

[19] Malcolm Muggeridge, "*Something Beautiful for God*." Mother Teresa of Calcutta. (Collins/Fontana Book: London, 1972), pp. 97, 99, 114,

[20] The word "hospital" also comes from the Latin "hospes" which, as we have seen, refers to either a visitor or the host who receives the visitor. From "hospes" came the Latin "hospttalia", an apartment for strangers or guests, and the medieval Latin "hospitale" and the old French "hospital."

It crossed the Channel in the 14th century and in England began a shift in the 15th century to mean a home for the elderly or infirm or a home for the down-and-out.

"Hospital" only took on its modern meaning as "an institution where sick or injured are given medical or surgical care" in the 16th century. Other terms related to hospital include hospice, hospitality, hospitable, host, hostel and hotel. The Hôtel-Dieu, a name often given to a hospital in France during the Middle Ages, is the hotel (of) God. http://www.medicinenet.com/script/main/hp.aspx.

Love of god, compassion for humanity, and concern for their own welfare encouraged people to build hospitals" (Kealy 82). With time, the houses adjacent to some monasteries evolved from shelters for the poor (**xenodochia**) into places where the sick were cared for by skilled physicians. The greatest development of hospitals occurred in the 12th century. http://www.intermaggie.com/med/healing.php

[21] The term **hospital** was vital and flexible. It encompassed hotels for travelers and indigent students, dispensaries for poor relief, clinics and surgeries

for the injured, homes for the blind, the lame, the elderly, the orphaned, and the mentally ill, and leprosaria for people of all ages and classes. Almost one half of the built hospitals were directly affiliated with monasteries, priories, and churches. Many hospitals, imitating religious communities, formulated precise rules of conduct, required a uniform type of dress, and integrated several worship services into their daily routine.

However, the traditional spiritual context of the hospital enhanced, but did not overshadow, their genuine therapeutic achievements. "Adopting a religious model was not only the tradition of the times, it was also an eminently successful therapeutic device. Through prayer, patients were supposed to help each other and, indeed, to assist their relatives and friends and people everywhere. Many hospitals had definite local community responsibilities - education and housing students, feeding paupers, maintaining bridges, and sponsoring commercial fairs. All this was both good theology and good psychology" (Kealy 97icine http://en.wikipedia.org/wiki/Medieval_medicine).

[22] Ibid.

[23] Ibid.

[24] *"Anesthetics...Used By Medieval Monks!"* MedicineNet.com: http://www.medicinenet.com/script/main/art.asp?articlekey=151.

[25] Ibid.

[26] Ibid.

[27] *"Shelter in old age"*, http://www.building-history.pwp.blue/yonder.co.uk/Bath/medieval/shelter.htm.

[28] Ibid.

[29] Ibid.

[30] http://www.building-history.pwp.blueyonder.co.uk/Bath/Medieval/Shelter.htm.

251

[31] *"Medieval hospitals of Bath"*. http://www.buildinghistory.org/bath/medieval/hospitals.htm.

[32] Ibid.

[33] *"Unclean! Unclean!"* by Maureeen Miller. History of Medicine. Summary One. website: members.tripod.com/-Millerm/medhist/unclean.pdf.

[34] *"Trying to embrace St. Francis' message"*, by Dan Ricks. http://www.chicagotribune.com/technology/developers/bal-md.rodricks30apr30,0,5593901.column.

[35] *"Were He Here"*, by Luke Eggleston. Catholic Sun. Sept.22-28, 2005. Vol 124, No. 32.

[36] *Leviticus* 13: vv1-3, 45-45, *New International Version*. Quotation from *King James Bible.*

[37] *Canon 23* relates to the organization of care for lepers. *Catholic Encyclopedia:* Third Latern Council. http://www.newadvent.org/cathen/09017b.htm.

[38] http://www.thewholeisgreater.comekklesia/archive/Ekklesia48.htm.

[39] "Almost from the beginning of monastic life, certain monks took upon themselves the care of the sick brethren, but it was with the founding of the monastery on Monte Casino by St. Benedict of Nursia (480-543) in 529 that a real interest in medicine awoke in the cloisters of the far-flung Roman Church". David Riesman, *The Story of Medicine in the Middle Ages* (Paul B. Hoeber, Inc. New York, New York, 1935), Chapter III"Monastic and Clerical Medicine", p.17.

[40] http://www.benecictine.org.au/hosp.htm. Various translations of the *Rule* exist. A modern translation is by Anthony C. Meisel and M.L. de Mastro, translators. *The Rule of St. Benedict.* Image Books, New York, 1975), Chapter 53, "The Reception of Guests". "All guests to the monastery should be welcomed as Christ", p.89.

[41] "Hospitality", http://www.benedictine.org.au/hosp.htm.

[42] Ibid.

[43] http://www.thedome.org. *The Rule of St. Benedict* by Sister Jane Michele McClure, OSB

[44] Article, *"Music for the Dying: Using Prescriptive Music in the Death-Bed Vigil",* by Therese Schroeder-Sheker. Noetic Sciences Review #31, Page 32, Autumn 1994. http://www.noetic.org/publications.com.

[45] Ibid.

[46] Ibid.

[47] Ibid.

[48] Ibid.

[49] Ibid.

[50] Ibid.

[51] J.C. Hokendijk. *The Church Inside Out* (Westminster Press, Santa Ana, Ca.1964).

[52] Ibid., p.71.

[53] Ibid., p.71.

[54] Ibid., p.83.

[55] Ibid., p.83.

[56] *"Commentary on Psalm 60",* quoted in Reflections on a Dying Life, by Donald X. Burt (Liturgical Press: Collegsville, Minnesota, 2004), p.1

[57] Ibid., p.vii.

[58] *"History of the Grand St. Bernard Pass".* http://www.Switzerlandisyours.com

[59] Ibid.

[60] Ibid.

[61] *"A Brief History of the St. Bernard Rescue Dogs"* http://www.smithsonian.com.

[62] *"The History of St. Bernard Dogs".* http://www.essortment.com/all//st-bernardsdog.com

[63] *St. Bernard Dog: The Great Rescuer Barry.* http://www.ezinearticle.com/?St.-Bernard-Dog Also see the book by Marilyn Singer, *A Dog's Gotta Do What A Dog's Gotta Do* (Henry Holt & Co. New York, New York, 2000. Chapter 4, "A Nose for Trouble".

[64] This description is taken from Philippe Aires, *The Hour of Our Death* (Alfred A. Knoff, New York, New York, 1981), Chapter 1.and "The Tame Death", sections "The Death Bed: The Familiar Rites of Death" and "The Public Aspect of Death"., 14-19.

[65] *"Viaticum".* http://en.wikipedia.org/wiki/Viaticum.

[66] Ibid.

[67] **"Blessed Gerard Tonque and His Everlasting G Brotherhood: The Order of St. John"**. The Foundation and spiritual roots of the Hospital Order of St. John of Jerusalem". 8/23/2007. http://www.ewtn.com/library/PRIESTS/ORDJOHN.TXT.

[68] **"Hospitallers and Hospital Sisters"**. Catholic Encyclopedia, pp.155-156.

[69] http://blessed-gerard.org/bgt_2a2g.htm.

[70] Ibid.

[71] Ibid.

[72] Ibid.

[73] The following description of life in a hospital of the Order is taken from this source: **"Blessed Gerard Tongue and His Everlasting G. Brotherhood"**. "The Order of St. John". http://www.ewtn.com/library/PRIESTS/ORDJOHN. TXT

[74] **"Flummery"**. http://en.wikipedia.org/wiki/Flummery.

[75] University of Nottingham historian Christina Lee. Second Conference on Disease, Diability and Medicine in Early Medieval Europe. **"Dark Ages view of ailments was pretty bright"**. http://www.msnbc.msn.com/id/19933945/

[76] **"Hospice in Historical Perspective"**. Encyclopedia of Death and Dying, http://www/deathreference.com/Ho-Ka/Hospice-in-Historical-Perspective. html.

[77] Faye Getz, **Medicine in the English Middle Ages.** (Princeton University Press: Princeton, New Jersey, 1998), p. 92.

[78] Quotation by A. E. P. Wall. On the back cover of Elaine Murray Stone, **Maxililiam Kolbe. Saint of Auschwitz.** Paulist Press: New York, 1997).

[79] Sandol Stoddard. *The Hospice Movement. A Better Way of Caring for the Dying.* (Vintage Books, New York, New York 1991), xx.

Chapter Nine. *Hospice Companioning in Modern Times*

[1] James A. Corrick, *The Early Middle Ages* (Lucent Books, San Diego, Ca, 1995), 11

[2] Quoted byJames A. Corrick, Ibid., p.11.

[3] A photo of a Paris hospice, "L'Hospice des Vieillards" exists as a black and white postcard in the DePaul Universities Libraries. Archives Number: archives-cml-1772.

[4] *"About the Society of St. Vincent de Paul"*. http://www.vincenter.org/tree/svdp/about.html.

[5] *"Saint Vincent DePaul, Priest"*. http://www.passionistnuns.org/Saints/StVincentdePaul/index.htm.

[6] Cathy Siebold. *The Hospice Movement. Easing Death's Pains* (Twayne Publishing: New York, New York, 1992), p.18.

[7] David Clark, *"Palliative Care History: A Ritual Process,"* European Journal of Palliative Care 7, no. 2. (2000), p.51.

[8] Ibid., p.20.

[9] Ibid., p.20.

[10] Ibid., p.20.

[11] *"Our Lady's Hospice Ltd. Harold's Cross& Blackrock"*. http://www.le/AboutUs/OurHeritage/index.html.

[12] Ibid.

[13] Ibid.

[14] Ibid.

[15] Cathy Siebold. *The Hospice Movement. Easing Death's Pains* (Twayne Publishing: New York, New York, 1992), p. 23.

[16] *"Our Life and Work"*. Website of Hawthorne Dominicans. http://www. hawthorne-dominicans.org.

[17] Ibid.

[18] Website of Calvary Hospital. http://www.calvaryhospital.org.

[19] Stephen Strack, *Death and the Quest for Meaning Essays in Honor of Herman Feifel.* (Jason Aronson, Inc. North Vale, NJ., 1997), front dustcover.

[20] Herman Feifel, editor. *The Meaning of Death* (McGraw-Hill. New York, New York, 1959).

[21] *"Thanatology"*. http://en.wikpedia.org/wiki/Thanatology.

[22] Stephen Strack, *Death and the Quest for Meaning Essays in Honor of Herman Feifel.* (Jason Aronson, Inc. North Vale, N.J., 1997), p.241.

[23] St. Christopher's Hospice website. http://www.stchristophers.org.

[24] *"The Power of Music in Therapy"*. http://www.camnewton.com/music_ therapy.htm

[25] Ibid.

[26] See the website: *"The Chalice of Repose Project"*. http://www.chaliceof-repose.org

[27] *"A Tribute to Dame Cicely Saunders"*, by Dr. Robert Twycross. http://www.stchristophers.org.

[28] Quoted in *"Science Hero: Dame Cicelely Saunders"*, by Barbara Field. The My Hero Project. http://myhero.com.

[29] Ibid.

[30] *"A Tribute to Dame Cicely Saunders",* by Dr. Robert Twycross. http://www.stchristophers.org.

[31] Ibid.

[32] Website of St. Christopher's Hospice. http://www.stchristophers.org.

[33] Quoted in: *"A Tribute to Dame Cicely Saunders"*, by Dr. Robert Twycross. http://www.stchristophers.org.

[34] *"Total Pain: The Work of Cicely Saunders and the Hospice Movement"*, by Marcia Meldrum. American Pain Society. APS Bulletin. Volume 10, Number 4, July/August 2000.

[35] Ibid.

[36] Ibid.

[37] Wesley J. Smith, *"Dame Cicely Saunders"*. *"The Mother of Modern Hospice Care Passes On"*. The Weekly Standard. July 19,2005.

[38] Quoted in: *"Total Pain: The Work of Cicely Saunders and the Hospice Movement"*, by Marcia Meldrum. American Pain Society. APS Bulletin. Volume 10, Number 4, July/August 2000.

[39] Ibid.

[40] Quoted in Ibid.

[41] Ibid.

[42] Ibid.

[43] *"Watch With Me: Inspiration for a Life in Hospice Care"*, by Cicely Saunders. http://www.obervatory-publications.net. This is a review of the book.

[44] Quoted in: *"A Tribute to Dame Cicely Saunders"*, by Dr. Robert Twycross. http://www.stchristophers.org.

[45] Ibid.

[46] Ibid.

[47] Quoted in *"As It Happens"*. Don Scumacher, President of the National Hospice and Palliative Care Organization. 8/25/2004.

[48] *"Hospice: A Historical Perspective"*. Hospice and Palliative Care Association of New York State. http://www.hpcanys.org/about_hp_historical.asp.

[49] Elizabeth Kubler Ross. *On Death and Dying* (Touchstone, New York, New York, 1969).

[50] *"The Stages in the Dying Process"*, Baxter Jennings, Charlene Gemnill, Brandie Bohman, Kristin Lamb. *"Critisisms of Kubler Ross"*. http://www.uky.edu/classes/PHI/350/KR.htm.

51 Website of the Connecticut Hospice. http://www.hospice.com.

52 Connecticut Hospice. http://www.hospice.com.

53 Ibid.

54 Cathy Siebold. *The Hospice Movement. Easing Death's Pains* (Twayne Publishing: New York, New York, 1992), p. 122.

Chapter Ten. A Spiritual Manifesto

1 Zelda Foster. Quoted on back cover of: Cathy Siebold. *The Hospice Movement. Easing Death's Pains* (Twayne Publishing: New York, New York, 1992),

2 The abiding spiritual theme of the Hospice Way through the years is expressed in the Latin root for the word *Hospes* which means both host and guest. The hospice spiritual tradition is a caring between practitioner and recipient, a radical sharing of hospitality. The Latin word emphasizes a dynamic interaction, or a process that is taking place between fellow humans, and not simply a physical location or one event. We see hospitality in hospice as dignified acts of caring that flow from a welcoming and inviting heart of the caregiver, and shared with the dying and their loved ones.

Seven basic practices form the Spiritual Art of Hospitality, with each practice expressed through the Spiritual Presence of the caregiver. These practices are:

1. Observe the Dignity of the Patient above all else.

2. Provide Palliative Care, Focusing on Pain Management and Symptom Control.

3. Offer Compassionate Care for the Family of the Dying and Empower the Family to Companion the Patient.

4. Provide Care Ideally in the Home of the Patient or a Home-Like Facility.

5. Let all Care Be Determined by the Needs of the Patient, as Much as Possible.

6. Provide Holistic Care Through a Health Care Team.

7. Foster Sacred Presence through Nature and All Creation.

Appendix II. *Reflections on St. Augustine and Companioning the Dying*

[1] Thomas F. Martin. *Our Restless Heart. The Augustinian Tradition* (Orbis Books. Maryknoll, New York, 2003), p. 91.

[2] Ibid., p. 91.

[3] Ibid., p. 25.

[4] Ibid, p. 25.

[5] Ibid, p. 26.

[6] Ibid, p. 26.

[7] Donald X. Burt, *Reflections on a Dying Life* (Liturgical Press, Collegeville, Minnesota, 2004), p.84.

[8] Ibid, p. 105.

[9] Ibid, p. 103.

[10] Ibid, pp. 134-135.

[11] Ibid, p. viii.

Appendix III. *Reflections on St. Benedict and the Hospice Way*

[1] Christine D. Pohl, *"Hospitality: A Practice and a Way of Life"*. Vision, Spring, 2002.

[2] Daniel Ward, *"Monastics: Life and Law"*. http://www.osb.org/aba/law/mll2.htm

Select Bibliography
Arranged by Subjects
Books and Printed Articles

Death and Dying

Aries, Philippe.1981. *The Hour of Our Death*. New York: Alfred A. Knoff.

Aries, Philippe.1974. *Western Attitudes Toward Death: From the Middle Ages to the Present*. John Hopkins University Press: Baltimore, Maryland

Becker, Ernest. 1997. *The Denial of Death.* Free Press: New York.

Callanan, Maggie and Kelley, Patricia. 1992. *Final Gifts.* Understanding the Special Awareness, Needs, and Communications of the Dying. Simon & Schuster:New York.

Coberly, Margaret. 2002. *Sacred Passage*. How to Provide Fearless, Com passionate Care for the Dying. Shambhala Publications: Boston, Massachusetts.

Ethedirge, Melissa. *"Elizabeth Edwards"*. Time Magazine. Friday, April 27, 2007. Available on the Web at: http://www.time.com/time/special/2007.

Feifel, Herman, Editor 1965. *The Meaning of Death*. McGraw-Hill Book Company: New York.

Kaufman, Sharon R. *...and a time to die.* How American Hospitals Shape the End of Life. University of Chicago Press: Chicago.

Kessler, David. 1997. *The Needs of the Dying.* A Guide for Bringing Hope, Comfort and Love to Life's Final Chapter. HarperCollins: New York, N.Y.

Ross, Elizabeth Kubler. 1997. *On Death and Dying.* First Scribners Classic Edition: New York, N.Y.

Singh, Kathleen Dowling.2000. *The Grace in Dying*. How we are transformed spiritually as we die. Harper: San Francisco.

Strack, Stephen, Editor 1997. *Death and the Quest for Meaning*. Essay in Honor of Herman Feifel. Jason Aronson, Inc: Northvale, New Jersey.

Webb, Marilyn. 1997. *The Good Death*. The New American Search to Reshape the End of Life. Bantam Books: New York, N.Y.

Yoder, Greg. 2005 . *Companioning the Dying.* A Soulful Guide for Care givers. Companion Press Center for Loss and Life Transition): Fort Collins, Colorado.

Gardens and Health Care

Gerlach-Spriggs, Nancy, and Kaufman, Richard Enoh, and Warner, Sam Bass Jr. 1998. *Restorative Gardens.* The Healing Landscape. New Haven, Connecticut,   Yale University Press.

Harvey, John H. 1981. *Medieval Gardens.* London: B.T. Batsford.

Landsberg, Sylvia. 1996. *The Medieval Garden.* New York: Thames and Hudson.

Marcus, Clare Cooper. 1999. *Healing Garden-Therapeutic Benefits and Design Recommendations*. John Wiley & Sons. New York.

Hospice

Byock, Ira.1997. *Dying Well.* Peace and Possibilities at the End of Life. Riverhead Books: New York, N.Y.

"Guidelines for Spiritual Care in Hospice" (Booklet).National Hospice and Palliative Care Organization. Alexandria, Virginia 2001.

Lattanzi-Licht, Marcia, with Mahoney, John J. and Miller, Galen W. 1998. *The Hospice Choice*. In Pursuit of a Peaceful Death.   The National Hospice Organization Guide to Hospice Care. Simon & Schuster, New York, N.Y.

Mango, Josefina B. 1993. *Midwife for Souls.* A pastoral care guide for hospice workers and all who live with the terminally ill. Boston: Pauline Book and Media.

Siebold, Cathy 1992. *The Hospice Movement.* Easing Death's Pains. Twayne Publishers: New York.

Singer, Marilyn. 2000. *A Dog's Gotta Do What a Dog's Gotta Do*. Dogs at Work. New York: Scholastic Inc.

Stoddard, Sandol. 1992. *The Hospice Movement.* A Better Way of Caring for the Dying Vintage Books. Random House, Inc: New York.

Verderber, Stephen & Refuerzo, Ben J. 2006. *Innovations in Hospice Architecture*. Taylor & Francis. Abingdon, Oxon, Great Britain, 2006.

Hospitality

Boersma, Hans.2004. *Violence, Hospitality and the Cross.* Baker Academic: Grand Rapids, Michigan.

Hay, Leslie A. Hospitality. *The Heart of Spiritual Direction*. Morehouse Publishing. Harrisonburg, Pa. 2006.

Homan, Daniel O.S.B. and Pratt, Lonni Collins. *Radical Hospitality.* Benedict's Way of Love. Paraclette Press. Brewster, Massachusetts, 2002.

Newman, Elizabeth. 2007. *Untamed Hospitality.* Welcoming God and Other Strangers. Brazo Press: Grand Rapids, Michigan.

Pohl, Christine D. 1999. *Making Room.* Recovering Hospitality as a Christian Tradition. William H. Errdmans Publishinging Company. Grand Rapids, Michigan.

Richard, Lucien. 2002 *Living the Hospitality of God.* Paulist Press: New York, New Jersey.

Rupprecht, David and Ruth. 1983. *Radical Hospitality.* Presbyterian and Reformed Publishing Company. Phillisburg, New Jersey.

Sawyer, Nanette. 2008. *Hospitality. The Sacred Art.* Discovering the Hidden Spiritual Power of Invitation and Welcome. Skylight Paths: Woodstock, Vermont.

"Shall We Dance?". Movie 2 004. Starring Richard Gere, Jennifer Lopez. Peter Chelsom Director. http://www.amazon.com.

Sutherland, Arthur.2006. *I Was a Stranger. A Christian Theology of Hospitality* Abingdon Press: Nashville, Tennessee.

Medical History

Brodman, James William.1998. *Hospitals and the Poor in Medieval Catalonia.* University of Pennsylvania Press.

Getz, Faye. 1998. *Medicine in the English Middle Ages.* Princeton University Press. Princeton, N.J.

Kiernan, Stephen P. *Last Rights.* Rescuing the End of Life from the Medical System St. Martin's Griffin: New York, N.Y.

Riesman, David.1935. *The Story of Medicine in the Middle Ages.* Paul B. Hoeber. New York. 1935.

Siraisis, Nancy G.1990. *Medieval and Early Renaissance Medicine.* U. of Chicago Press, Chicago Illinois.

Towsend, John A. 2006. *A Painful History of Medicine. Bedpans, Blood & Bandages.* Raintree. Chicago, Illinois.

Middle Ages

Brooke, Christopher. 2003. *The Age of the Cloister.* The Story of Monastic Life in the Middle Ages. Hidden Spring. Paulist Press. Mahwah: New Jersey.

Corrick, James 1995 A. *The Early Middle Ages*. Greenhaven Press: Farmington Hills, MI.

Newman, Paul B. 2001. *Daily Life in the Middle Ages*. McFarland & Company, Inc.: Jefferson, North Carolina.

What Life Was Like in the Age of Chivalry. Medieval Europe AD 800-1500. Time-Life Books.

Spirituality and Theology

Augustine of Hippo.2004. *The Monastic Rules* New City Press: Hyde Park, New York.

Burt, Donald X. 2004. *Reflections On A Dying Life.* Order of St. Benedict. Liturgical Press: Collegeville, Minnesota.

Frossard, Andre (1987). *Forget Not Love*. The Passion of Maximilian Kolbe. Ignatius Press. San Francisco. 1987.

Mango, Josefina B. (1993). *Midwife for Souls*. A pastoral care guide for hospice workers and all who live with the terminally ill.

Meisel, Anthony and del Mastro, M.L.1975. Translation, Introduction and Notes. *The Rule of St. Benedict.* Image Books, Doubleday: New York, N.Y.

Hoekendijk, J.C. 1964 *The Church Inside Out*. The Westminster Press, Philadelphia, Pennsylvania.

Martin, Thomas F. 1970. *Our Restless Heart.* The Augustinian Tradition. Orbis Books :Maryknoll, New York.

Muggeridge, Malcom.1971. *Something Beautiful for God*. William Collins and Sons Ltd., London.

Mother Teresa. 1995. *A Simple Path.* Ballantine Books. New York.

Nouwen, Henri J.1994. *Our Greatest Gift.* <u>A Meditation on Dying and Caring.</u> Harper Collins: New York, N.Y.

Nouwen, Henri J. 1975. *Reaching Out.* Doubleday Publishing: New York, N.Y.

Pohl, Christine D. *Making Room.*1999. <u>Recovering Hospitality as a Christian Tradition.</u>William H. Errdmans Publishing Company. Grand Rapids, Michigan.

Pompey, Henrich. *"Biblical and Theological Foundations of Charitable Works"*. Paper presented at the Acts of the World Congress on Charity. Rome. 12-15 May, 1999.

Smith, Jeremiah J. O.F.M. Conv. 1998. *Saint Maximillian Kolbe . Knight of the Immaculata*. Tan Books and Publishers, Inc: Rockford, Illinois.

Stone, Elaine Murray. 1997. *Maximilian Kolbe. Saint of Auschwitz.* Paulist Press: New York.

Muggeridge, Malcolm. 1986 *Something Beautiful for God.* Harper & Row, New York, N.Y.

Newman, Elizabeth. 2007. *Untamed Hospitality.* <u>Welcoming God and Other Strangers</u>. The Christian Practice of Everyday Life Series. Branzos Press, Grand Rapids, Michigan.

Thompson, Marjorie J 1995. *Soul Feast.* <u>An Invitation to the Christian Spiritual Life</u>. Westminster John Knox Press: Louisville, Kentucky.

Tolle, Eckhart. 1999. *The Power of Now*. New World Library, Novato, California.

Tolle, Eckhart. 2005. *A New Earth. Awakening to Your Life's Purpose*. Penguin Group, New York, N.Y.

Vardey, Luicinda.1995.Mother Teresa. *A Simple Path.* Ballantine Books: New York.

Web Sites and Internet Articles

Death and Dying

"A Profile of Death and Dying in America". 6/1/2008. http://www.nap.edu/ readingroom/books/approaching/2.html.

Encyclopedias

Catholic Encyclopedia. http://www.newadvent.org/cathen

Wikipedia. http://www.wikpedia.org.

Gardens and Health Care

"The Mary Garden". in "Medieval Gardens". http://www.stmarydehaura. org.uk/gardens.html.

Ulrich, Roger S. 2002. *"Health Benefits of Gardens in Hospitals"*. Paper for Conference, Plants for People". International Exhibition Florida, http://www.greenplantsforgreenbuildings.org.

Hospice

Allen, Kathleen Ann. *"The Hospice Concept in Health Care"*. http://www2.sunysuffolk.edu.

Blue Ridge Hospice. Mai Amy Ha, MD. *"Physician Newsletter"*. November, 2007. http://www.blueridgehospice.org.

Calvary Hospital. 6/1/2008. *"About Us"*. http://www.calvaryhospital.org.

Connecticut Hospice. http://www.hospice.com.

Field, Barbara. *Science Hero: Dame Cicely Saunders.* http://myhero.com.

"Hospice in Historical Perspective". 8/10/2007. Encyclopedia of Death
and Dying. http://www.deathreference.com/Ho-Ka/Hospice-in-
Historical-Perspective.html.

Hawthorne Dominicans. *"Our Life and Work"*. 6/1/2008.
http://www.hawthornedominicans.org.

"Hospice: A Historical Perspective". Hospice and Palliative Care Association of New York State. http://www.hpcanys.org.

"Hospice Caring, Inc." Reading List. http://www. Hospicecaring.org.

"Kubler-Ross and other Approaches". PH350: The Stages in the Dying
Process. http://www.uky.edu/classesPH350/kr.htm.

Our Lady Hospice. Harold's Cross. *"Our Heritage"*. http://www.olh.le/
aboutus/OurHeritage/index.html.

Ross, Elisabeth Kubler. Website. http://www.elisabethkublerross.com.

Saunders, Cicely. *"Watch with Me: Inspiration for a life of hospice care"*
http://www.observatory-publications.net.

Saint Christopher's Hospice. http://www.stchristophers.org.

Twycross, Robert. *"A Tribute to Dame Cicely Saunders"*. http://www.
stchristophers.org

St. Joseph's Hospice. John Scott, *"The Early Days"*. 9/24/2007.
http://www.stjh.org.

Hospitality

"Benedictine Hospitality". http://www.benedictine.org.au/hosp.htm.

"Spiritual Practices: Hospitality". Spiritual & Practice. Website. http://www.spiritualityand practice.com.

Pohl, Christine D. *"Hospitality, a Practice and a Way of Life"*. Vision, Spring 2002. http://www.mennonvision.org.

Medical History

"Anesthetics…Used By Medieval Monks!" 7/5/2008. http://www.MedicineNet.com.

Markham, Margaret. *"Medieval Hospitals"*. Van and Downland Museum-Local History Series. http://www.wantage.com.

"Medieval Medicine". *"Healing and Hospitals"*. http://www.maggietron.com/med/healing.php.

"Morpheus" (mythology). http://en.wikipedia.org/wiki/Morpheus_ (god).

Yousif, Jason. *"The Progress of Ancient Medieval Medicine"*. http://students.ou.edu/Y/Jason.S.Yousif-1/episode_3_medieval. html.

"Total Pain: "The Work of Cicely Saunders and the Hospice Movement". http://www.ampainsoc.org.

"WHO Definition of Palliative Care". http://www.who.int/cancer/pallia tive/definition/en/.

Middle Ages

"A life apart: leper hospitals". http://www.building-hsitory.pwp.blueyon der.co.uk/Articles Heritage2.htm.

"Blessed Gerard Tonque & the early history of the Order of Malta. "The Works of Charity Hospitality". 9/10/2007. http://blessed-general. org/bgt_2a2g.htm.

"Blessed Gerard Tonque and His Everlasting G Brotherhood: The Order of St. John. "The Foundation and spiritual roots of the Hospital Order of St. John of Jerusalem".8/23/2007. http://www.ewtn. com/library/PRIESTS/ORDJOHN.TXT.

"Medieval hospitals of Bath". http://www.buildinghistory.org/bath/medi eval/hospitals.htm.

Miller, Maureen. *"Unclean! Unclean!"* History of Medicine. http://millerm.tripod.com/medhist/unclean.pdf

"Shelter in old age". Medieval Hospitals. http://www.building-history.pwp. blueyonder.co.uk/Bath/Medieval/shelter.htm.

Silverman, Benjamin C. (Spring 2002). *"Monastic Medicine: A Unique Dualism Between Natural Science and Spiritual Healing"*. HURJ, Spring 2002. Issue 1. http://www.jhu.edu/hur.

"Third Lateran Council" (1179). Catholic Encyclopedia. http://www. newadvent.org.cathen/09017b.htm.

Music and Hospice Care

Cassidy, Ann. *"Helping Patients Die a Good Death"*. Music Thanatology. The Catholic University of America Online Newspaper. November 5, 2004. http://inside.edu.

Hillard, Russell E. *"Music Therapy in Hospice and Palliative Care: a Review of the Empirical Data.* Advanced Access Publication. 7 April, 2005. ecam.oxfordjournals.org/cgi/content/abstract/2/2/173".

The Chalice of Respose Project. 6/12/2008. The Voice of Music-Thanatolo gy. http://www.chaliceofrespose.org. Coleman, Korva.

"MusicTherapy May Help Ease Pain". NPR. "Your Health" June 3, 2008. http://www.npr.org.

Rund, Even. ***"Music Therapy-History and Cultural Contexts"***. "Two Major New Texts on Music Therapy". Voices 1(3). http://www.voices.no/mainissues/Voices1(3)Ruud.html

Schroeder-Sheker, Therese. ***"Music for the Dying: Using Prescriptive Music in the Death-Bed Vigil"***. <u>Noetic Sciences Review #31</u>, Autumn 1994.06/11/2008. http://www.noetic.org.

Spirituality and Theology

"Blessed Maximilian Kolbe-Priest Hero Of A Death Camp". http://www.ewtn.com.

Brenner, Paul R. ***"Spirituality in Hospice"***. The Park Ridge Center for Health, Faith, and Ethics. http://www.parkridgecenter.org.

"Charity and Hospitality" World Scripture. A Comparative Anthology of Sacred Texts http://origin.org/ucs/ws/theme141.cmf.

"Eckhart Tolle Retreat at Omega" October 2002. Part 1. Manuscript. Eckhart Tolle: a fan site. http://www.inner-growth.

"Eckhart Tolle Interview: The Power of Now and the End of Suffering". 02/14/2007.Sounds True. http://store.soundstrue.com/interview_tolle.html.

"Frequently Asked Questions: Seven Corporal Works of Mercy". University of Leicester (Great Britian). http://www.le.ak/arthistory/seedcorn/faq-scwm.html.

"Interview With Eckhart Tolle". Interview at Omega Institute. Fall 2003. Ecomall. http://ecomall.com/greenshopping/eckhartole.htm.

"An Interview with Eckhart Tolle, by Michael Bertand. Eckhart Tolle: a fan site. http://www.inner-growth.info/power_of_now.

"Maximilian Kolbe". Patron Saints Index. http://www.catholic-forum.com/saints/saints/saintm01.htm.

Marytown. The National Shrine of Saint Maximilian Kolbe. Conventual
  Franciscan Friars of Marytown, Libertyville, Illinois. http://mary
  town.com.

Ward, Daniel.7/12/2008. ***"Community/Common Life in Monastic Life and
  Law".*** http://www.osb.org/aba/law/mll09.htm.

ABOUT THE AUTHOR

Ken Patrick, Master of Divinity, Doctor of Ministry, and graduate of The Shalem Institute for Spiritual Formation as well as the U.S. Army Chaplain School, is a spiritual teacher and compassionate social activist. He has devoted his life to providing hospitality and companioning for those in need.

He is currently a hospice chaplain and parish minister. Ken has hiked the Appalachian Trail solo over 2, 139 miles to help open the RAM House, a day shelter for the homeless in Roanoke, Virginia. In 2007, the shelter provided emergency financial aid to 5, 141 people and served 41,346 nutritious midday meals. The thru hike resulted in the privately published book, *Mountain Meditations, My Walk With Christ on the Appalachian Trail* (available through www.xlibris.com).

Ken has extensive knowledge of spiritual traditions, both East and West. He is a graduate of Kubasaki High School, Okinawa. He has also done graduate study at New College, The University of Edinburgh, Scotland.

Ken is available to design a workshop or offer a talk to meet the specific needs of your group or organization. You may contact him through his website: www.thehopsiceway.com. Ken would love to hear from you, and he answers all correspondence.

Blessing on your journey to the end of life. May the depth and wonder of life unfold for you on this path.